ARCHAEOLOGY OF THE
ROMAN EMPIRE

ARCHAEOLOGY OF THE
ROMAN
EMPIRE

ARCHAEOLOGY OF THE
ROMAN EMPIRE

ANTHONY KING

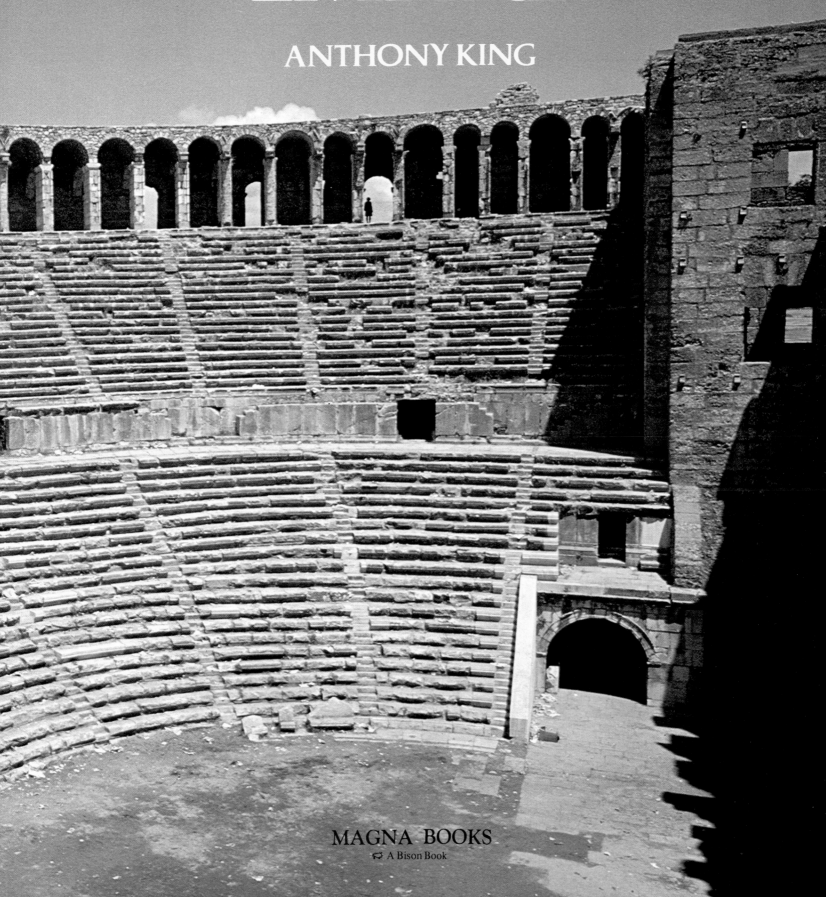

MAGNA BOOKS

A Bison Book

Published by Magna Books
Magna Road
Wigston
Leicester, LE8 2XH

Produced by Bison Books Ltd.
176 Old Brompton Road
London, SW5 0BA
England

ISBN 0 948509 46 5

Printed in Hong Kong

Reprinted 1988

CONTENTS

To my parents, who first took me to visit
Roman sites and fostered my
interest in archaeology.

PAGE 1 Julius Caesar, 100–44 BC.
PAGE 2–3 Theater at Aspendus, Turkey,
second century AD.
PAGE 4–5 Exterior of the Colosseum,
Rome.

A cameo of Augustus, the
first Roman emperor,
27 BC to AD 14.

6

CHAPTER I
THE RISE OF ROMAN SUPREMACY

Rome was not founded in 753 BC, as is commonly believed. This is a date made up by a Roman historian in the first century BC and based on spurious calculations. Also, Romulus was almost certainly not the founder of the city, for the name means simply 'man of Rome' and is now generally accepted as fictitious. However, these shadowy snippets of information do have some basis in reality. Archaeological investigation shows that there was a settlement in Rome in this early period, but the present evidence indicates an earlier date for the first occupation of the site, from the tenth century BC rather than the eighth century. The notion that the settlement was ceremoniously founded by one man may well be a reflection of some ritual designed to bind the original settlers on the site into a single coherent body. Certainly, in later periods there were complicated rites associated with the foundation of colonies sent out from Rome, and it is assumed that these were similar to the rites originally used for the mother city.

Perhaps of more importance to the history of Rome is the simple fact of the existence of these foundation myths. They indicate that Romans of later generations felt strongly about the origins of their city as an independent political state, and were proud of their ancestry. How much better it must have been to have built up the Roman Empire from such humble beginnings in the remote past, than to admit that outside influences played any part in the rise of Rome.

Yet there were outside influences throughout the early history of Rome, and none were more powerful than those of the Etruscans. These people, of disputed ancestry, but with their own distinctive version of Greek culture, were dominant in the affairs of central and northern Italy throughout the early centuries of Rome's existence. Several of the kings of Rome are acknowledged to be Etruscans, and it appears that Etruscan expansion toward the fertile lands of Campania in the seventh century BC had been the original source of contact between the two communities, for up until that period Rome had been more or less on the southern periphery of Etruria. The excellent geographical position of Rome was one of the main reasons for Etruscan interest, for the town commanded several important land and river routes, especially those between Etruria to the north and Latium to the south, and the 'salt way' or *via salaria* down to the coast.

The most obvious manifestation of the Etruscans in Rome was their direct political control of the town by means of a succession of kings. There was a great inflow of cultural ideas as well; architecture started to reflect Etruscan styles, and their gods were introduced to be worshipped alongside the traditional deities of the local region. It was during this period that Rome began to

emerge as a city, as opposed to a rather scattered community of settlers. The population grew and their houses spread down from the hills into the lowlying areas, which were drained and paved over.

The original culture of the Romans was not submerged by the arrival of the Etruscans, however. Most importantly, Latin remained the native tongue for everybody except the rulers themselves and their immediate followers. It is apparent that Etruscan culture was restricted to the upper classes and that most of the inhabitants of the town remained hostile to the kings. This ultimately led, after about 125 years of Etruscan rule, to the overthrow of the last king, Tarquinius Superbus ('the proud'), and the establishment of a republic in *circa* 510 BC.

Historical records seem to indicate that this was not an isolated democratic act on the part of the Roman people. Elsewhere in the region, Etruscan influence was waning and the other towns in the Latin-speaking area south of the Tiber were also throwing off Etruscan rule. It was this area rather than Etruscia that was of crucial importance to Rome in the years following its achievement of independence. Several of the other towns had cause to be apprehensive of Rome's intentions, and banded together in the Latin League. After a battle in 496 BC, Rome became allied by treaty to the League, and for a short while the League itself was the most important political unit in the area. Its existence helped to preserve the autonomy of the Latin-speaking peoples, particularly in the face of the threat from the hill tribes of the Apennines, who were jealous of the rich agricultural resources of the coastal peoples. Gradually Rome became dominant in the League, and although its subsequent influence on Roman affairs remained very strong, it was ultimately submerged completely as an independent political force.

Rome's rise during this period seems to owe much to two very different factors. First, its army was organized along the lines of a Greek infantry force and, together with Greek styles of armor, proved superior to the old-fashioned cavalry armies of the Latins and the disorganized bands of the hill tribes. Second, it was Roman policy to transfer the religious cults of defeated communities to Rome. This had the effect on the very pious peoples of the region of reducing the morale of the defeated community and, to a certain extent, assimilating its political power to that of Rome itself. This process of assimilation continued throughout Roman expansion.

At the same time as these events in Latium were absorbing Rome's attention, the Etruscans to the north of the Tiber began to reassert their presence. Soon after the establishment of the Republic there were attempts to recover the city by the Etruscans, most notably by Lars Porsenna of Clusium. However, the major threat came from the city of Veii, 14 miles to the north. This community was more completely Etruscan than Rome had ever been under the kings, and its well-organized command of agricultural resources meant that it was the main rival to Rome in the region. After a disastrous Roman defeat in 476/5 BC, Veian territory was extended to the far bank of the river Tiber, and this provoked the Romans, after a few years of truce, into retaliatory action. This rapidly developed into a full-scale war, culminating in the siege of Veii itself. The strong natural fortification was eventually breached by a small band of Romans who cleared an old agricultural land-drainage tunnel that ran under the defenses; the town was partially destroyed and the population evicted. This was the first time that an enemy city had been treated in this way and served as a precedent for the future. After this war, Rome's territory was almost doubled and

it became evident to the other members of the Latin League that Rome was the senior ally, capable of acting more or less with impunity. Peoples in Italy and elsewhere now began to take notice of the burgeoning power in their midst.

There were, however, other peoples in Italy at this time who regarded Rome less with trepidation than as a plum ripe for picking. These were the Gauls, who were moving south on a plundering expedition under their leader Brennus in 387/6 BC. They abandoned the siege of Clusium just to the north of Rome and turned on the city itself. A force of 10–15,000 Romans, apparently the majority of the able-bodied men, was sent out to meet this threat, but it was decisively defeated by the superior arms and tactics used by the Gauls. Most of the Romans drowned while crossing a small stream near the battlefield. After this disaster, the city lay undefended for the Gauls to march inside,

RIGHT The founding of Rome was almost certainly accompanied by ceremonies for blessing the city and its inhabitants. This sculpture from the Roman colony of Aquileia, north Italy, shows the plowing of the foundation furrow round the future site of the town, a ceremony that originally took place in Rome.

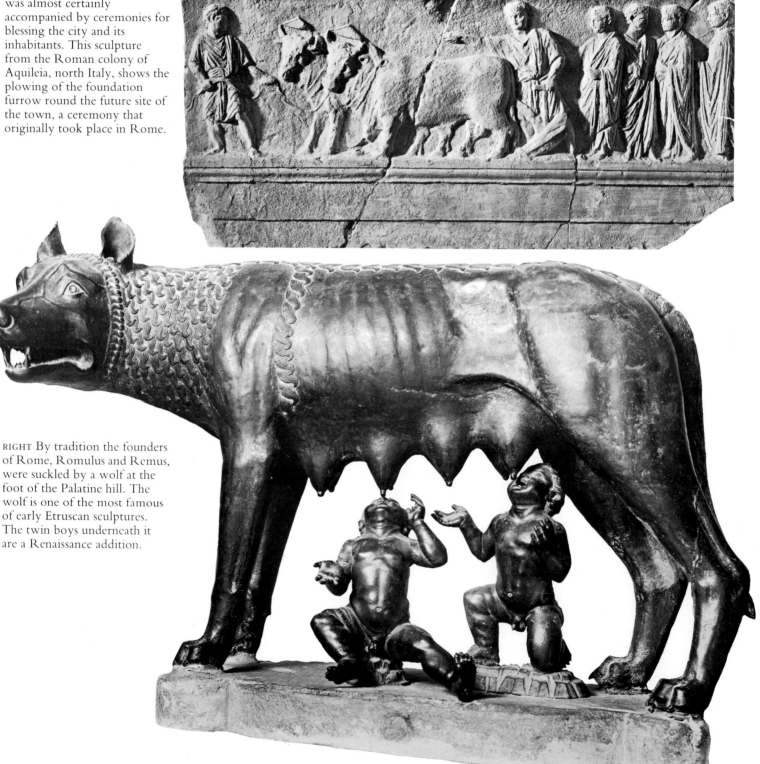

RIGHT By tradition the founders of Rome, Romulus and Remus, were suckled by a wolf at the foot of the Palatine hill. The wolf is one of the most famous of early Etruscan sculptures. The twin boys underneath it are a Renaissance addition.

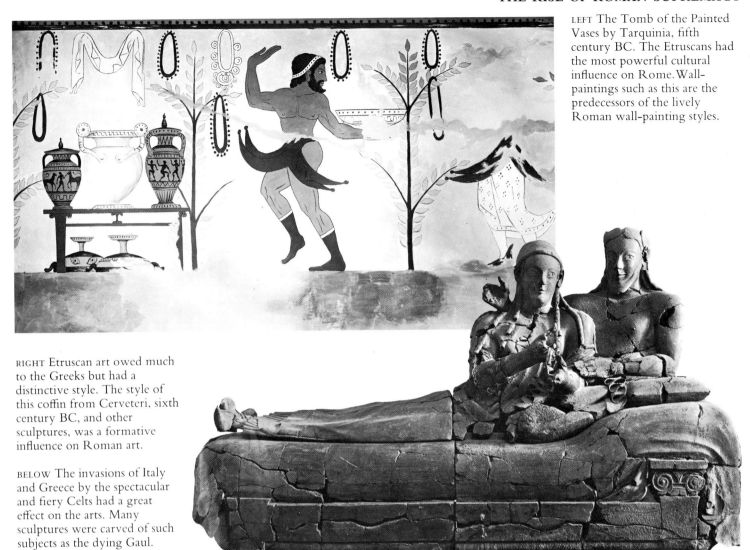

LEFT The Tomb of the Painted Vases by Tarquinia, fifth century BC. The Etruscans had the most powerful cultural influence on Rome. Wall-paintings such as this are the predecessors of the lively Roman wall-painting styles.

RIGHT Etruscan art owed much to the Greeks but had a distinctive style. The style of this coffin from Cerveteri, sixth century BC, and other sculptures, was a formative influence on Roman art.

BELOW The invasions of Italy and Greece by the spectacular and fiery Celts had a great effect on the arts. Many sculptures were carved of such subjects as the dying Gaul.

where they looted and burned the temples and houses, as archaeological remains in the area of the forum testify. Roman fortunes were at the lowest point in the whole of their history up to that time, and such an attack on the city was not to be repeated for 800 years.

To the great relief of the Romans, however, the Gauls soon left, since their homelands in the Po Valley were under attack. One positive result of this traumatic experience was the building of a strong defensive wall which enclosed the traditional seven hills and an area of 1000 acres, which made Rome by far the largest town in Italy.

Its resilient civic pride soon led to a reassertion of Rome's presence on the political scene. Conflicts were brewing with the other members of the Latin League, culminating in the war of 340–38 BC, after Rome attempted to intervene in the affairs of Campania to the south of the Latins. The defeat of the Latins was followed by the breaking up of the League and the absorption of their territory. Significantly, in the aftermath of this war Rome, unlike many of the other ancient powers, was not vindictive to the defeated (despite the precedent of Veii), and granted many of the communities partial or complete Roman citizenship. This was a politically astute move that pleased the Latin cities, for it gave them the right to trade in Rome and to marry Romans. Complete citizenship also conferred voting rights. In return, Rome gained control of foreign policy and had the right to levy troops from the citizens. The latter aspect was doubtless one of the most important reasons for Rome's seemingly lenient attitude. Another reason became more apparent later, namely that Rome wanted to share the benefits and advantages (as it saw them) of Roman culture with the other peoples of Italy, and subsequently outside Italy too. This could almost be called the 'manifest destiny' of Rome's expansion, and it took the form politically of the desire to expand the city territory so that, nominally, the greater part of conquered land was part of the city of Rome itself. In effect, the Roman Empire was a gigantic city state, whose population was theoretically able to enjoy the fruits of Roman civilization.

Those fruits were initially available only to the upper classes, however. The early centuries of the Roman republic, besides seeing the remarkable expansion of Roman rule throughout Italy and beyond, are also witness to long and sometimes ferocious struggles for political recognition of the lower class, or plebs. At first, all power resided in the hands of the patricians, an hereditary ruling caste composed of a few families only. The Senate, or council of elders, was made up of patricians, and the elected heads of state, the two consuls, were also drawn from the same group of people. Theoretically, all Roman citizens voted for the consuls, but many elections were, in effect, rigged by the patricians to give power to their favored candidate. The rigging was carried out by means of the client system, under which poor citizens were protected by wealthy senators in exchange for political support. This allowed the richest men to acquire a great deal of political influence and their chosen candidates were usually elected.

Problems arose with the increasing prosperity, through trade, of some of the plebs. These men did not want protection any more, but their own say in affairs of state. Debt afflicted much of the lower class, and they partly attributed this to abuses of power by the patricians. Add to this the realization by the plebs that they were indispensable to the smooth running of Rome and its army, and the quest for power by the lower class may be seen as a concerted and genuine political move for fairer access to positions of importance. Their first success was the Senate's recognition of the *tribuni plebis* (tribunes of the people) as officials elected by the plebs to protect their interests as a class. The tribunes eventually acquired the right to veto any legislation proposed by the Senate, and thus the posts became very powerful and sought-after. Further progress was rapid: the law was codified (the Twelve Tables) so that everybody knew their rights and duties; plebs and patricians were allowed to marry; and in the early fourth century BC, plebs were allowed into the Senate and to become consuls. Eventually, the assembly of the plebs was recognized as a law-making body in 287 BC, and this brought the class struggle to a virtual close. Although not democratic in any modern sense, the transformation of Rome's political system had been a remarkable one, for it changed from an oligarchy drawn from a self-perpetuating caste to a fairly accessible system of government that was elected and open to nearly all ranks of society.

Italy during the Republic

LEFT At first, Rome's influence was confined to the region immediately around the city itself. However, after casting off Etruscan domination and expelling the kings, Rome began to threaten the Latin-speaking peoples just to the south. They formed the Latin League to counteract the threat, but although Rome became allied to the League in 496 BC, this did not prevent the gradual assertion of power by the Romans. Eventually the Latin League was absorbed by Rome – beginning the city's territorial expansion. Next the Etruscans were pushed back from cities such as Veii, and lands to the south of the Latin League were also conquered. By the third century BC Roman possessions extended over most of central and southern Italy, bringing the city into conflict with the rich Greek colonies on the south coast. Battles were fought against king Pyrrhus of Epirus for control of the south. Eventually the area fell into Roman hands. By the end of the third century all of Italy including part of the Po Valley in the north was under Roman control.

ABOVE The walls of the acropolis of Saguntum in Spain, where the dispute that led to the great war between Rome and Hannibal originated.

Returning to the foreign affairs of Rome, expansion was continuing throughout this period, and after annexing much of southern Italy, Rome came in contact with the Greek colonies that had been planted around the 'heel' and 'toe' of the country. For the first time, Rome had to fight an army from a foreign land, for the colonies called upon King Pyrrhus of Epirus in western Greece to help them against the Roman threat. Pyrrhus' first battle against the Romans, at Heraclea in 280 BC, was won by his use of elephants, which frightened the Roman horses into stampeding. However, many of his own men were killed, and a costly success became known as a 'Pyrrhic victory.' After further fighting, and more Pyrrhic victories, the Greek army decided to return home, leaving the colonies in southern Italy under the control of Rome.

Carthage was the next foreign power to come into contact with Roman military might. However, the scale was altogether different from previous wars, and the outcome was crucial in deciding which of the two states should control the western Mediterranean. There were three Carthaginian wars between 264 and 146 BC, after which Rome was undisputed ruler of the Mediterranean.

Rivalry for dominance of the Mediterranean was the underlying reason for conflict with Carthage, but the immediate cause of war was trivial and the result of complex local politics. Essentially it revolved around who was to control the straits of Messina between Sicily and Italy. The people of Messana, the town that dominated the narrows, at first invited Carthage to protect their interests, but subsequently changed their opinion and asked Rome for help instead. A Roman army was transferred to Sicily, and began to occupy the eastern part of the island. At this stage the Senate realized that further successes would be impossible without a fleet to ensure supplies. Some 140 ships were built, forming the nucleus of a Roman navy, which immediately engaged the much more experienced fleet of the Carthaginians in a series of battles. Initial successes were spectacular and it was decided to invade North Africa, a move that proved rather costly as the invading force was defeated and a relieving fleet wrecked by a storm. However, these setbacks were only temporary and, after further victories at sea, Carthage sued for peace in 241 BC. Two points deserve mention about this war; Rome had built up naval supremacy from nothing in a remarkably short space of time, and thereafter was in overall control of most of the western part of the Mediterranean seas; secondly, Sicily was incorporated as the first overseas province of Rome, directly administered from the city. Soon after, Sardinia and Corsica were annexed from Carthage and made into a second province.

Carthage's reaction to these defeats was to build up its power in the rich colonies it owned in Spain, and it was in this region that the greatest general to oppose Rome rose to power. Hannibal expanded the territory under Carthaginian control until it reached further north than Saguntum, a nominally independent town on the Mediterranean coast. The Saguntines appealed to the Romans for help and envoys were sent to the Carthaginians. However, this did not deter Hannibal, thus forcing the dispatch of a Roman force to resolve the issue. In addition it was decided to invade North Africa in order to strike at the Carthaginian heartland. These moves were counteracted by Hannibal's brilliant and audacious decision to invade Italy.

This surprised the Romans, but they were confident that the difficult Alpine crossing in autumn would prove too much for the Carthaginian army. However, Hannibal arrived in Italy successfully, an event that should have warned Rome of the mettle and persistence of his army. Unfortunately the warning went unheeded, and after a series of disastrous defeats, Rome itself lay open to attack. However, Hannibal did not lay siege to the city, which with hindsight can be seen as the one major error of his entire campaign. Yet it is possible to perceive some of the reasons why he turned away from a siege. Hannibal had no siege equipment with him and, more importantly, he had no base in which he could construct it. This was because none of Rome's Italian allies had defected to his side, displaying the remarkable success of Roman social policy in the face of this severe test. Lastly, Hannibal could not rely entirely on Carthaginian help in his enterprise, as the elders were suspicious of his personal intentions. In all probability he decided to gain support in southern Italy before returning to defeat Rome finally. In the south, he was shadowed by Roman armies but not engaged in battle until, after a change in leadership in Rome, it was decided to confront him on the plain of Cannae near the 'heel' of Italy. Despite their numerical strength, the Battle of Cannae, in 216 BC, was the worst defeat the Romans ever suffered. Their force was almost totally annihilated in a pincer movement by Hannibal's troops.

At last some of Rome's allies started to defect to Hannibal. Yet he still did not attack, probably because he was waiting for

his brother Hasdrubal to bring reinforcements from Spain. In 209 BC Hasdrubal managed to evade the Roman army which had been pinning him down there, and reached Italy not long after. However, the two armies never met, for the Romans found out where their rendezvous was to be and wiped out Hasdrubal's army in an ambush near the river Metaurus. This turned the tide of the war, and Hannibal was forced to retreat to southern Italy to recoup his losses. At the same time rapid gains were being made in Spain by the young Roman general Publius Cornelius Scipio, who proved to be a general of similar stature to Hannibal. By 206 BC Spain was largely a Roman possession, and was made into a province. Two years later Scipio invaded North Africa, thus forcing Hannibal to retreat from Italy to protect his homeland. The final battle took place in 202 BC at Zama, not far from Carthage. Hannibal was defeated, and terms imposed on the Carthaginians. Their lands were to be restricted

Elephants were used by Pyrrhus against the Romans in 280 BC, and became part of Rome's weaponry thereafter. A campanian plate, third century BC.

to the hinterland of the city, their navy was to be no larger than 10 ships and, finally, they could not wage war without the consent of Rome.

The dominant personality of the war had been Hannibal. His qualities of leadership and generalship were obviously outstanding, and many Roman histories have respectful assessments of his achievements. Even that most loyal of historians, Livy, wrote:

It is difficult to decide whether he was more remarkable in success or failure. He waged war far from his home, in enemy territory, for 13 years with varied fortunes, at the head of an army not of his own country, but a mixed force from all peoples, differing in customs, law and language, and having nothing in common in behavior, dress, arms and religion. Yet he bound them together as if with a chain, so that there was never any internal dissension or mutiny against their leader, even though money and supplies were often lacking.

Flushed with success after the Carthaginian war, the Romans soon began to interfere in the affairs of other states in the Mediterranean. This happened most obviously in Greece, where an alliance was made with some of the Greek cities against the kingdom of Macedonia to the north. In addition, a couple of the smaller Greek states convinced Rome that Macedonia was a threat to the balance of power in the east. An ultimatum was issued, rejected by Philip of Macedon, and war declared in 200

BC. The framing of the ultimatum marked a departure from Rome's normal foreign policy, for this war was very much an aggressive act, based on suspicions whipped up by third parties with strong ulterior motives. Hitherto Rome could claim, with some justification, that all its wars had been defensive and just, even if they did result in an expansion of territory.

The outcome of this war was a Roman victory in 197 BC, after which the Greek cities were declared to be 'free,' which meant in practice that they were allies under Rome's thumb. At first the Greeks were jubilant, but when they realized that they had simply swapped one form of domination for another, they appealed to another eastern magnate, Antiochus, of the Seleucid Empire. An aggressive stance by Antiochus led to fighting with Rome, most notably at the famous pass of Thermopylae where he was defeated in 191 BC, and forced to evacuate Greece. Final defeat followed the next year, after Roman troops had landed in Asia Minor.

With the defeat of Macedonia and the Seleucids, both inheritors of Alexander the Great's vast empire, there was a power vacuum in the eastern Mediterranean, which Rome soon found itself filling. Nevertheless, Rome did not openly annex and form provinces in the east, but preferred to rule by means of treaties. Continued resistance in Macedonia, however, led to a revision of this policy and a tax-paying province was created there in 148 BC. Even in the treaty areas, Rome's rule was strengthened by acts that were, on occasion, quite ruthless and barbaric. Most

BELOW A temple at Cosa, one of Rome's outpost colonies in Etruria.

After the Romans entered the east in the late third century BC, Greek influences flooded into Rome. Greek theaters, such as this one at Dodona in western Greece, were the forerunners of Roman theaters.

notably, the city of Corinth was razed to the ground and its inhabitants sold into slavery in 146 BC, after some Roman envoys, while trying to quash anti-Roman riots, were beaten up.

The year 146 BC also saw the final destruction of Carthage, in a very similar fashion, which marked the end of the third Carthaginian war. This war had been brought about largely through xenophobia in the Roman Senate, inflamed by the hatred of one of the more conservative senators, Cato, who saw no peace for Rome while Carthage survived. The pretext for war was the breaking of the terms imposed after the second war, since the Carthaginians had taken up arms to defend their territory against the unscrupulous encroachments of a neighboring king. Despite requests to Rome to settle the issue by the imposition of new terms, the price was so high that Carthage, in desperation, turned to armed resistance. The war lasted for four years, culminating in the destruction of 146 BC and the incorporation of Carthage's old territory as the province of Africa.

In little more than 250 years, Rome had transformed itself from a local Italian town under threat from external forces such as the Gauls, into the capital of the most powerful empire in the ancient world, with control of most of the Mediterranean lands, either directly or through dependents. Rome's remarkable success was due to many different factors, the most important of which were the single-mindedness of the ruling classes, coupled with an efficient army and vast reserves of manpower on which to draw. In addition, when under threat from Hannibal, other qualities show through, notably tenacity of purpose, and the loyalty of the Italian allies.

However, by the late second century BC, cracks were beginning to show in the consensus view held by the aristocracy. Political divisions started to appear within the Senate, and the tensions that ultimately led to the destruction of the Republic started to surface. Two brothers, Tiberius and Gaius Gracchus, were in many ways the initiators of these tensions. Both were tribunes of the people who attempted to introduce reforming measures favoring the poor, the merchants and non-Roman citizens – all classes in society very badly represented politically and for whom the Senate, generally speaking, did very little. Not surprisingly the Senate opposed these measures, causing the

RIGHT A Gaulish charioteer on a coin.

LEFT Coin celebrating Caesar's assassination.

tribunes and the popular assembly to bring in the legislation without reference to the Senate, which they were legally entitled to do. Unfortunately, this so displeased the Senate that violence flared, and both brothers were killed in separate incidents. Gaius' death was a direct result of a motion being passed in the Senate that declared the state to be imperilled. The motion was obviously an overreaction by the Senate, but it set the tone for the politics of the next century.

Another development during these years was the increasing intrusion of the army into public affairs. The general Marius is thought to have been responsible for making the army a more professional body. At the same time, the army also came to show its loyalty more to the commanding general than to the Roman state as a whole, especially since the general often undertook to look after the men after their retirement. The first major involvement of troops in Roman politics occurred when Sulla was superseded as general for a campaign in the East by Marius, whereupon Sulla gathered his troops together and led an attack on the capital. This was the first act of civil war in Roman

history and set a dangerous precedent for the future.

After this, government in Rome was on the verge of anarchy for several years. Squabbles and assassinations alternated with strong-arm rule backed up by military force. During the late 70s BC, two men emerged as capable of overriding the Senate and using the state to increase their own personal prestige and influence. These were Gnaeus Pompeius (Pompey) and Crassus. They secured for themselves political positions and military commands, in particular Pompey, who cleared the Mediterranean of pirates in a spectacular campaign lasting three months, using 120,000 troops and 500 ships. Pompey then went on to assume an eastern command and was outstandingly successful in solving the manifold problems of all the minor states in Asia Minor, and extending Roman control in the East.

On Pompey's return from the East, he asked for money to settle his retired troops and for ratification of his actions in the field. For obscure and short-term reasons the Senate opposed this request, which led Pompey to band together with Crassus and another ambitious politician, Julius Caesar, in a secret accord or 'triumvirate' with the aim of concentrating power in their hands. In this they were extremely successful, and the power of the Senate was on the wane from this time on.

Caesar was elected consul in 59 BC, and pushed through a number of reforms in a manner that was technically illegal. This laid him open to prosecution after he laid down his office, and so he took up the command of a provincial army immediately after his consulship ended in order to continue his official position. The command was in Gaul, and Caesar decided to use his talents as a general to expand Roman territory in the province. He did this partly to impress the Senate and persuade them to extend his period of command, which they did, and partly because he wanted to emulate Pompey's exploits, at that time regarded as one of the highest military achievements of any Roman.

Gaul reeled under Caesar's blows and virtually the whole of the country came under Roman control in two years. However, this control was not very strong, because it had been imposed so quickly, with the result that six further years of fighting were necessary to consolidate the early gains and quash rebellions. In addition, Caesar used his command to make explorations of the surrounding lands, notably Germany and Britain. No doubt these expeditions were designed merely to impress the Senate, but they are important to us, as Caesar's commentaries provide the first eye-witness accounts of these countries.

Rome did not receive Caesar back from his campaigning in triumph, however. The political climate had turned against him: Pompey had been wooed by the Senate, having abandoned his old ally, and the Senate, suspicious of Caesar's attempts to gain another consulship on his return to Rome, and jealous of his enormous popular following in Rome, declared that the state was imperilled by Caesar. Together with his army, Caesar crossed the river Rubican into Italy and advanced on Rome. The most traumatic upheaval in Roman history had begun.

The orator Cicero commented, 'I was horrified at the sort of war Pompey envisaged, cruel and total, of a kind which men do not yet comprehend.' Pompey commanded the senatorial forces against Caesar, and his first act was to make a strategic retreat to Greece, where he could recruit more troops and fight in an area traditionally loyal to him. Accordingly Caesar occupied Rome, and set about consolidating his hold on the west, where his own power base lay. After defeating Pompeian strongholds in Spain and Marseilles, and after declaring himself dictator in order to carry out administrative reforms in Rome, he pursued Pompey in Greece. The result was the battle of Pharsalus in 48 BC, one of the largest battles fought between Roman forces, which is described in detail on p. 49. Pompey

RIGHT Julius Caesar, born 100 BC, died 44 BC.

After Augustus' victories over the tribes of the Alps, he characteristically set up this vast victory monument at La Turbie, overlooking the sea near Monte Carlo.

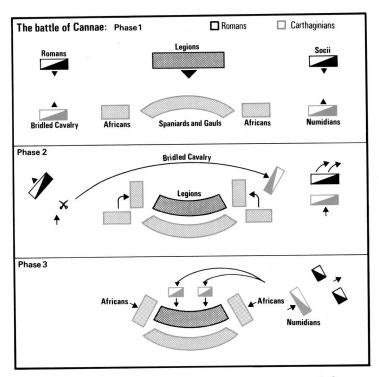

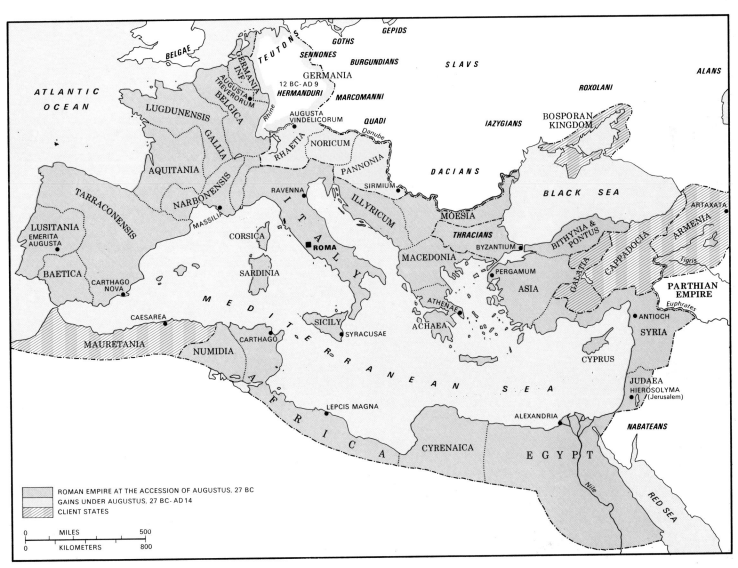

ABOVE The Battle of Cannae, 216 BC, was Rome's worst defeat, because Hannibal's pincer movement surrounded the Roman infantry. After this disaster, the Roman army never made the same mistakes and became virtually invincible.

BELOW The extent of the Roman empire at the time of Augustus.

lost, but escaped to Egypt where he was assassinated by the local politicians, presumably because they perceived that Caesar was likely to win and they wanted to be on the winning side.

The death of Pompey did not end the civil war, for hostilities continued in North Africa and Spain for another three years. However, Caesar was sufficiently in control to begin to make administrative reforms. He settled thousands of retired soldiers in colonies, both in Italy and, more importantly, in the provinces. These colonies became bastions of the empire, and as is seen later, important agents of 'Romanization' in the new provinces. He also built many splendid new monuments in Rome, including a new forum and basilica.

Caesar's self-glorification, reflected in his building program and in other decisions, such as allowing his head to be shown on coins – the first time a living Roman had ever been portrayed on the currency – stuck in the gullets of other members of the aristocracy, and there was a rising tide of resentment against him. He chose to ignore this, even declaring himself perpetual dictator, a move that denied other senators the chance of real executive power and explicitly ratified Caesar's superior position. Eventually, when it was learned that he wanted to leave Rome for a military campaign in the East on 18 March 44 BC, a group of 60 discontented senators resolved to assassinate him. On 15 March, the Senate met to be addressed by Caesar and there he was killed, being left to die at the foot of a statue of Pompey.

The Roman world was plunged into civil war once again. Mark Antony and Octavian, Caesar's devoted follower and his heir respectively, pursued the leading assassins and defeated them at the battle of Philippi. The two then divided control of the provinces between them, Antony taking the East and Octavian the West, but strains soon began to show as both men jockeyed for ascendency and, ultimately, sole control. One of the sources of tension was Antony's famous liaison with Cleopatra, which flew in the face of his marriage to Octavia, Octavian's sister. The fighting that followed soon after this culminated in the sea battle of Actium in 31 BC, in which Antony and Cleopatra were defeated and forced to retire to Alexandria. The following year Octavian captured Egypt and they committed suicide, leaving him sole ruler of the Roman empire. After a generation of fighting, civil war had come to an end, but the result was not the restoration of the republic as it had been, but what was, in effect, a monarchy under Octavian.

The reasons for the end of the republic seem to be rooted in the failure of the Senate to adjust to the changed circumstances of Roman politics and economics from the second century BC. Wealth was pouring into Roman coffers from the newly acquired provinces, but was passing into the hands of the richest and most influential men alone and the bulk of the population, even including some of the poorer senators, did not at first reap any benefit. The best way of acquiring the most fabulous sums was to command an army, which all the most ambitious men did. Such a combination of military might and ambition proved fatal to orderly government, for even if the general did not actually march on Rome, as Sulla and Caesar had done, the Senate found that it could not assert its authority in the face of such a compelling alternative source of power.

Octavian was well aware of the power that the backing of the army gave him. He was careful to keep the control of the army in his own hands or those of trusted generals. He also brought in a series of other measures, which in a very subtle fashion enabled him to exercise complete power without appearing to do so. The Senate was given extra administrative tasks, which had the effect of reducing its political role. Octavian took over the government of all the military provinces, leaving only the more peaceful inner provinces in the hands of the Senate. He also gave many more people of relatively humble backgrounds the chance to serve the state, particularly in provincial and central administration. This resulted in the spread of the fruits of the new empire, now vastly increased in size as a result of the civil war. Octavian's measures were also helped by this wealth, which gave the Roman people an unprecedented standard of living, and contrasted sharply with the ravages of war. Rome was ready for peace and quite willing to accept it under an emperor.

Octavian is, of course, better known by the name of Augustus, the honorific title given him in 27 BC, a date often regarded as the symbolic beginning of Imperial rather than Republican Rome. The most remarkable thing about the new constitutional arrangements is that they survived Augustus' death, but it was part of his genius that the Senate and people were happy to agree to his wish that his stepson Tiberius be his successor, despite the fact that this acknowledged his family to be hereditary rulers (the Julio-Claudian dynasty).

One of Augustus' achievements was the setting up of dozens of towns and cities throughout the empire, and their embellishment with many fine public buildings. It would be fair to say that it was Augustus, more than any other Roman, who was responsible for the establishment of Roman culture in the provinces, using the towns and the roads that linked them as a springboard. In confirmation of this, from this period onward there is good archaeological evidence of the presence of Roman art and artifacts in the provinces.

The world of the new empire in the first and second centuries AD was the culmination of the long rise to dominance of Roman civilization from its remote origins nearly a thousand years earlier. The establishment of the empire is also a suitable point at which to break off the historical narrative and turn to consider the details of Roman civilization as it existed during the empire, and the physical remains that survive today. The thread of history will be resumed in the final chapter, but it has a different theme – the gradual decline of Roman power and the crumbling of its civilization.

BELOW The *ara pacis* (altar of peace) set up by Augustus in 13 BC as a symbol of the stability he had restored to the Roman world.

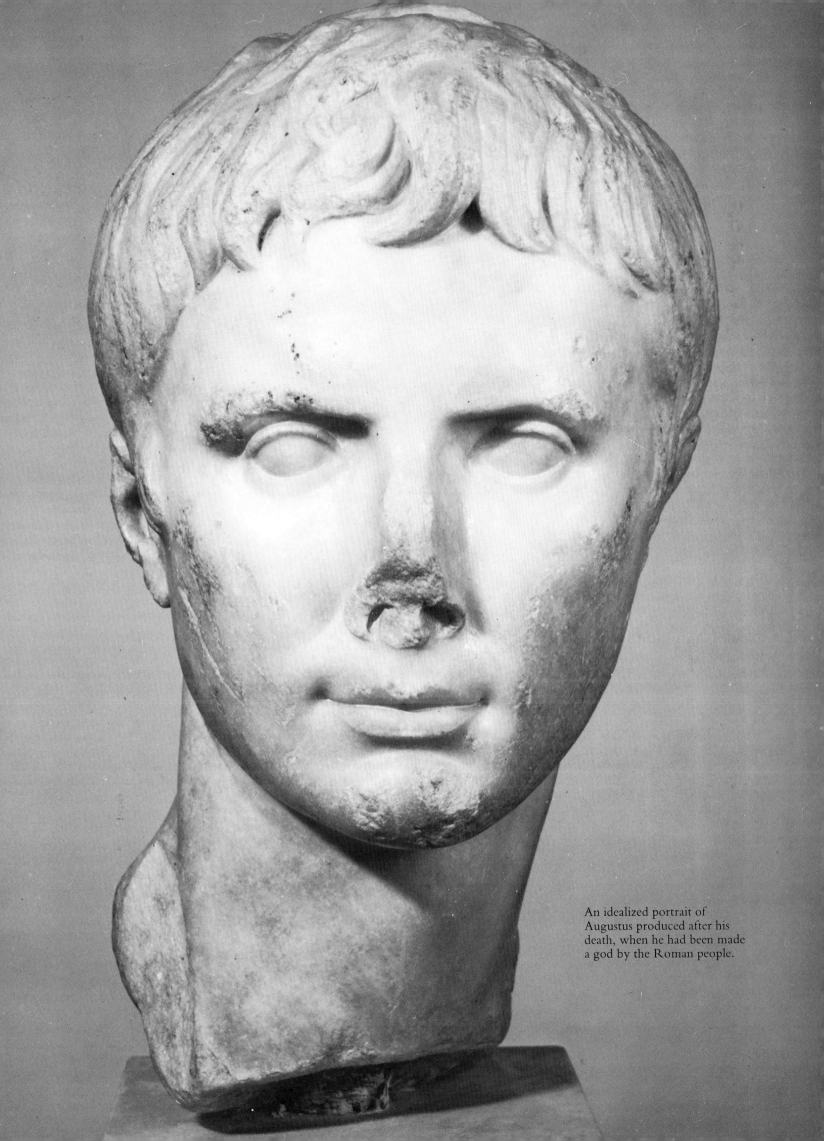

An idealized portrait of
Augustus produced after his
death, when he had been made
a god by the Roman people.

THE ROMAN CONSTITUTION

The historian Polybius commented that 'the share of power in the whole state has been regulated with such a regard for equality and equilibrium that no one could say for certain, not even a native, whether the constitution is an aristocracy or a democracy or a monarchy. No wonder, for if we confine our observation to the consuls we should regard it as monarchical; if to that of the Senate, as aristocratic; and finally, if we look at the power held by the people it would seem a clear case of democracy.' This sums up the Roman constitution brilliantly, and demonstrates how the constitution attempted to provide for all shades of opinion in a fairly balanced system of three parts, each able to check on the other.

Consuls were the chief magistrates of Rome. There were two, elected by the people for a year only from 1 January each year. They were in charge of all the other officials save the tribunes, and in theory could disregard the Senate when issuing decrees, but rarely did so. They led the army and had absolute control over it, except for its pay which was in the hands of the Senate. Under the Roman Empire the consuls were presided over by the emperor who habitually took one of the consulships for himself or for a member of his family. In addition they lost their military powers to the emperor, but otherwise retained their prestige. Provincial government was sometimes carried out by a proconsul.

Other magistrates in Rome were the praetors, the quaestors, the aediles and the tribunes. Praetors were responsible for administering justice, and deputized for the consuls while they were away from Rome with the army. At first there was only one praetor, elected by the people, but additional men were appointed as Rome's area of jurisdiction increased. A praetor peregrinus dealt exclusively with foreigners, and praetors held power in each province. Quaestors were financial officials, in charge of the aerarium (official treasury). There were several of them, since some were stationed in other parts of Italy to deal with Roman interests outside the city. Others were sent to the provinces. In Imperial times actual power was almost entirely removed from the quaestors and given to the civil service.

Aediles were a different sort of magistrate, being appointed originally from the plebs rather than the patricians, which was the case with the other posts. An aedile oversaw the care of the public buildings in Rome, the preservation of the state archives, the food supply and the public games. This last duty became the aediles only responsibility during the empire, as the civil service took over the other functions, and because of this the post became very popular with those who wanted to curry favor with the public for future elections to higher offices. Tribunes of the people were also plebian magistrates, with wide powers of veto over the acts performed by the other officials, including the holding of elections and the passing of laws. They were similar to modern ombudsmen, but much more powerful, and consequently the posts were extremely sought-after. Naturally, under the empire, their power to undermine legislation was vastly curtailed, and the emperors ensured that their laws could be enacted smoothly by permanently assuming the tribunician powers for themselves.

All these magistracies were part of the *cursus honorum* (official career structure) of Roman politics. By the late Republic, laws had been passed to make it compulsory for a praetor to have been a quaestor, and a consul a praetor. It was customary for an ambitious young man to

ABOVE A Roman senator or magistrate from the first century AD, believed to be the philosopher Dogmatius.

ABOVE An early statue of a Roman senator, possibly Aulus Metellus, dating from about 200 BC.

enter politics as an aedile or a tribune, then have a spell in the provinces in a junior military post, then return to Rome for the quaestorship, go again to the provinces in a higher military rank, and return for the praetorship (sometimes held in the provinces also). The process of alternating between Rome and the provinces continued higher up in the career structure too. A man might be appointed governor of a small province, then be appointed consul in Rome, returning afterward as a governor of a more important province. Finally, in his old age he might become a censor, whose responsibility was to make a list of citizens every five years, at the same time assessing everyone's morals and their property qualifications for the different classes of Roman citizen (ordinary citizens, *equites* [knights] and senators). The censors' powers were assumed by the emperor in the first century AD, and they became more moralistic in tone. The least common office was a dictatorship which was the only Roman position to be held by one person at a time. Only used during a crisis, the dictator was appointed for no longer than six months to sort out a problem. It tended to be a military post, and went to the best-suited ex-consul. After the early Republic it became rare.

The *cursus honorem* (career structure) open to a wealthy Roman wanting to serve the emperor.

Initially— **VIGINTIVIRATE**
(junior posts in Rome, 20 in number, held for one year in late teens)

then— **TRIBUNUS MILITUM**
(second in command of a legion, about 20 posts, held for at least a year in early twenties)

then— **QUAESTOR**
(financial and other duties in Rome or in the provinces, 20 posts, held for one year after age 24)

then— **PRAETOR**
(judicial duties in Rome or the provinces, up to 18 posts, held for a year after age 30)

then— **LEGATUS LEGIONIS**
(command of a legion, sometimes held before the praetorship, about 24 posts, usually of three years duration)

and/or— **PRAEFECTUS, CURATOR, IURIDICUS** or **LEGATUS**
(administrative posts in Rome or the provinces, 25 or more in number, held for about three years).

and/or— **LEGATUS AUGUSTI, PROCONSUL**
(governor of a minor province, about 20 posts, usually held for three years)

then— **CONSUL**
(senior minister of government, two posts with about eight assistants known as *consules suffecti*, held for a year after age 41, but sometimes earlier)

then— **LEGATUS AUGUSTI, PROCONSUL**
(governor of a major province, about 12 posts, usually held for three years)

and/or— **CURATOR AQUARUM, PRAEFECTUS URBI, CENSOR** and similar posts
(senior administrative duties in Rome and Italy, six or more in number, held for at least two years, sometimes for life)

The Senate, consisting of about 600 senators, was the other major body in Roman administration, as it issued advice (*senatus consulta*) which was not legally binding but was invariably followed. Senators were chosen from those who had the right property qualification (1,000,000 *sesterces*), and who had held one of the junior magistracies. They debated topical and important issues, often moving a resolution at the conclusion of business and, more importantly, they also deliberated on the spending of money by the magistrates. The Senate was, in effect, Rome's council of elders, whose deliberations reflected the wishes and opinions of the upper classes.

Popular assemblies reflected the opinions of the ordinary people. There were several different assemblies, concerned with elections, military conscription, legal cases and the making of laws (*plebiscita*). The tribunes were the representatives of the popular assemblies in the Senate. The power of the people was greatest at election times, and when they were called on to declare war on an enemy or ratify a treaty. Of course, in Imperial times, these privileges dwindled to virtually nothing, as effective power was assumed by the emperor.

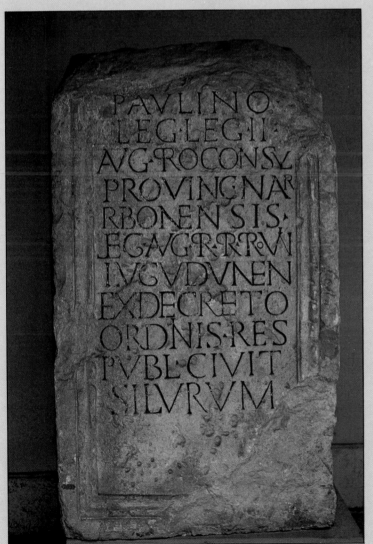

LEFT An inscription relating to the man's career. Paulinus had been legate of the Second Augustan Legion, proconsul of the province of Narbonensis and Imperial Governor of Lugdunensis.

BELOW Iron model of the *fasces* (bundle of rods and axe) that the lictors carried in front of magistrates as a symbol of their authority. It dates from the 7th–6th century BC, and is from an Etruscan tomb.

CHAPTER II
ROME,
THE SEAT OF POWER

A glance at a physical map clearly shows the importance of the geographical position of Rome. The early settlement was perched on the summits of several small steep-sided hills overlooking the river Tiber. The hills were in the best defensive position on the lower reaches of the river, and commanded all movement up- and downstream. Since the Tiber was the major river in central Italy and led directly into the heart of the rich agricultural lands of Etruria, it was soon apparent that whoever held the site of Rome was in a position of considerable strength and power. In addition, there was an important land route crossing the river at this point, somewhere near the island or *insula*, that connected Etruria with the equally rich lands further south in Campania. Another significant route was one that led from the hills down to the salt pans on the coast: salt was a vital commodity in ancient times, as today, and its collection from evaporation ponds was an important summer activity.

All these factors help to account for the location of Rome in its present position but other considerations provide an insight into Rome's later expansion. Most importantly, the area around Rome was lacking in natural resources, such as metal ores or high-quality agricultural land. This may well have forced the city to seek these resources elsewhere once the population had grown beyond a size capable of being sustained by the local region alone. Rome's early development was virtually ignored by the wealthy but rather inward-looking agricultural societies on either side, particularly to the north in Etruria. This left the Romans free to develop a distinctive culture of their own, so that when the Etruscans did eventually force their attentions on the city and imposed their kings on the population, Roman identity survived and the kings were eventually evicted. That identity was also strong enough to be capable of absorbing the best aspects of other civilizations, which was no doubt another facet of the expansionary nature of Roman culture, and one of the reasons for its success.

Such geographical and cultural explanations for Rome's growth go some way toward accounting for the city's extraordinary success in building up an empire. However, this chapter describes the city as it appeared after the empire had been built up, when it had become by far the largest and most resplendent urban center in the ancient world.

The center of Rome was the two hills of the Capitoline and the Palatine, together with the valley between them, where the forum and monumental center were situated. These hills were

the original occupied areas of the city, and tradition has it that the wolf suckled the twins Romulus and Remus in a cave at the foot of the Palatine. Certainly the original city boundary was drawn around the Palatine and forum areas, and excavations have uncovered the remains of rectangular wooden huts dating from the ninth century BC on the southwest part of the Palatine. This is precisely the area where the Romans thought that the community was first established, and they preserved and continually rebuilt one of the huts as the *casa Romuli* (house of Romulus).

The Palatine was principally a residential area, and it seems to have been the most sought-after part of the city by senators and politicians, who found it conveniently close to the forum. Owing to this, in Imperial times it became the natural spot for the residences of the emperors. Augustus was the first, setting up his home not far from the *casa Romuli*. To judge from the surviving remains and from descriptions by his biographers, Augustus' life style was modest and he strove to keep his house more or less the same as those of other senators. However, in order to make room for his secretariat and to conduct public business he expanded into adjacent houses, and this formed a precedent for future emperors. His successors, Tiberius, Caligula and Claudius, lived in a large house nearer the forum, which may have originally consisted of several private houses joined together, but rapidly grew until it occupied much of the northwest corner of the hill. Although very little has been excavated, it had a unified plan with a large courtyard or peristyle in the center, and may have been a large dwelling house rather than a palace.

That development had to await the erection of the *domus Augustana* (house of the emperors) in the reign of Domitian. This enormous building occupied most of the hill-top and became the Imperial residence from that time on: it is from this that the word palace comes, because it was positioned on the Palatine hill. Designed by the architect Rabirius in the so-called baroque style, it had two parts: that on the forum side being for official business, and that on the more secluded far side being the private rooms. In this building we can see Domitian's taste for autocratic rule to the full. The vast audience chamber was about 130 by 107 feet in floor area, and may have been about 97 feet high with a vaulted roof. There were niches along the walls with colored marble statues, and doubtless the room was embellished with marble inlays from the different provinces of the empire – a demonstration, if one was needed, of the extent of Roman power. The private rooms were more modest, although even these include some surprising features, such as the enclosed garden or peristyle in the shape of a stadium or horse-racing track, which may have been used for exercise.

LEFT A model of Rome as it was during the empire. The Colosseum can be seen in the foreground, behind it the Palatine hill, the Imperial palace, the Great Circus and the river Tiber. The model can be seen in the Museo della Civiltà Romana, Rome.

On the other main hill of Rome stood the Capitoline, the religious heart of the capital. It is usually also assumed to have been the best defensive site for the early community as there is a sheer face on nearly every side. Certainly its ancestry is at least as old as the Palatine's and early pottery has been found there. The main temple on the site, to the Capitoline triad of Jupiter, Juno and Minerva, was first built by the Etruscan kings when they occupied the city. Remains of its terracotta decoration have been found, and its stone podium was 205 by 173 feet, making it the largest known temple in the Etruscan world. It must have dominated the rest of the city in much the same way as a medieval cathedral did its surrounding community. This early temple stood until it was destroyed by fire in 83 BC, after which it was rebuilt in a newer style in marble. This too was destroyed, by two fires in AD 69 and 80, a fact that reflects the inadequate provision for fighting fires in the city and the overcrowded housing near the Capitol, through which a fire could easily spread.

Two other buildings on the Capitol were important to city life. One was the mint beside the temple of Juno Moneta (Juno 'the admoniser'), where Rome's coinage was produced, and from which comes the word 'money.' The other was the *tabularium* (state archive) where all the official records were kept on bronze tablets. This was an imposing building of several stories which was positioned on the side of the Capitol facing the forum, and it effectively closed the view down the forum toward the hill.

The forum itself was originally a marshy area between the high ground on each side, except to the southwest where it was drained by a stream into the Tiber. It could not at first be used for habitation, and early burials have been found there, indicating that it lay outside the city area. However, after the Etruscan kings came to Rome, a sewer (the Cloaca Maxima) was laid to drain the marsh properly, and a pavement was laid out. This became the meeting place for the population, when they wanted to conduct business or, in Republican times, when they voted in the *comitium* (popular assembly), which was situated in the forum

just beside the *tabularium*. The political aspect was what the forum was justly famous for, since much of the commercial business tended to be conducted nearer the river where the harbors were, or in the later Imperial Fora.

Originally the area of the forum was simply an open space, but it swiftly became cluttered with monuments, whether of a religious or mythological nature, such as the *lapis niger* (black stone) or *lacus curtius* (pool of Curtius), or administrative such as the *milliarium aureum* (golden milestone) on which were marked the distances to the principal cities of the empire, or commemorative such as the equestrian statue of Domitian and the various triumphal arches. There were also buildings in the forum, of which the earliest was the *regia*, which was originally the house of the king Numa according to tradition, but was used as a small religious shrine to Mars and Ops, and as a store for the sacred shields which were carried by the Salian priests. The house was rebuilt several times, but always in exactly the same form, so that conserves the shape of a building of the sixth century BC despite its late-Republican date of construction. This reflects the venerable nature of the cult with which it was associated, for Mars and Ops were some of the earliest gods associated with Rome. They appear to have been fertility deities particularly concerned with crops, although Mars is usually thought of as the god of war. The warrior priests of Mars performed wild, leaping dances to make the crops grow by sympathetic magic; the crops were supposed to sprout like their leaps.

Next to the *regia* was the temple of Vesta, the goddess of the hearth, and the house of the vestal virgins who tended the shrine and made sure that its sacred fire did not go out. This cult also had its origins in the time of the kings, and was one of the most important in Rome – the fire was the hearth of Rome and a symbol of its existence. The six vestal virgins were the only women priests in Rome, and had to remain virgin throughout their 30-year service, which they entered at the age of six to 10 years. The penalty for breaking this rule for the woman was death by being immured alive, and the man was beaten to death

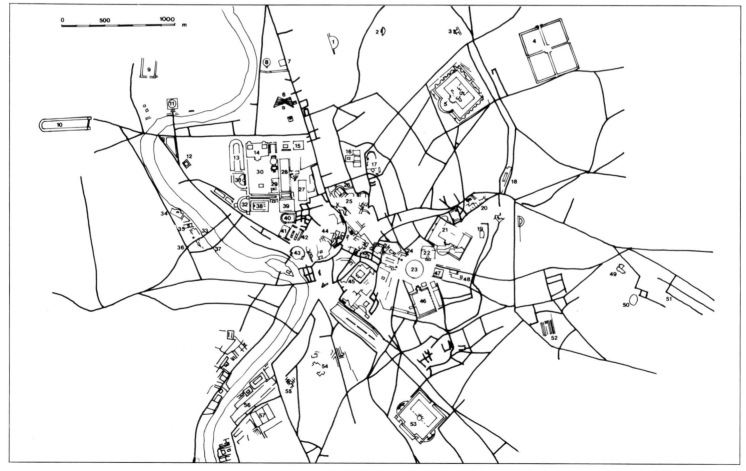

RIGHT A fountain and pool in the Imperial palace on the Palatine hill. Successive emperors, particularly in the first century AD, enlarged their residences until by the time of Domitian the palace covered most of the hill.

BELOW RIGHT The Tiber was the commercial lifeline of Rome, and wharves lined its banks. By the Capitoline hill was an island in the river, part of which can be seen on the left, connected to the main bank by the Roman *pons Fabricius* (bridge of Fabricius). The island was one of the features that drew the original townsfolk to the site.

LEFT Major monuments of Rome. 1 Horti Lucullani. 2 Domus Pinciana. 3 Nymphaeum. 4 Castra Praetoria. 5 Thermae Diocletiani. 6 Horologium. 7 Ustrinum Domus Augustae. 8 Mausdeum Divi Augusti. 9 Castra Praetoria. 10 Circus Gai et Neronis. 11 Mausoleum Hadriadi. 12 Ara Ditis. 13 Stadium. 14 Thermae Neroninae Alexandrinae. 15 Templum Matidae. 16 Templum Serapidis. 17 Thermae Constantini. 18 Macellum Liviae. 19 Piscina Domus Aureae. 20 Porticus Liviae. 21 Thermae Traianae. 22 Thermae Titi. 23 Amphitheatrum Flavium. 24 Colossus. 25 Forum Triani. 26 Templum Triani. 27 Divorum Divibitori. 28 Saepta Iulia. 29 Thermae Agrippae. 30 Porticus Boni Eventus. 31 Odium Domitiani. 32 Theatrum Pompeii. 33 Pons Agrippae. 34 Domus Clodiae. 35 Cellae Vinariae. 36 Porta Septimiana. 37 Pons Aurelius. 38 Porticus Pompeiana. 39 Templum Bellonae. 40 Circus Flaminius. 41 Porticus Philippi. 42 Porticus Octavia. 43 Theatrum Marcelli. 44 Capitolium. 45 Aedes Caesarum. 46 Templum Divi Claudii. 47 Ludus Matutinus. 48 Ludus Dacius. 49 Thermae Heleninae. 50 Amphitheatrum Castrense. 51 Circus Varianus. 52 Posterula. 53 Thermae Antoninanae. 54 Thermae Decianae. 55 Lucus Stimulae. 56 Portus Aemalia. 57 Horrea Galibana.

with sticks in the *comitium*. In compensation vestal virgins were given rights that raised them to the same status as men – they could own property, make a will and they had places reserved for them in the amphitheater. Their house was luxurious and in no way can they be compared to a convent of nuns, as they might appear to be superficially. The cult and the house continued to be used right up to the abolition of pagan religion in AD 391, which is an indication of the reverence with which this spot was regarded.

There were other temples in the forum, of which the most significant is probably that of the deified Julius Caesar. After his assassination his body was taken to the spot in the forum where the temple was later erected and cremated. Augustus, his successor, adopted the eastern custom of deifying heads of state, and put up the temple. This set a precedent, and several other temples were built to dead emperors, both in the forum and elsewhere in the city.

Buildings of a secular nature were also set up in the forum by rich citizens and various emperors. These included the meeting house of the Senate, the *curia*, which survives virtually intact because it was converted into a church in the seventh century. It was a small building, about 91 by 59 feet and had seats on each side with a space in the center. As such it resembles the British House of Commons in layout, but that is as far as the comparison can be taken, for the two facing rows of seats did not have opposing parties in them as there were not really any political parties. After a speech by a leading senator, those who agreed with him would move to sit behind him in the upper tiers of seats. Owing to this, the political complexion of the chamber was always changing, since sides were taken only for separate issues, not for complete programs of policies.

Julius Caesar was responsible for putting up the *curia*; he also set up the *basilica Julia* and a new forum. The former was a large hall used for court hearings and for business transactions, chiefly banking. The latter was a new open space, like the old forum just next to it, designed principally for legal business. In his *Art of Love* the poet Ovid describes the lovesick advocates practicing in front of the temple of Venus in this forum.

Apart from glorifying his name, Caesar built a new forum because the old one was becoming too small for efficient use: the population had grown, business was expanding and the increasing number of monuments and buildings was making less rather than more space available. This trend continued and even intensified after his death, which led other emperors to follow his example and build new forums. The culmination of this process took place under Trajan when he built his massive forum and basilica beside the others put up by Augustus, Vespasian and Nerva. Together they form one of the masterpieces of ancient town planning, and were rightly considered one of the marvels of the city.

Each forum had a different purpose. Augustus' contained the temple of Mars Ultor (Mars 'the avenger'), and also a large number of statues to Roman heroes. Several of these were of members of Augustus' own family, the Julians, and it can be seen that the forum was a subtle piece of propaganda for his claims to be *princeps* (the principal Roman). It also was meant to be a celebration and shrine to Roman success at arms, and Augustus decreed that the Senate should meet in the temple when questions of war were to be discussed. Generals were ceremonially escorted there, presumably for the inspiration of the deeds of the dead heroes that surrounded them, before being sent out on their commands. By contrast, the forum of Vespasian went by the more common name of the Temple of Peace, and it seems to have had formal gardens laid out in it that were adorned with statues and works of art by the Greek masters. There were libraries next to the temple itself, the wall of one having a very

LEFT Emperor Marcus Aurelius, veiled in his capacity as chief priest, offering a sacrifice in front of a temple.

RIGHT One of several Imperial triumphal arches that adorned the forum and surrounding streets of the city. This one was set up by Titus on the *via sacra* near the House of the Vestal Virgins. On the frieze inside the arch can be seen the seven-branched candlestick (*menorah*) from the Temple in Jerusalem, which came to Rome after Jerusalem was sacked in AD 70.

LEFT Trajan's Column, the centerpiece of that emperor's forum. It depicts his Dacian wars (AD 102–6) in a scroll unfurling from the bottom of the column. The sculpture provides a unique portrait of the Roman army.

ABOVE The Temple of Vesta in the foreground, and the Temple of Antoninus and Faustina behind, two of the most prominent remains in the Roman forum.

RIGHT The *curia* (Senate house), as rebuilt by Diocletian. It is in the forum, and has only survived because of its conversion to a church in Medieval times.

accurate marble city plan laid on it. However, even here there were spoils of war – the temple contained the Jewish temple treasures from Jerusalem, including the cult image and the famous seven-branched candlestick given by Solomon. Nerva's forum was also known as the Forum Transitorium (the passage-way) because it linked those of Augustus and Vespasian and was also one of the main thoroughfares to the old forum just to the south.

Trajan's forum surpassed all these in size and in architectural conception. It marks the high point of Imperial confidence and achievement, for its central monument, a sculpted column narrating Trajan's war against the Dacians, was set up at a time when the empire was at its fullest extent. The main theme of the forum was military; apart from the column itself, the basilica was decorated with sculpture and friezes that glorified the achievements of the Roman army, and it was surmounted by a sculpture of Trajan in a quadriga (four-horse chariot). In fact, it has been pointed out that the overall layout of the forum is very similar to the headquarters of a Roman fort. However, it was not devoted entirely to the army, for there were two libraries on either side of the column, one for Latin and the other for Greek scrolls. The southern end of the basilica was known as the *atrium libertatis* (hall of liberty) because it was here that slaves could be officially freed by their masters.

Just to the north of Trajan's forum, but built at the same time as it, was a series of shops and a covered market terraced into the hillside. Doubtless these represent some attempt on the part of the emperor to compensate the dispossessed citizens who had been moved away from the ground where his forum was to be built. They survive largely intact and are among the best examples of utilitarian architecture anywhere in the empire. Also, they are evidence of one of the results of the vast expansion of the area of the forums over the previous 150 years – ordinary shops and day-to-day trade were gradually pushed out from the central area of the city to be replaced by services such as banking, legal advice and teaching. As the city adapted to being the hub of an empire, so the roles its citizens played became more complex and more ordinary activities began to take second place.

Another area of the city just outside the central district also became a monumental zone, with temples, arches, theaters and

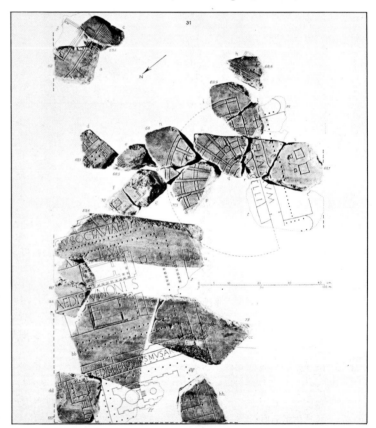

ABOVE Part of the building scheme of Trajan's forum was the provision of shops and covered markets in surrounding streets for traders. Shown above are some of the shops in the *via Biberatica*.

ABOVE RIGHT A section of the remarkably accurate marble map of Rome, at a scale of 1 in 300, originally put up in the Temple of Peace in Severan times. It shows the theater of Marcellus (see opposite).

RIGHT The ordinary housing in Rome consisted of crowded tenement blocks. This model is of a tenement block in Ostia.

columns adorning it. This was the Campus Martius, just to the west of the Capitoline hill on a flat area enclosed by a bend in the river Tiber. It was traditionally a public open space where the people could assemble for voting, for army conscription and for exercise. The earliest buildings were associated with these activities, the most important being the Saepta where voting for the consuls and other magistrates took place, and the Villa Publica where the censors counted the Roman people every five years. However, from the second century BC a mass of other structures began to be built over the campus, never totally covering its large area, but nevertheless confining the open space more and more. Some of the new buildings were for entertainment, such as the horse-racing track or *circus* under the modern piazza Navona, or the three theaters of Pompey, Balbus and Marcellus. The majority were religious, however. Since it was outside the official city limits, burials could take place in this area, and so there were several important tombs, to emperors such as Augustus and Hadrian (just over the river), and the *ustrina* (funeral pyres) on which their bodies were cremated.

Besides these, there were many temples, of which the most famous is the Pantheon. This building survives almost exactly as it was in the Roman period, because Emperor Phocas presented it to Pope Boniface VIII in AD 608 and it was subsequently preserved as the church of St Mary ad Martyres. It is one of the most impressive of Roman monuments anywhere and once held the record for the largest dome ever built, with a diameter of 140 Roman feet. However, ancient literary references to it are scarce and contradictory, with the result that it is not

entirely clear why it was dedicated to 'all gods' as its name suggests. Even its date of construction is a source of confusion, for over the porch is an inscription that reads M AGRIPPA L F COS TERTIUM FECIT (Marcus Agrippa, son of Lucius, built this when consul for the third time – that is 27–25 BC), yet the circular building is of later date, from the time of Hadrian. We do not know why Hadrian decided to rebuild the temple, nor why he changed its shape from an ordinary temple to the one we can see today, nor why he altered the entrance from one end of the building to the other. There are also some intriguing mysteries about its internal details. For instance, the distance from the top of the dome to the floor is the same as the diameter of 140 feet. This allows a sphere of that size to be just fitted inside. In addition, there are seven divisions in the dome, including the open *oculus* right at the very top, and seven niches for the planetary gods. These numbers and proportions were obviously deliberate features of the construction, but their significance eludes historians, except that they are probably astrological in some way. As the poet Shelley wrote 'it is, as it were, the visible image of the universe.'

From the parts of the city looked at so far, it would be very easy to think that Rome consisted of nothing but temples and forums. Of course there were also people, around 1,250,000 to 1,500,000 of them, according to modern estimates. The city was filled with tenement buildings, often up to five- or six-stories high, and by all accounts was vastly overcrowded, with rabbit warrens of narrow winding streets that were filled with pushing crowds during the day and by rumbling and clattering carriages at night. That, at least, is the picture painted by poets such as Martial and Juvenal, whose satires and epigrams on daily life are such a valuable complement to the mute evidence available from archaeology.

BELOW The theater of Marcellus, still largely intact under medieval and modern buildings. It could hold about 14,000 people.

The Colosseum, Rome's famous
amphitheater, built by Vespasian and Titus
on the site of the gardens of Nero's infamous
Golden House.

One of the large tenement blocks has been excavated, and is visible just below the Capitoline hill on the side facing the Campus Martius. Excavated is perhaps the wrong word, because it was preserved, remarkably, within modern buildings, that were removed to expose the ancient remains. At ground level there was a series of shops, with mezzanine floors above them and a portico in front to shade passers-by. Above these two floors were at least another three of living quarters, divided into small *cenacula* (flats). The number of occupants is estimated to

LEFT The large public baths were often adorned with sculpture. The Punishment of Circe was in the Baths of Caracalla.

have been 380, living in far from comfortable conditions, with no water supply or sanitation. There was also the constant fear of fire or collapse owing to the poor state of repair of the tenements.

The bread was handed out by the state to the poor free citizens of Rome, who for the most part had no work. In Julius Caesar's time 150,000 received it, and the number rose dramatically after that, so that by the third century AD up to 1,000,000 had free bread, and also oil and occasionally pork. Its supply was a major undertaking. A port was specifically developed at the mouth of the river, at Ostia, to cope with the enormous inflow of supplies from different parts of the empire. At Ostia goods were moved from sea-going vessels to river barges which then transported the goods upstream to warehouses in the city. The banks of the Tiber were lined with storage facilities, and there were large markets such as the forum Boarium and the forum Holitorium for dealing in the goods. One of the most impressive remains of all this activity is the Monte Testaccio (Hill of Sherds) which is a large mound about 100 feet high and five-eighths of a mile in circumference. It is completely artificial, consisting entirely of broken pieces of *amphorae*, the containers used to transport oil and wine in bulk. It is next to the river-side warehouses, and presumably was a rubbish dump for these containers after they had been unloaded from the barges. An estimate of the quantity of *amphorae* has never been made, but their numbers must run

BELOW In AD 272 Emperor Aurelian started to build a new defensive wall, here seen at the Porta Appia.

into millions, and they provide a glimpse of the extraordinary organization needed to provide food for all the hungry mouths living in the ancient world's largest city.

Since most of Rome's population was unemployed, or at best only occasionally working, the emperors felt it necessary to provide entertainment as well as food, in order to insure against public disorder. Hence the *circenses* (horse-racing) and other public spectacles, which by the time of Trajan took place every other day. Several different sorts of sport formed the core of these spectacles, which were ostensibly religious celebrations. The most popular were shows of wild beasts and gladiators in the amphitheater, and there were often lavish and, to us, barbaric displays in which scores of animals were killed in the arena. For instance, after the Colosseum was completed in AD 80, 5000 wild animals were killed during the hundred days of dedicatory games.

The other favorite sport was horse and chariot racing, the most famous of the surviving tracks being the Circus Maximus, which the ancient writer Pliny said was capable of holding 250,000 spectators. The riders were divided into 'factions,' each with a different color, with, of course, similar divisions among the spectators. The factions were sharply divided and sometimes violently partisan, much like a modern football crowd, although the divisions in Roman times were taken further and eventually began to take on the character of mob political parties that were a threat to imperial authority. However, little was done about them, as the emperors relied on the support of the mass of citizens living in Rome to keep them in power. They often introduced popular measures in order to curry favor from the people, which had the secondary effect of reducing the power and influence of the Senate. In this way the emperors were able to maintain themselves in power while their support from the Senate and from people living outside Rome was at a low ebb. Another, more dictatorial, way was to use the army, an organization examined in more detail in the following chapter.

LEFT Coin of Nero showing the harbor at Ostia built by Claudius.

RIGHT The interior of Hadrian's Pantheon, painted by G B Pannini in 1749.

BELOW Lining the roads leading from the city were tombs, such as this one of Caecilia Metella on the Via Appia. Burials were not allowed within the city limits for religious reasons.

INTEREST IN ARCHAEOLOGY

Modern interest in the remains of ancient civilizations is part of the long history of the preservation of the memory of the Greeks and Romans. This history begins, in effect, after the fall of the western Roman Empire in the fifth century. At that time Latin was still the sole language, at least among the learned classes, and it was to continue as such for some time thereafter. Manuscripts of the classics were preserved, and copies made, in order to teach Latin grammar and literature. The task of making the copies and handing on the knowledge of Latin fell to Christian monks, who were actively setting up monasteries throughout Europe from the sixth century as centers of learning and Christianity.

Charlemagne was the first medieval ruler to revive interest in the Roman period, which he did as part of a deliberate policy of putting forward his own kingdom as the natural inheritor of Roman power and greatness. Later in the Middle Ages, however, the ancient world receded from the popular consciousness, and the study of classical texts languished. The next major upsurge in interest was, of course, during the Renaissance. Starting with such scholars as Dante, Petrarch and

Boccaccio in the fourteenth century, the monastic libraries were quarried for their classical texts. New editions of the ancient authors came out, with studious commentaries on their style and contents. Classical ideas of learning and philosophy spread rapidly, with the result that a new spirit of enquiry into history, science and medicine emerged. One of the new interests was archaeology.

In the fifteenth and sixteenth centuries, students who were actively pursuing the study of the ancient texts widened their scope of enquiry to include the actual remains left behind by the Greeks and Romans. At first, the surviving buildings in Rome, such as the Pantheon, the Colosseum and the Baths of Caracalla, and artifacts dug up from sites, such as statues and coins, were used as examples of the buildings and objects in use at the time that the texts were written. In other words, the ancient texts ruled supreme as the main focus of study – archaeology was subordinate, at this time merely an illustrative appendix. The emergence of archaeology as a subject worthy of study in its own right was to come later, in the late seventeenth and eighteenth centuries. The origins of modern archaeology are, however, to be seen in this shift away from the texts alone to the physical remains as well. Mercati in the sixteenth century was

the first to write a treatise on what we would regard today as archaeology. At the same time, academic societies were being founded to promote the investigation of natural phenomena, including archaeology.

The next stage in the emergence of Roman archaeology was the development of an esthetic appreciation of ancient art and architecture. Artists such as Palladio, Piranesi and Winkelmann drew and recorded surviving buildings and sculptures. Out of Palladio's architectural work came much of the inspiration for the neoclassical revival of the eighteenth century. Winkelmann is best known as an art historian, whose judgments on ancient art were to color opinions about the Greeks and Romans for most of the neoclassical period. He maintained that Roman art was inferior to Greek as it slavishly copied the Greek originals. As can be seen in chapter eight, this judgment may be true up to a point, but at the time it prejudiced many people against Roman art, and Roman archaeology became less popular as a result.

Excavations of ancient sites started in the eighteenth century with the ransacking of Herculaneum and Pompeii for statues and other works of art. At the same time, expeditions were being organized by such groups as the Society of Dilettanti

LEFT Manuscripts, such as this one of Vergil's *Aeneid*, were preserved by Medieval monks. Later, they were rediscovered by Renaissance scholars, with the result that interest in the Roman world revived.

BELOW The Arch of Titus by d'Overbeke, 1709. Compare its present state as illustrated on page 29.

ABOVE The Arch of Septimius Severus, engraved by du Pérac, 1575, which helped arouse interest in Roman art.

ABOVE RIGHT Modern excavations, as here at Hayling Island Roman temple, uncover large areas of ground.

for the purpose of carrying off sculpture and ancient art objects for private and public collections in northern Europe. Museums such as the British Museum were founded and soon filled to bursting with material of all kinds, including Roman finds. The accumulation of artifacts, and the increasingly enthusiastic appreciation of the ancient world by the leisured classes, led to a more rigorous historical approach on the part of scholars, exemplified by Edward Gibbon's *Decline and Fall of the Roman Empire* (1788). More scientific excavations started with the planned program of King Murat to uncover all of Pompeii in the 1810s, which he decided to do not only to recover works of art, but also to discover the ancient town plan. Upstanding monuments elsewhere started to be conserved and treasured as part of Europe's heritage.

After the early years of the nineteenth century, public interest in the ancient world changed. No longer were the Greeks and Romans used as the inspiration of contemporary writings, architecture and art, for fashions were changing from the neoclassical to the romantic and the Gothic revival. Roman history and archaeology became a more academic discipline, with such great scholars as Theodor Mommsen laying the foundations of the modern study of the subject. The archaeological contribution to Roman history began to realize its true potential, especially in the provinces outside Italy, where large-scale excavations at the end of the nineteenth century led to a much clearer understanding of the great differences between the various regions of the empire. A good example is the complete excavation of the Roman town of Calleva (Silchester, Hampshire, England), by the Society of Antiquaries.

From the beginning of the twentieth century, excavations have been carried out in every part of the Roman world, usually for sound academic reasons, but occasionally for political ends, such as Mussolini's identification of his own government with the greatness of the Roman Empire, and the consequent rather hasty excavation of large areas of ancient Rome. The techniques in use made steady progress; in the 1920s Sir Mortimer Wheeler developed and applied the concepts of archaeological stratigraphy, with the result that excavators could date and understand their sites much more accurately. More recently, scientific techniques of analysis such as carbon dating, and ever closer control of the process of excavation have meant that archaeologists now have the ability to recover the most fragile of objects, and to record and understand what was happening in ancient times in minute detail.

Public interest in Roman archaeology has become ever stronger in recent years. The growth of tourism is the main reason for this, because it is now possible to visit the major sites of the Roman world relatively cheaply and comfortably. Archaeological societies, too, play their part by encouraging excavations and active participation in the discovery of new sites. Such activities, and the interest in Roman archaeology, will continue to expand with the increasing leisure time available in the modern world.

LEFT The neoclassical revival led to the construction of many buildings in Greek and Roman style. Greek architecture was preferred, as here at The Grange, Hampshire (1809), largely because of Winkelmann's unjustified condemnation of Roman art.

CHAPTER III
THE IMPERIAL ARMY

It has been said that the Roman imperial army was so successful that the Senate and the emperors were constantly trying to catch up with the problems of administering the areas conquered by the legions. The Roman army was a fighting force without parallel in the ancient world, and it remained undefeated in any major campaign which was adequately manned and competently led. In addition, there are numerous records of outnumbered Roman units inflicting defeats on enemy forces. Such successes are not easy to explain, but possible reasons are explored in this chapter.

The structure of the army must have made a major contribution to its success. Its most important unit was the legion, approximately the equivalent of the modern regiment. Legions formed the mainstay of any expeditionary force and were under the command of a high-ranking officer or, quite often, the emperor himself. There were about 30 legions by the time of Augustus' reign, each made up of 6000 infantry when fully manned. There were 10 cohorts in a legion, each of six centuries 80 to 100 men strong.

The centuries were commanded by centurions, men promoted out of the ranks, and who were the key to one of the organizational strengths of the Roman army. The rank of centurion was the highest of the permanent posts in the army, more senior officers having short-term appointments only. The centurions were quite often elected by the men from out of their own ranks, and were generally the most courageous and respected men in the legion. Besides having responsibility for training and discipline, they led the centuries into battle, often being commended by their generals for prowess in the forefront of the fighting. For instance, in a telling passage on the rivalry between two centurions, Pullo and Vorenus, for the post of senior centurion (equivalent of sergeant major), Caesar gives us an insight into the ambitions that motivated such men into heroic acts.

'In the thick of the fighting by the ramparts, Pullo said, "Why hesitate, Vorenus? What sort of chance are you waiting for to prove your courage? Today will be the judge of our rivalry." As he said this, he climbed down the ramparts and threw himself upon the most closely packed group of the enemy. Vorenus followed close behind, in fear of what the men would think if he did not.'

This spirit of obtaining personal recognition and promotion through bravery was obviously one of the factors in the success of the army, although the discipline of training made it rare for such acts to be foolhardy.

The upper ranks were all drawn from the senatorial classes and the *equites*, and usually held their posts for a few years only, continuing, to a certain extent, the early tradition of an army that was formed anew for each summer fighting season. Tribunes commanded each cohort, and a legionary legate was in overall charge of the legion. Since these posts were never in the hands of one person for very long, there was a continual replenishment of talent for leadership and tactics. This ensured that legions did not become stale, and if there was incompetent leadership, a replacement could easily be made. However, it was the long-term service of the men themselves (usually 20–25 years) that provided the essential continuity of tradition and practice necessary for a fighting unit to sustain its morale.

The legions formed the core of the army, but a major contribution to Rome's fighting capability was made by the auxiliary troops. These were originally men provided by the Italian allies of Rome during the Republic, but in imperial times they were usually drawn from newly conquered provinces. In this way recent enemies could be made use of, and not left idle to foment rebellion. They were formed into small units of 500 or 1000 men, and could be infantry, cavalry or part-mounted. One of the inducements to joining the auxiliaries was the award of citizenship after completion of service, and the men often retained the use of their native dress and weapons, such as the units of Syrian archers or Balearic slingers. The main use of the auxiliaries was to provide assistance on the flanks of the legions during battle, and to patrol and garrison frontier regions. As time wore on during the empire, and there were fewer and fewer new conquests, defense became an increasingly important part of the army's role. This meant that the auxiliaries came to assume a dominant position in the army, which eventually led to the eclipse of the legion as a fighting unit.

Other units that formed an integral part of the army were the *exploratores* (scouts), the small unit of 120 cavalry attached to each legion to help with reconnaissance, the *numeri* or *cunei* of irregular troops, who were often mercenaries, and the navy, which ensured supplies.

The navy did not form a major part of Roman military strength, for unlike the Greeks, the Romans had no naval tradition. It was regarded very much as the junior branch, its men receiving lower pay (indeed some were slaves), and its role

LEFT Praetorian guardsmen in full regalia. They were the élite bodyguard of the emperor, based in Rome, and the only troops in Italy for most of the period of the empire.

43

was largely to supply the army and suppress piracy. Nevertheless, there were occasions when the navy played a more dominant part, for instance in sea battles, the most famous being at Actium in 31 BC, or in seaborne invasions, such as that of Britain in AD 43. Even in sea battles, however, the actual fighting was usually done by legionaries.

The navy's warships were all rowing craft of Greek type, usually with a sail for assistance, and equipped with a prow for ramming and sinking enemy vessels. There were also smaller patrol craft, which were sometimes camouflaged.

The supply role of the navy is very well illustrated by the results of excavations in Britain. In the Weald, in southeast England, numbers of iron-smelting furnaces have been found that are connected with the *classis britannica* (British fleet). It seems that the iron was being extracted to make weapons for the army stationed further north. The fleet also made roofing tiles for military buildings, and was responsible for shipping troops, supplies and official passengers across the Channel.

The role of the navy allows us to see that the army as a whole was very well organized. Presumably it had to be, in order to be able to push deep into enemy territory or sustain a military campaign far from base. One aspect of their organization was the degree of standardization. Equipment appears to have been made to specific patterns at Imperial *fabricae* (workshops), and routines and instructions were carefully worked out and written down in military manuals so that, as far as possible, practices were always carried out in the same way wherever the army was. Some of these manuals have survived and, together with papyri and other sources of information, they give a detailed picture of the soldier as part of a disciplined and well-oiled system, which presumably operated in very much the same way in every part of the empire. This made it easy for the men and units to be

ABOVE The tombstone of Caecilius, a centurion who died in the defeat in Germany in AD 9. Note the vine stick, his symbol of office, and the medals on his breastplate.

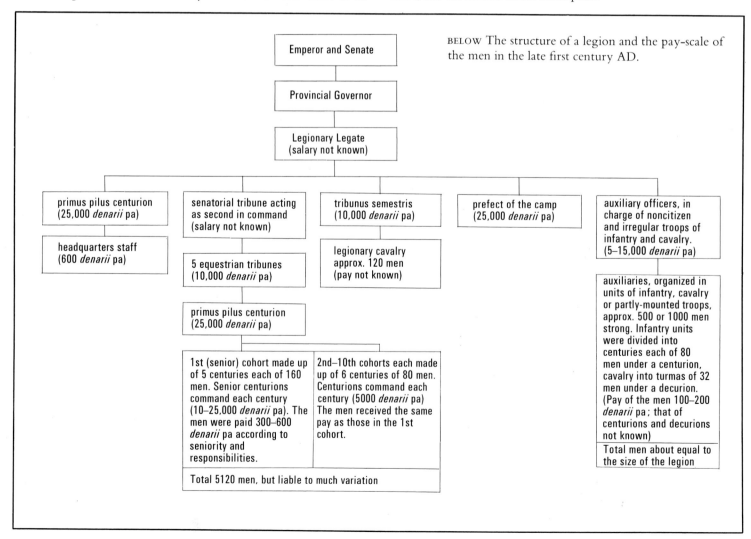

BELOW The structure of a legion and the pay-scale of the men in the late first century AD.

Emperor and Senate

Provincial Governor

Legionary Legate (salary not known)

| primus pilus centurion (25,000 *denarii* pa) | senatorial tribune acting as second in command (salary not known) | tribunus semestris (10,000 *denarii* pa) | prefect of the camp (25,000 *denarii* pa) | auxiliary officers, in charge of noncitizen and irregular troops of infantry and cavalry. (5–15,000 *denarii* pa) |

headquarters staff (600 *denarii* pa)

5 equestrian tribunes (10,000 *denarii* pa)

legionary cavalry approx. 120 men (pay not known)

primus pilus centurion (25,000 *denarii* pa)

| 1st (senior) cohort made up of 5 centuries each of 160 men. Senior centurions command each century (10–25,000 *denarii* pa). The men were paid 300–600 *denarii* pa according to seniority and responsibilities. | 2nd–10th cohorts each made up of 6 centuries of 80 men. Centurions command each century (5000 *denarii* pa) The men received the same pay as those in the 1st cohort. |

Total 5120 men, but liable to much variation

auxiliaries, organized in units of infantry, cavalry or partly-mounted troops, approx. 500 or 1000 men strong. Infantry units were divided into centuries each of 80 men under a centurion, cavalry into turmas of 32 men under a decurion. (Pay of the men 100–200 *denarii* pa; that of centurions and decurions not known)

Total men about equal to the size of the legion

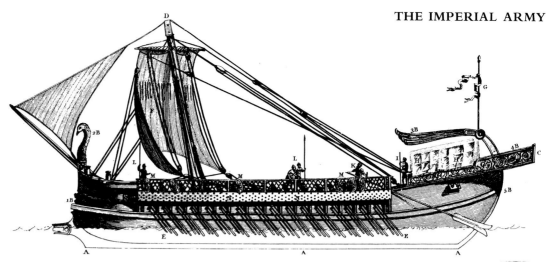

RIGHT Although the Romans used sail on long passages, it was oars which gave them speed and maneuverability in battle.

BELOW A battle scene from Trajan's Column.

BELOW RIGHT Another scene from Trajan's Column showing the troops crossing a bridge at the start of the Dacian wars.

BOTTOM Legionaries and cavalrymen in a display organized as a mock battle.

posted to where they were needed with the minimum of fuss. Another conclusion to be drawn from the apparent conformity of the army to a specific set of rules and a fairly standardized personal kit is that this helped the individual soldier to feel himself part of a coherent unified body. This was very different from the armies of most of Rome's opponents, and may well have contributed to the long-term success of the army.

Good training was another factor in the effectiveness of the imperial forces, and it began as soon as a recruit applied to join a legion. After a check that he was a Roman citizen and medically fit, he was sent for basic training, which consisted initially of route marching – 20 Roman miles ($18\frac{1}{4}$ modern miles) in five hours. This was followed by physical training and marching with heavy packs, all of which must be depressingly familiar to anyone who has himself served in an army. Modern and ancient training

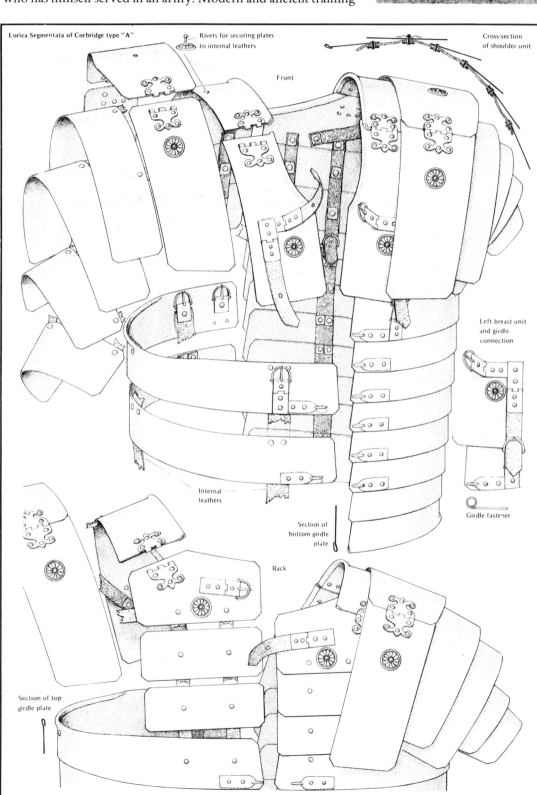

Lorica Segmentata of Corbridge type "A"
Rivets for securing plates to internal leathers
Cross-section of shoulder unit
Front
Left breast unit and girdle connection
Internal leathers
Girdle fastener
Section of bottom girdle plate
Back
Section of top girdle plate

ABOVE Reconstruction of a *ballista* (mechanical cross-bow), which was part of the equipment of every legion. The box-like frame on the machine contained the twisted sinews that provided the motive power.

LEFT A legionary's *lorica segmentata*. Since it was made of iron hoops and strips, it gave far better protection than the armor of most of Rome's enemies.

BELOW A *pugio* (dagger) was one of the standard weapons, together with a *gladius* (sword) and a *pilum* (throwing spear)

ABOVE A highly decorated cavalry sports helmet from Ribchester.

begins to differ, however, when weapons start to be used, for the sword, not the rifle, was the basic piece of equipment in Roman times. Vegetius, the writer of a military manual, says that recruits were trained with

'round wickerwork shields, twice as heavy as those of service weight, and wooden staves instead of swords, again of double weight. With these they were made to practice at the stakes both morning and afternoon. No man has ever distinguished himself as invincible in armed combat who was not carefully trained and instructed at the stakes.'

These stakes were firmly placed vertical poles about six feet high, and were dummy adversaries for target practice.

Training was progressive, and the recruit moved on to the use of real weapons and human opponents. After mastering the sword, the throwing spear was introduced, and after this the two weapons were combined in single exercises. This training in weapons continued throughout a soldier's length of service,

besides which there was regular marching in full kit, and practice in laying out and building overnight camps.

The kit that a soldier carried while on the march seems to have been about the same weight as that carried by modern soldiers, about 66 lb. Judging from depictions of soldiers on sculpture, supplemented by the many archaeological finds, it was made up of his weapons (a *gladius* or short stabbing sword, a *pilum* or throwing spear and a *pugio* or dagger), his defensive armor (a *scutum* or large rectangular or oval shield, a *galea* or iron helmet, and a *lorica* or suit of body armor) and lastly his other kit (bedding, cooking pans and foraging equipment such as a *dolabra* or axe). Each century also had donkeys or mules to carry heavy equipment such as the leather tents and the stones for grinding corn. In addition a fully equipped century would have had a *carroballista* (large crossbow).

Two items of equipment are of greater interest, as they show quite clearly how well the legionaries were provided for, in order to improve their fighting capability. Body armor and helmets were issued to each man (paid for by money deducted from his pay). The easiest type of armor to make, and therefore in use from an early date, was made of small iron or bronze scales, each about one inch by one-and-a-half inches, threaded together onto a leather jerkin. Generally speaking, the jerkin was short sleeved and protected the chest and abdomen only, arms and legs being left free to allow for easy movement. Chain-mail and laminate plated armor were introduced later. Interestingly, it seems that chain mail was not first developed by the Romans, but by the Gauls; it is a case of the Romans borrowing from their enemies in order to improve their own effectiveness. The suit of *lorica segnentatu* (laminated plates) was, however, a Roman development of the Early Empire, and it became the typical garb of the legionary in action.

Among the more interesting aspects of the Roman army is that of pay. The surviving records form the only complete pay scale from the ancient world, and they give a fascinating insight into the relative levels of wealth in the Roman Empire. The most important point that can be made is the enormous difference between the pay of the lower ranks and that of the permanent officers. By comparison, the average pay of the more lowly-paid modern workers is only in the order of 10 times less than the pay of chief executives. Obviously, the rich in the Roman world were very rich, and the poor very poor; and the army's pay was a reflection of that state of affairs. One of the other important points is the possibility of a private soldier being promoted to one of the officer posts and thereby raising his social status. In fact it

was possible for an ambitious soldier to accumulate enough money, if he became a senior centurion, to be accepted into the ranks of the *equites*. The Roman army offered the chance of social advancement, difficult to obtain in other walks of life.

The principal role of the army during the empire was to invade and occupy new territory, which inevitably meant fighting many battles. In common with the other armies of the Mediterranean powers, Roman forces were largely composed of infantry, and it was the tactics of fighting on foot that dominated military thinking. In battle formation, infantry normally took the central zone, with cavalry and auxiliaries guarding the flanks. The infantry was positioned in three ranks, so that there were always two groups of fresh men behind the front line. Each man was allocated a lateral space of three feet and, for a typical battle, there was generally an infantry force about 10,000 strong arranged in a rectangle about 1500 by 12 yards.

For the atmosphere of a Roman battle, it is best to turn to Caesar's writings, as his commentaries on the Gallic and Civil Wars give a vivid account of what it was like to be in the thick of the fighting. In this passage he relates a surprise attack by one of the Celtic tribes of northern France in 57 BC.

'The Nervii advanced at such incredible speed that it looked as though they were at the edge of the woods, in the river and on top of us all in the same moment. They swarmed up the opposite hill toward our camp and onto the troops building the fortifications.

BELOW AND RIGHT Skeletons of Britons from Maiden Castle, Dorset. The body in the foreground has a Roman *ballista* bolt lodged in its spine that entered from the front (in detail, right).

I had to do everything at once – raise the flag, sound the trumpet for action, call the men away from their work, form them into battle order, address them and give the signal for attack. As the enemy was almost upon us there was no time to do most of these things, but we were helped by two factors; first, the training and experience of the troops enabled them to dispense with orders and judge for themselves what should be done; and second, since the commanders were with their units supervising the fortification work, they were able to do what they thought best on their own initiative, without waiting for my orders.'

As might be expected, Caesar went on to defeat the Gauls decisively. Another account, from the Civil War, gives a good idea of the tactics of a battle, this time against Pompey's troops at Pharsalus in 48 BC.

'Our men, on the signal, ran forward with javelins levelled, but when they saw that Pompey's men were not running to meet them, they stopped, so as not to be worn out. After a while they renewed the charge, threw their javelins and, as ordered by Caesar, quickly drew their swords. The Pompeians did not fail to meet the occasion. They stood up to the hail of missiles, kept their ranks, threw their javelins and then resorted to their swords. At the same time their cavalry all charged forward, as instructed, from Pompey's left wing, and the archers rushed out. Our cavalry failed to withstand the onslaught and were dislodged from their position. Pompey's cavalry pressed on more hotly as a result and began to surround our line on its exposed flank. Observing this Caesar gave the signal to the fourth line, which was formed of single cohorts. They ran forward swiftly to the attack, and charged at

Pompey's cavalry with such force that none of them could hold ground. They all turned and fled headlong to the hills. Their withdrawal left the archers and slingers exposed, and, unarmed and unprotected, they were killed. In the same charge the cohorts surrounded the Pompeians who were still fighting and putting up a resistance on the left wing, and attacked them in the rear. At the same time Caesar gave orders for the third line to advance; it had stayed in its position doing nothing up until then. Consequently, because fresh and unscathed troops took the place of tired ones, while others were attacking from the rear, the Pompeians could not hold out, and they all turned and fled.'

There are records of many of the battles that the Romans fought, either against an enemy or among themselves. The chief source for their location is the writings of ancient historians, as few battle sites have ever been detected through archaeology. This is probably because the victorious troops and local scavengers usually removed all the bodies and equipment after a battle.

In addition to fighting battles, an important part of any ancient army's capability was to be able to lay siege to a town or fort, and few sustained campaigns were completed without one. By far the best-known Roman siege is that of Masada, where the last of the Zealots resisting Roman rule were entrenched in a superbly defended fortress overlooking the Dead Sea. After Jerusalem fell in AD 70, this fortress became the base from which the Zealots could harry the Romans and so, in AD 72, the Roman general Flavius Silva laid siege to it with the Tenth Legion, its associated auxiliaries and thousands of Jewish prisoners of war. Silva was faced with enormous problems – Masada is an isolated

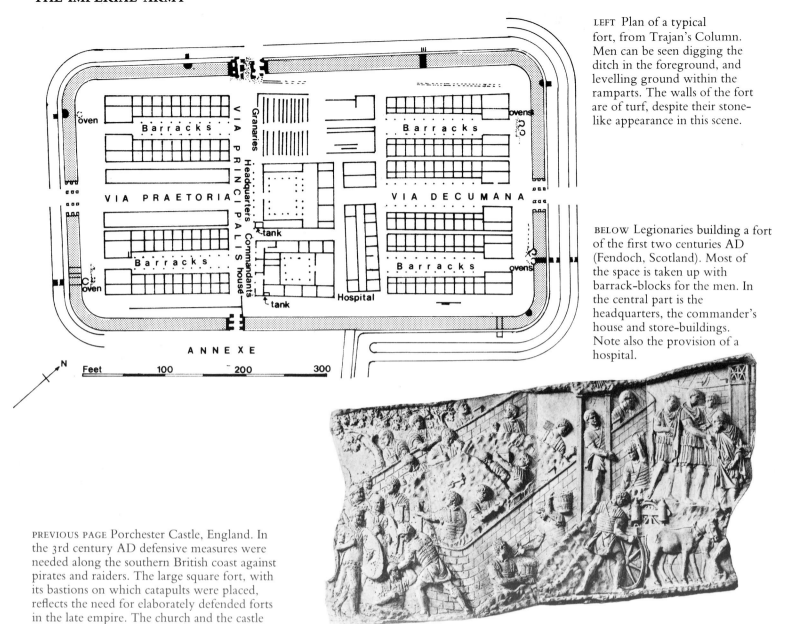

LEFT Plan of a typical fort, from Trajan's Column. Men can be seen digging the ditch in the foreground, and levelling ground within the ramparts. The walls of the fort are of turf, despite their stone-like appearance in this scene.

BELOW Legionaries building a fort of the first two centuries AD (Fendoch, Scotland). Most of the space is taken up with barrack-blocks for the men. In the central part is the headquarters, the commander's house and store-buildings. Note also the provision of a hospital.

PREVIOUS PAGE Porchester Castle, England. In the 3rd century AD defensive measures were needed along the southern British coast against pirates and raiders. The large square fort, with its bastions on which catapults were placed, reflects the need for elaborately defended forts in the late empire. The church and the castle keep in the left-hand corner are Norman.

flat hill-top with steep cliffs on every side, rising about 1200 feet from the floor of the desert-like Dead Sea basin. It was also fortified with a wall running around the rim of the cliffs. Accordingly he followed the standard practice of enclosing the hill in a circumvallation to prevent the defenders from breaking out, or new supplies being brought to them, and settled down to wait for the Zealots' submission. The wall was 3800 yards long and six feet thick, with towers at intervals. Doubtless it was also built to lower the morale of the defenders, as the surviving remains indicate that the wall was much stronger than it needed to be for tactical reasons alone. In addition to the wall, eight camps were built at various points around its perimeter, two large ones for the legion, and the smaller ones for the auxiliaries. Owing to the desert conditions, these camps are almost perfectly preserved and it is still possible to see the stone emplacements on which the tents stood, and the stone benches within the tents for sleeping and eating.

The considerable effort put into the wall and camps is over-shadowed by the work undertaken by Silva to breach the defenses on top of Masada. He constructed an enormous earth ramp on the western side, about 650 feet long and 350 feet high, on which to push up a siege tower against the walls of the fortress. This tower would have been wooden with iron-plate armor, and was designed to overshadow the defense towers. From the siege tower the Romans could drive the defenders from the

defenses, meanwhile using a battering ram in the base of the tower to breach the wall. In the graphic account of the siege by the Jewish historian Josephus, we are told that this is what in fact happened, but that the defenders promptly built another wall within the first, made of earth so that it could not be battered down easily. However, Silva managed to set fire to the timbers which held the earth wall together, and the strong wind from the south quickly spread the fire throughout the rampart. At this stage Silva retired, resolving to capture the fortress the next day. The Zealots could not take any effective measures to counter this planned assault, and so they decided that the Romans should not take them alive. In the most dramatic move of the whole long siege, 960 men, women and children committed suicide, leaving only two women and five children to greet the Romans as they clambered over the defenses on the following day. In Josephus' words, 'The Romans could not do other than wonder at the courage of the Zealots' resolution, and at the immovable contempt of death which so many of them had shown when they went through with such an action.'

Masada was by no means the bloodiest siege in Roman history, that dubious honor probably going to the siege of Jerusalem three years earlier, but it is certainly the best documented, both by Josephus' account and by the remains still to be seen. It is also a remarkable testimony to the logistical strength of the Roman army, as well as to the dedicated resolve of the defenders.

The camps set up by Flavius Silva at Masada are good examples of the accommodation provided for the troops while on campaign. Each night the army was supposed to build a temporary defense, particularly while in enemy territory, and written records show that the order of march was arranged so that these camps could be laid out with the minimum of fuss and confusion. Each century was allocated a stretch of defenses to build, and the tents for the men and officers were always laid out in the same way, as illustrated. If the terrain allowed, a playing-card shape was adopted, with four or six gateways. In the center was the *principia* (headquarters building), the *praetorium* (commander's quarters), *horrea* (store buildings), sometimes a *valetudinarium* (hospital) and other buildings such as *fabricae* (workshops). The men were placed at each end of the camp, in century and cohort order. Each single row of tents equipped a century, the centurion and his orderlies occupying a big tent at the end and the remaining, rather smaller, tents for a *contubernium* (mess) of six to eight men each. The space allocated to the different ranks varied enormously, in very much the same way as the pay scale.

Although the arrangements just described are for temporary camps, they apply equally well to more permanent forts, such as those set up to garrison frontier regions. Large numbers of these forts are known, either because the remains survive, or through excavation. The better preserved structural remains allow archaeologists to add some details to the camp layout given above. For instance, each *contubernium* was divided into two, the rear part for sleeping and the front part for eating and storage. Bread ovens and corn-grinding emplacements were provided for each century. The ovens were placed in the ramparts as they were a fire risk; the ramparts also housed the latrines for sanitary reasons. Often the forts were supplied with running water diverted from a nearby stream, and the waste water was flushed through the latrines before it was drained out of the camp. The same care can be seen in the construction of granaries, which were built with raised floors to keep the grain dry and as some protection against infestation. That they were not always successful has been demonstrated in the recent excavations at York, where a large quantity of weevils was found in a Roman grain store.

Outside the defenses of a fort there were often annexes, for the bathhouse and for coralling animals and housing extra stores. In hostile areas the annexes were often as strongly defended as the forts. In addition, many forts attracted civilian settlement, mainly the houses of people closely connected in some way with the garrison. It is known that despite the regulation forbidding soldiers from marrying, many of them did, and that their wives and children often lived outside the fort. Other people connected with the civilian settlements were merchants, veterans and, in all probability, prostitutes.

Nearly all the known forts are in the frontier regions of the Roman Empire, and are concentrated in those areas that resisted Roman domination most strongly. Large numbers have been found in northern England, Scotland, Wales, the Rhineland (especially in the area around Mainz), in Dacia (modern Rumania), along the Danube, in Israel, Tunisia and Algeria. In areas that were pacified, the forts were abandoned and the garrisons withdrawn. For instance, in Spain, where intense fighting had gone on during the Middle and Late Republic, the end of hostilities after the civil wars led to the reduction of the garrison to a single legion for the whole province.

In addition to the forts, frontier regions often had other works designed to control the movement of peoples across the frontier and to deter invasions. In many areas this was simply a network of watchtowers and roads to give advance warning to the garrisons of any attack. This was the sort of defense that proved adequate in desert areas or where there was a dominant natural feature such as a mountain range or a large river. However, if the possibility of attack was high, artificial barriers were built, of which the best known and most developed example is Hadrian's Wall. Generally speaking these were walls, palisades or banks, along which the soldiers patrolled, with watchtowers at intervals to look out for enemy attack and to communicate with the forts. In addition, there were gates through the barrier, often defended by small fortlets holding a century or so. These gates allowed civilians to cross the frontier and they doubtless acted as frontier posts, but their most important function was to give soldiers access to enemy territory, for it was Roman practice to counter attacks before they reached the frontier, rather than rely on the barrier itself to keep the invaders out. Apart from Hadrian's Wall, there are a number of other barriers known from different parts of the empire. Further north in Britain there was the Antonine Wall, in Germany there was a continuous barrier from

RIGHT Design for a siege machine, taken from an eleventh century manuscript illustration of the late Roman military tract *De Rebus Bellicis*.

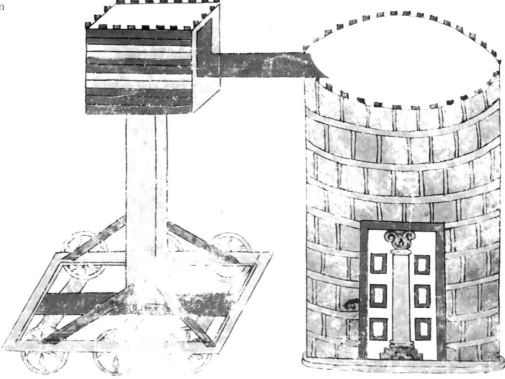

LEFT The siege ramp at Masada. In order to bring their siege machines up to the wall of the fortress, the Romans built a vast ramp of earth against the sheer cliff, about 650 feet long and 350 feet high.

RIGHT Defenders at the walls of a town throwing missiles down on the besieging force.

BELOW Two of Flavius Silva's camps constructed during the siege of the Jewish fortress of Masada in AD 72. One camp is to the right of the stream-bed, with the circumvallation wall that surrounded Masada running along in front. The other camp, partially reconstructed, is beside the car-park.

the area around Mainz to the upper valley of the Danube, and there were others in Yugoslavia, Rumania, at the mouth of the Danube, and along the edge of the Sahara desert in North Africa, this last one for the control of raiding and movement by the nomadic Berbers. In addition to providing defenses in areas where there was not a good natural barrier, they also helped to mark out the limits of the empire, and they made it easier to collect taxes and customs duties.

So far, the army being described here is essentially that in existence during the first two centuries of the empire. However, from the reign of Emperor Severus at the beginning of the third century AD, the army underwent a period of profound change lasting over a century. The legions declined and the cavalry reasserted itself as the most important force in the army.

One of Severus' reforms was to grant the soldiers permission to marry. This was perhaps the official recognition of what had in fact been happening previously, but one of the effects was that many soldiers married in the areas in which they were stationed, and they were loathe to be transferred elsewhere at a later stage. In other words the army, and especially the frontier garrisons, became increasingly static and interested in local rather than empire-wide matters. This tendency was compounded by the fact that both legions and auxiliary units were recruiting new troops from their local regions by this time.

In the mid-third century Gallienus introduced reforms designed to break down the class divisions within the legions. Men were permitted to rise to any rank, according to their ability, and the old distinction between officers and men was dropped. Thereafter, the upper classes played little part in the

army, and it became common for ambitious men to attain very high ranks indeed. The most famous example is Diocletian, who rose from obscurity in the army stationed in the Danubian region to become a general, and ultimately, emperor. As well as this reform, Gallienus made use of an elite force of troops that accompanied him to the various trouble-spots of the empire. Ultimately, under Constantine the Great, this force was organized into regular field armies that were responsible for virtually all the active fighting in the empire. Known as *comitatenses* and composed of both infantry and cavalry, these troops took valuable resources of both equipment and manpower away from the frontier garrisons of legions and auxiliaries, which became increasingly unable to repel more than the lightest of barbarian incursions. As a result the frontier regions became battlefields, and it was the usual practice in the fourth century for the frontier garrisons to retreat to their strongly fortified defenses if they could not push the barbarians back themselves, and to send signals for the *comitatenses* to come and deal with the situation. Owing to this, much of the land near the frontier was abandoned, and such buildings as grain stores had to be fortified in order to ensure supplies for the field armies.

Another change in the army that is increasingly noticeable through the fourth century is the recruiting of barbarians, either by a treaty with a tribe, by hiring mercenaries or by allowing barbarians to settle on abandoned lands within the empire in exchange for providing military service. Germans especially were recruited, and some of them reached high positions of power and influence, the most famous being Stilicho, who was supreme commander of the army in the western empire at the end of the fourth century, and had almost total control over the weak Emperor Honorius. It is often suggested that this 'barbarization' of the army was one of the causes of the downfall of the Roman empire. This will be examined in more detail in the final chapter.

LEFT The foundations of the granary of Housesteads fort on Hadrian's Wall. The floor was raised on stone blocks to keep the grain dry.

BELOW A late Roman outpost at Qasr Halabat, overlooking the Syrian desert.

Hadrian's Wall, the northern frontier of the empire. The wall can be seen in the foreground, with a milecastle, one of the guard-posts at intervals along the wall, in the background.

HADRIANS WALL

One of the most impressive remains left by the Romans is Hadrian's Wall, a stone barrier running from the Tyne to the Solway in northern Britain, and an intimidating symbol of Rome's military might. It was designed to separate the native peoples north of the wall from those within the empire to the south, and it marked out the northern limit of the province of Britain for tax and customs purposes. However, it is as a military structure that it is best known. It is apparent that Hadrian, although not the first builder of such static, defensive frontiers in the Roman Empire, decided that it was time to end the rapid expansion of the empire that had occurred under his predecessors and he consolidated the frontiers at the limits of the existing territory. He strengthened the frontier areas by building new forts, roads and watchtowers, and by redeploying troops to places where they were most needed. In addition, he built continuous barriers where there were no satisfactory natural boundaries, in North Africa, Germany and Britain, the most highly developed of all.

The wall was built by detachments from the legions stationed in Britain, and it is possible to deduce from inscriptions and from the differences in the design of gateways and other features, which legion was responsible for which section of the wall. Work probably began in AD 122,

shortly after Hadrian's inspection of the province, and continued for several years.

The original scheme that Hadrian commissioned was to have a wall of stone, 10 feet thick and 15 feet high, for the eastern 45 (Roman) miles, and a turf wall, 20 feet thick at the base and the same height, for the western 31 miles. Small fortlets, known as mile castles, were built at mile intervals and every third of a mile were watchtowers or turrets. In front of the wall was a ditch, except where the rock was too hard to dig it out or where the crags were too steep. The main forts were positioned a little way behind the wall, but could be signalled to by the men in the watchtowers. Access through the wall for troops and civilians was permitted at the mile castles, whose north gates opened directly onto the ground beyond the wall. There is a good deal of evidence to suggest that this scheme was rigidly adhered to while the wall was being built, for some of the turrets are poorly positioned, in order to preserve their exact distance from the next turret, and some of the mile castle gates open directly onto cliff edges.

However, before the original plan could be completed, major modifications were made, probably in response to the need for greater security on the frontier. The forts were moved up to the wall itself, and in some cases sat astride it so that three of their six gates opened onto enemy territory. In this way the troops, who were all auxiliaries, could be deployed quickly in an emergency. A *vallum* (double bank and ditch) running parallel

to the wall a short distance to the south provided additional protection in the rear. This had the effect of creating a narrow military zone alongside the wall, and greatly reduced civilian access from the south. Together with a military way linking the forts that was added later, this was the complete system. It is not known how long it took to build, although it has been suggested recently that building work and initial modifications took up to 15 years, on the basis of an inscription of AD 136/7 in one of the last forts to be built.

Tactically, the wall seems to have served mainly as a deterrent. It was not used as a fighting platform, for the parapet walkway would have been too narrow to deploy troops effectively, and the ancient

BELOW LEFT Reconstruction of the turf wall and a stone turret at Chesterholme.

BELOW The bath-house in the civil settlement at Vindolanda.

military manuals frown on such a use of defenses. They prefer men to advance in front of the defenses in order to meet an attack before it reached the wall. The preferred tactic was possibly to use a pincer movement by two sallies from different gates, so as to trap the enemy up against the wall.

Ironically, as Hadrian's Wall reached its final stages, Hadrian died and his successor, Antoninus Pius, launched a new offensive into Scotland. Hadrian's Wall was abandoned and a new one built between the Forth and the Clyde estuaries, now known as the Antonine Wall. However, this wall, although held by a greater concentration of troops than Hadrian's Wall, was in its turn abandoned after a few years, and by the end of the second century the northern frontier of Britain once again became Hadrian's Wall, where it was to remain until the end of the Roman occupation of Britain.

RIGHT The *vallum* (boundary ditch) to the south of Hadrian's Wall itself.

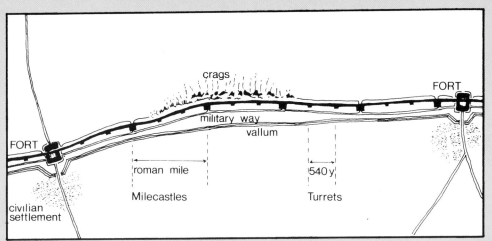

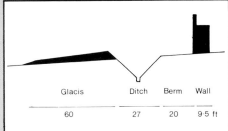

LEFT AND ABOVE Diagram of the layout of Hadrian's Wall and a section across the main defenses.

BELOW The fort at Housesteads. Note the civilian settlement and traces of Roman cultivation to the left of the fort.

CHAPTER IV
TOWNS AND CITIES

The cities of the Greek and Roman world were regarded as the supreme achievement of civilization by the people who lived in them. The splendor of the monuments and quality of civic life were matters held dear by the townsfolk of each city, and any rights and privileges granted by the government were jealously guarded. Indeed, in Greece the whole system of government revolved around the cities, each of the major ones being an independent, self-sustaining state or country. This idea of the city-state was strongest in classical Greece when cities such as Athens, Corinth and Sparta were flourishing. However, the idea continued into Roman times and it is possible to say that the Roman Empire was simply the logical development of that idea on a scale never seen before. In other words, Rome was the biggest city-state of all, absorbing all the others in the process of its expansion. Of course, other cities continued to exist, and in fact most of them reached new levels of prosperity, owing to the prolonged periods of peace that the Roman Empire brought.

There were a great number of cities in the empire, with astonishingly varied characters and development. In some areas, particularly around the coast of the Mediterranean, dense concentrations of towns existed, and virtually everybody was a town dweller. In the east, towns and cities were usually much older than in Italy and the west, many having peculiar layouts and positions to Roman eyes, because of their foundation in very different historical circumstances. When the Romans penetrated to the east, they found a fully developed city-based society already in existence. There was little they could do to change these cities, except by embellishing them with new monuments. Few new cities were founded, except for colonies of Roman citizens in some of the more sparsely populated regions in the east, such as the upper Euphrates valley in modern Syria and Turkey.

In the west, however, the Romans had a much freer hand, for many of the peoples of Spain, France, Germany and Britain were unused to living in large conglomerations and towns and cities were few and far between. Even where there were fledgling towns, such as the Iron Age *oppida* of pre-Roman Britain, these were smothered by the new foundations that the Romans made in most areas of these provinces. Thus it is in the west that the purest expression of Roman civic ideals is seen.

Those ideals were quite simple: a town should be a mirror of

the greatness of Rome itself. It should have a forum or market place and a basilica or hall of justice as the town center, just as the forums of Rome were the natural focus of the capital. There should be temples, particularly one to the Imperial cult, the deified Augustus and the goddess Roma. The housing should be similar architecturally to the houses in vogue in Rome and Italy, and the street grid should be regular, as befitted an orderly plan. Each city was also to be a capital in its own right, although usually of the local region only.

One of the most striking things about Roman towns was that they were organized in a hierarchy, according to the civil rights that the citizens enjoyed. At the top was, of course, Rome itself, together with the colonies of Roman citizens that were planted in the provinces. These were regarded as part of the mother-city and accordingly were treated as the most important towns in any given area. Of secondary status were colonies with Latin rights, which was a slightly inferior grade of citizenship granted initially to the towns surrounding Rome that had alliances with her. This was a category often conferred on existing towns, which were known as *municipia*, and it was an honor eagerly sought by the local inhabitants through petitions to the emperor, since it allowed the magistrates to receive Roman citizenship after they had held office, and gave legal and commercial privileges. They enjoyed a status fairly close to that of Rome and her colonies, and greatly superior to the third category, *civitates stipendiariae* or *peregrinae* (tax-paying or 'foreign' cities). This was another reason why the emperor was constantly receiving petitions from the provincial cities requesting the elevation of their status by his conferring Latin rights. Of course, this competition for privileges and status was in part deliberately engineered by the emperor, since it was a very useful way of controlling cities in areas without a strong military garrison, and it encouraged town councils to set up Roman-style monuments and generally conduct themselves in a more 'Roman' way.

Most towns of the empire, however, belonged to the lowest category, at least in the early days of imperial rule, but large numbers were promoted as time passed. They were at a considerable disadvantage compared with cities of higher status, for the citizens were not allowed to marry Roman citizens or to trade with them, and they contributed a large proportion of total imperial revenue in the form of land and poll taxes.

The way in which this complicated system worked in practice can be seen in Gaul, where the tribes were given different treaty terms by Caesar according to whether they opposed him,

LEFT Colonnaded marketplace in Jerash, Jordan, second or third century AD. The town was an important caravan city for routes to Persia.

BELOW The town of Cuicul (modern Djemila, Algeria), an uncommon example of unregulated planning in the Roman world. The result is much more lively than the four-square planning of many Roman colonies.

BOTTOM In a prominent position in most Roman towns was the *capitolium*, a temple dedicated to the major Roman gods, Jupiter, Juno and Minerva. This example comes from Thugga.

remained neutral or made an alliance with him. All his opponents received peregrine (foreign) status, and so their towns and the countryside (*territorium*) that went with each town, roughly corresponding with the old tribal area, were penalized both politically and financially. They ended up becoming the poorer regions of the province. Most of the other tribes received Latin status, with the favored few becoming Roman colonies or acquiring that honor later. In Britain nearly all the towns were of the lowest status, which goes some way toward explaining why the province was so poor in comparison with the rest of the empire.

So much for the important but rather intangible question of the political background to Roman towns and cities. It is time to consider what they actually looked like. The average town was largely made up of houses, just as modern ones are, but the essential complement to them was civic amenities such as market places, whereas modern towns may consist almost exclusively of housing. New Roman towns were usually laid out on a grid pattern, with the central squares devoted to public buildings and the surroundings to the houses. The tradition of a regular plan goes back to Greek practice, where new colonies or extensions to existing ones were often laid out with rectangular or square blocks. One of the most famous Roman examples is the colony at Timgad on the edge of the Sahara desert. This was a specialized town, established in AD 100 to house military veterans after they had retired from the Third Augustan Legion based at Lambaesis, 12 miles away. The layout is very much like an army fortress, but with square blocks for houses instead of the long rectangular barrack-blocks. The town occupied a large square of about 25 acres with the forum and basilica at the junction of the two main streets. Behind it was a theater, built into the side of a small hill, and scattered about the town were several sets of public baths, temples and a library. The original foundation was obviously very successful, for within a century settlement expanded outside the original area, this time on a much less regular basis without the Roman's supervision. The town must have been a thriving bastion of Roman culture in an area that the Romans held rather precariously against both the nomadic tribesmen and the inroads of the desert itself.

A special feature of Roman colonies was that they extended

the concept of regular planning out into the countryside as well. The land around a colony was often divided into squares in a process known as centuriation, and the squares were allocated to each colonist by lot. This ensured a fair distribution of land, although a few unlucky people ended up with a square that had a river running through it or some other disadvantage. Vast areas of land were divided in this way, including most of the Po Valley, modern Tunisia and the south of France.

To return to the towns themselves, or rather to the individual parts that made it into a town, the most important element was the forum, the center of all ancient towns. The forum of Timgad and other towns served much the same functions as in Rome. It was a meeting place for the townspeople, where news and official business was given out, where law suits were heard (although they were also heard in the basilica) and where private deals were negotiated and goods traded. In appearance the forum was an open space with a colonnade running around its edge. Behind the colonnade were stone-built stalls and shop counters, and often there was a second storey to provide an extra set of shops. Temporary stalls were set up in the central space, which with the permanent shops provided nearly all the town's provisions. In hot countries fresh food, particularly meat, was often kept separate, however, and sold in a cool, covered *macellum* to help prevent it rotting.

Apuleius provides a lively description of buying food in the market in his *Golden Ass*:

'Then I went towards the baths, first visiting the provision market to buy something for my supper. There was plenty of fish for sale, and though I was first asked 200 *drachmae* (Greek equivalent of a *denarius*), eventually I beat a fishmonger down to 20, paid him and walked off with my purchase. As I left, a man named Pythias, who had been one of my fellow students in Athens, happened to be walking in the same direction.

"Why, if it isn't my friend Lucius! Tell me, my dear fellow, what in the world brings you here?"

'We must have a long talk tomorrow. But, Pythias, what's this I see? A magistrate's robe, and a posse of constables armed with truncheons, marching behind you?'

He explained: "I am now Inspector General of Markets, so if I can be of any service in helping you to buy something for your supper, please call on me."

'How kind of you! But I have just bought myself a few pounds of fish.'

"Let me have a look at them." He took the basket from me, shook the fish about so that he could inspect them more closely, and then asked: "Do you mind telling me what you paid for this refuse?"

'It took me a long time to beat the fishmonger down to 20 *drachmae*.'

"Which fishmonger? Point him out to me."

I pointed at a little old man seated in a corner of the market. Pythius at once began abusing him in his severest official tones:

ABOVE A typical market scene in a colonnaded forum or street. Cloth and cushions are for sale, being inspected by a potential customer.

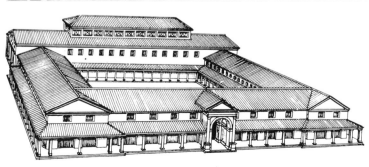

LEFT Reconstruction of the square type of forum and basilica (to the rear of the forum) found in Roman Britain.

"Hey you, is this the way to treat the Inspector General's friends, or for that matter any visitor who comes to buy in the provision market? Asking no less than 20 *drachmae*, 20 *drachmae* indeed, for these absurd little tiddlers! Hypata is the most prosperous town in all Thessaly, but with fellows like you forcing up food prices to such a preposterous height we might as well be living in a rocky wilderness."

He emptied the basket on the ground, ordering one of his constables to jump on the fish and squash them into paste on the pavement. Beaming moral satisfaction with his own severity, Pythias advised me to go home. "All is well now, Lucius," he said cheerfully. "You need say no more. I am satisfied that the little wretch has been sufficiently humiliated."

My wise old fellow-student! Flabbergasted at having lost both my supper and my money as a result of his kind intervention, I went on to the baths where I spent the afternoon resting.'

(Graves' translation, slightly abridged)

The forum also housed temples, which served as the center of religious worship. Processions and ceremonies would have been seen on feast days, when all the stalls would have been shut and cleared away. Thus, the forum was used for a wide variety of purposes and, except during the afternoon siesta, would have always been alive with people discussing, buying or celebrating.

The basilica was usually on one side of the forum, and served much the same purpose as the Assembly Rooms of an eighteenth-century town. Legal cases and meetings were held there, and in most of the smaller towns the council probably met there too, although a town with enough money at its disposal usually built a separate chamber for the purpose. A typical basilica was a large open hall, with columns down one or both sides that divided it into a nave and aisles. It commonly had an apse at each end, giving

LEFT Stone measuring block in the market at Leptis Magna, Libya. Each town would have provided standard lengths, weights and volumes in the market place, to ensure that trading was fair. The measures would also have acquainted visitors with the local standards, since there was a great deal of variation from area to area.

RIGHT View down one of the streets in Pompeii, looking from the walls toward the forum. On each side are the remains of houses, standing in places up to roof level. The roof tiles visible on some of the houses are, however, restored, for the weight of ash from the eruption of Vesuvius and the intervening centuries have together ensured that the Roman roof-beams have collapsed and decayed. Excavations to uncover Pompeii have gone on since the seventeenth century, and about two-fifths still remains buried.

LEFT The basilica at Leptis Magna, partially restored. It had three aisles and an apse at each end. Built by the emperor Severus in AD 216, it is one of the most distinguished and well-preserved basilicas anywhere in the empire. In the sixth century AD it was converted into a church.

BELOW In the Po Valley, vast areas of the modern landscape still preserve the lines of the Roman *centuriation* (square land-division). It was originally surveyed in the early second century BC, when squares of 20 by 20 *actus* (774 by 774 yards) were laid out. A single square is contained within the black circle on the photograph, its area originally divided into plots for 20 colonists.

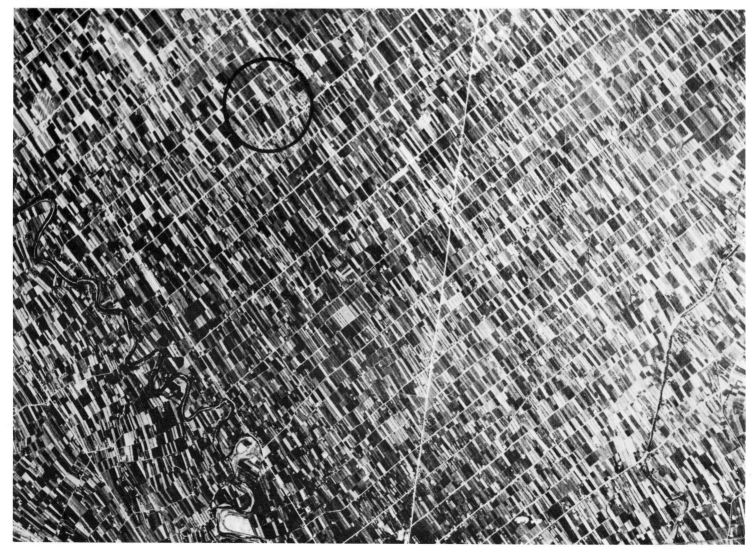

it the appearance of the Christian church, which is not surprising since it is very likely that the early Christians developed the architecture of churches from the large buildings that they saw around them, such as basilicas.

One of the important points to note about the public buildings in Roman cities was that, in general, they were set up with private rather than public finance. It was traditional for wealthy citizens to build such amenities as basilicas, theaters, baths and aqueducts during their tenure of official posts on the town council. Only very rarely was public subscription or council decree responsible for such buildings, and the monuments they did build were usually such things as statues commemorating the generous patrons of various building projects. Whole towns were established by private finance, since most of the colonies during the Republic were the result of the action of some rich senator or consul. This continued in the Empire, although now it was the emperor who took over the role of city founder, using his private purse to build colonies and civic amenities throughout his vast domains. The main reason for this public-spiritedness on the part of the leading citizens was the desire to be elected to offices on the council. A candidate would offer to build an amphitheater and hold lavish games in it if he were elected. Another reason for the building activity was that there were virtually no personal taxes, with the result that the rich became very rich and most of the rest of the population remained very poor. Spending money on public works was regarded as a duty toward the poorer citizens according to the moral standards of the time.

Apart from the forum and basilica, the most important features of most towns were the defensive walls and the water supply. Wall building was considered essential in some parts of the empire because of raids by bandits or barbarians across the frontiers. Even in cities at the heart of the empire, political events sometimes seemed to threaten their tranquillity and prosperity, with the result that walls were often built at times of crisis, such as civil war, or, after the second century AD, the threat of invasion. By the fourth century, most towns had defenses of one form or another. Generally, the walls had a walkway along the top for the town's militia to patrol, and towers at intervals and at corners to serve as look-out posts and to give defenders a height advantage during an attack. The gateways were especially stoutly defended, with ingenious systems of portcullises and inner courtyards to impede assailants. Few of these defenses were in fact used, merely providing a deterrent. However, long and bloody sieges did take place on occasion, and sometimes spectacular archaeological finds trace such a siege. For instance, at Dura Europos in the Euphrates valley one of the towers was undermined during an attack and the grisly remains of the bodies of the sappers were found in a tunnel under the rubble.

An adequate water supply was essential in ancient towns, and the number of aqueducts or public fountains was often taken as an indication of the importance of a town. Rome itself had 11 major aqueducts and at least 20 altogether. The development of the aqueduct was a gradual affair, since in early times nearly all towns were amply supplied by rivers or wells. However, the expanding population in Rome led to the building of the Aqua Appia in 312 BC, in the form of a tunnel. At this date the technology did not exist for constructing a channel on arches, which is the familiar form of aqueduct. There was also the risk of an enemy poisoning the water if the channel was exposed. Arched aqueducts were first built in the second century BC and were set up in many parts of the empire thereafter. Generally speaking, an aqueduct tapped a stream in the hills near a town, and then brought the water direct to the town, or occasionally to the town's fields for irrigation purposes. Many were 50 miles or more in length, and in their details of construction, their gradual slope to ensure even flow and the ingenious use of inverted

ABOVE A street in Herculaneum, showing the lead pipes that supplied water to the houses. Citizens paid to tap the supply.

BELOW The aqueduct at Tarragona, 200 yards long and 250 feet high, as it crosses a river valley.

The Pont du Gard, part of the 31-mile long
aqueduct that supplied Nîmes in France.
The proportions are simple and harmonious
– the small arches are one unit, the central
arches four units and the total height six
units.

LEFT Colonnaded street in
Palmyra. Many eastern cities
provided cool colonnades as
protection against the sun. Note
the brackets on which statues
could be placed.

BOTTOM The public lavatories
of the Roman colony of
Philippi in northern Greece.

BELOW The town wall of
Pompeii, with mason's marks
visible on several of the stones.
Walls were generally built at
times of insecurity, this one
dating to the fifth century BC
and reinforced in the first
century BC.

siphons to cross valleys, aqueducts can justly be regarded as the best-known and most public of the achievements of the Roman engineer. Of course, not all towns had need of an aqueduct, and many that did contented themselves with an open water channel that followed the contours of the hills, such as a canal does, without being raised on arches.

When an aqueduct reached the town the water was usually sent into a *castellum aquae* (water-distribution tower), where sediment was allowed to settle out, and where the single inlet was divided in several channels for the different parts of the town. Most of the water flowed out of public fountains, forming the sole source of supply for the vast majority of the populace. Only the rich could afford to pay the levies for a private supply, and even in large houses water only came to the ground floor, as there was generally not enough pressure to supply taps at a higher level. Baths were the other major consumer of water.

After being used the water was drained into the sewer system. This was the opposite end of the equation of water supply, for the drains had to be capable of carrying as much water away as was brought into the town or else floods would occur. Most towns had a comprehensive network of arched drains running under the streets, ultimately debouching into the nearest stream or river. No attempt was made to treat the sewage, or at least, no filters or treatment tanks have been found. However, this does not mean that they may not be found in the future, for the rather unglamorous study of Roman drainage is still largely unstarted.

Before the drains were led out of a town they were often diverted to flush out the public lavatories. They did this by flowing continuously through the waste channels of the latrines, a notably advanced and hygienic design in the ancient world. In other respects, however, these lavatories were completely unlike their modern counterparts. Privacy was entirely lacking, and small wet sponges were used instead of paper. It seems that public lavatories were jovial, social places, where conversation and business could carry on uninterrupted from the forum, to which they were often adjacent. Latrines were also incorporated in bath buildings, but were not particularly common in apartments or houses. Much like access to drinking water, washing and personal toilet were communal affairs, only the rich having privacy if they wanted it. However, to judge from the popularity of places

like the public baths, privacy was not necessarily sought after.

Baths, theaters and amphitheaters together form the remaining group of public amenities that were expected in a Roman town. The details of their construction and day-to-day working are dealt with elsewhere, and it need only be said here that such buildings were not frivolous additions to the urban scene, but were always considered an essential part of daily life; baths for obvious hygienic reasons, and for their use as places for socializing; amphitheaters and theaters for reasons of entertainment and religion.

Houses made up the remainder of the space in Roman towns. The different types of house and their architecture are of major importance in understanding the structure of Roman society, and the house types in different towns give us our clearest indications of the wide variations of wealth that could occur. The best evidence for Roman houses comes from three towns in Italy: Ostia, Herculaneum and Pompeii, which were all in one way or another abandoned and covered with a protective mantle of soil. This has ensured that a fantastic wealth of evidence survives for modern archaeologists to uncover.

Pompeii, of course, is the best known of these towns because of its destruction by the eruption of Vesuvius in AD 79. About two-thirds of the area within the walls was occupied by private buildings – houses, shops, workshops and inns. It is often very difficult to distinguish these four categories in the archaeological remains that survive, for businesses were often based in the home, and shops and industries tended to be closely connected with the houses of the owners and landlords.

BELOW Plan of the House of the Menader, Pompeii.

The most distinctive type of house in Pompeii was based around an *atrium* (partially covered courtyard). All the larger houses in the town were of this type, and many had a second courtyard at the back called a *peristilium* and sometimes also a garden or *hortus*. The plan occupied a good deal of space since it was usually on one level without a second storey. Sometimes an entire *insula* (block) was taken up by a single house. The House of the Faun initially occupied the southern end of its block, but by purchasing the property to the north the owners eventually managed to construct a garden in the rest of the rectangular space. The size of this house, the largest in Pompeii, was 302 by 112 feet.

There were poorer houses in Pompeii too, as would be expected. These ranged from the one- or two-roomed box, which often had a shop counter on the street front, to the type of house that copied the architectural style of the larger houses on a small scale, and sometimes incorporated workshops such as bakeries or fulling vats within them. The best illustration of all these different types of Pompeian house can be seen in the *insula* that contains the House of the Menander, so-named after the wall-painting showing the poet Menander in an *exhedra* (niche) in the peristyle. It was owned by Quintus Poppaeus, a relative of Nero's second wife.

Originally this *insula* contained several houses of roughly equal size, dating from the third century BC, not long after this part of Pompeii was first occupied. The only one of these to remain without drastic alteration is the House of the Lovers in the southwest corner. One of these original houses opened onto the street in the center of the north side, and this later became the large building that gives its name to the block. Initially it would

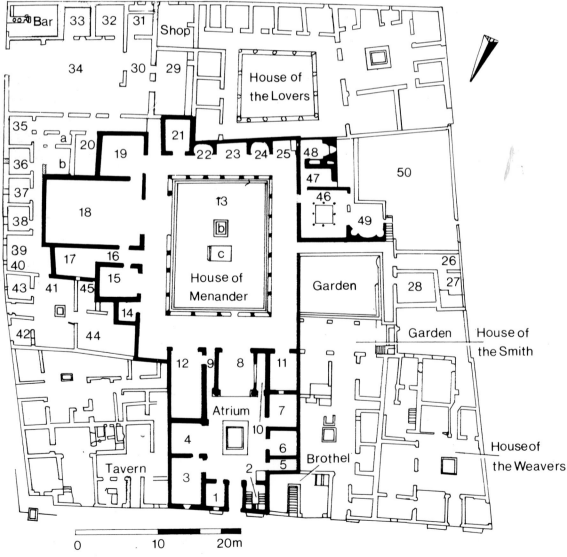

1 Door keeper's lodge.
2 Staircase to upper floor.
3 Bedroom later used as workshop. 4 'Ala.' 5 Storeroom.
6–7 Bedrooms. 8 Tablinum.
9 Corridor. 10 Cupboard.
11 Green oecus. 12 Large exhedra. 13 Peristyle garden.
14 Store. 15 Red oecus.
16 Corridor. 17 Bedroom.
18 Dining room (triclinium).
19 Yellow oecus. 20, 35–40 Servants' quarters. 21 Day bedroom/library. 22–24 Exhedrae. 25 Exhedra with images maiorum. 26–28 Kitchens. 29 Stable. 30–34 Farm quarters. 41–45 Steward's lodging. 43 Bedroom.
44 Garden. 46 Vestibule to bath suite. 47 Warm undressing room (apodyterium). 48 Hot room (calidarium). 49 Sun terrace. 50 Kitchen garden.
A Household shrine (lararium).
B Fountain basin. C Wooden dining area (triclinium).

have consisted of the *atrium* alone, with a garden plot behind it. The *atrium* was a high-ceilinged, airy room with an open rectangular hole in the roof to allow rain-water to drain off the roof into the *impluvium* (pool) below. In the days before public water supply was a regular service, this pool would have been the main source of drinking water for the household. Sometimes the *impluvium* was connected to a large underground cistern if it was important to store large quantities of water for the summer drought, but this was not the case in the House of the Menander, for its *impluvium* is a purely decorative feature. The entrance to the house opened onto the *atrium* and there were several rooms ranged around its edge, which would have been for eating, sleeping and storage. Undoubtedly there were also kitchens and slaves' quarters, but these did not survive the major alterations that took place in the second and first centuries BC.

In its altered form the house took up much more space, which must have been the result of purchases of the neighboring properties. The main development was the addition of a large peristyle to the rear of the original nucleus. This was an open space, usually with a formal garden, surrounded by a colonnade that created a cloister-like portico looking onto the garden. Around the peristyle were various rooms, including additional dining rooms and bedrooms to those in the *atrium*. One or two may have been day bedrooms in which the owner and his family would take their siestas. All of these rooms were richly decorated with mosaics and wall paintings.

On the west side of the peristyle was a small private bath building and a sun terrace overlooking what was probably a kitchen garden. Under the baths were a set of basement rooms, in one of which the excavators found the family treasure in two large chests – 118 pieces of silver, cups, bowls and similar items, together with some gold jewellery and 46 gold and silver coins. This is a rare find, even in Pompeii, for many of the houses were looted soon after the eruption had died down. The total weight of this hoard is 53 lb and it is probably fairly typical of the sort of treasure that a wealthy Roman would be expected to own.

Next to the kitchen garden was the kitchen itself, in what must have been rather an inconvenient position, since the main dining room was down a long corridor and on the far side of the peristyle. Perhaps the owners were not as concerned at having lukewarm food as is usual today! The main slaves' quarters were behind the dining room on the east side of the house. They were at a lower level and a narrow flight of stairs provided access to the peristyle. At the far end of the corridor of these quarters was a more spacious suite of rooms with its own small *atrium*, which was the steward's lodging. He was called Eros, and he seems to have been one of the few people to stay at his post at the time of the eruption, for his body was found lying on a bed in one of the rooms.

The remaining part of the house was in the southeast corner of the block, and in many ways is one of the most revealing parts of the building. It appears to have been farm quarters, with an open yard in the center in which was found the remains of a two-wheeled cart. There was stabling and storage space. The farm quarters must give us some clues as to the income of the household, or at least, one of the sources of income, for it is likely that some of the slaves were farm workers and went out to the fields surrounding the town every day to farm the land that belonged to Poppaeus. The farm quarters were the storage space within the walls, doubtless coupled with other buildings on the farm land itself. To judge from the 15 vine-pruning knives found in Eros' rooms, growing vines and making wine was one of the farm's activities. This could be a highly lucrative enterprise.

On the very corner of the block where the farm quarters were situated, was a small street-side bar, with a counter and large storage jars for wine set in it. Doubtless this part of the House of the Menander was let for a profit or, if Poppaeus was generous,

ABOVE Plaster cast of the entrance door to a Pompeian house.

ABOVE The peristyle of the House of the Gilded Cupids, Pompeii.
BELOW Tower-tombs outside the city of Palmyra.

given to one of his elderly retainers to eke out his retirement. The corner of a block was the most sought-after position for a bar, of which Pompeii seems to have boasted more than a hundred such sites altogether.

The opposite corner of the *insula* was not part of the House of the Menander, but consisted of two small *atrium* houses. These were originally small residences, like the House of the Lovers, but after the disastrous earthquake Pompeii suffered in AD 62 prior to the eruption, seem to have been converted into workshops. One was a weaving establishment, to judge from the large number of loom weights found in the *atrium*. A *graffito* scratched on the wall by the entrance to the house records the name of the gladiator Minucius, who appears to have owned the weaving shop. Next door was a similar house in which were found chisels, hammers, a foot rule, a saw and a pair of compasses. The unfinished remains of wooden, bone and stone objects also indicate that this was a mason's and carpenter's yard.

Between this house and the entrance to the House of the Menander was a very interesting establishment. On the ground floor was a fuller's shop where clothes, especially togas, were taken to be cleaned with fuller's earth and urine (which bleached the cloth!). Over this was a brothel, its purpose betrayed by the variety of obscene messages scratched on the wall by the entrance, and the women's names. The entrance led directly upstairs to a set of rooms that have not survived, but may have been over the bedrooms of the *atrium* to the House of the Menander. This part of the block seems to have been the only place where there was a second storey, apart from the peristyle of the House of the Lovers which had a second floor and set of columns running round the courtyard.

The northeast corner of the block also housed shops. The house next to the House of the Menander was a *caupona* (hot-food shop). It would have served meals and hot drinks to the many people who did not have cooking facilities of their own, such as the women in the brothel. An interesting *graffito* records the love of Sucessus, one of the weavers in the house on the corner, for the servant of the shop, Iris. Other *graffiti* give the name of his rival for the girl, Severus. The last house in the block, very small but with its own *atrium*, is one of the type that sought to emulate the larger houses, but was in reality extremely unpretentious, probably being inhabited by a well-off slave or a freedman (freed slave).

The general impression given by houses such as those just described is that they are very inward-looking. Few have windows looking onto the street and a passer-by would have been confronted by long stretches of blank wall, particularly on the west and south sides. This was partly to guard against theft, but also because rooms were lit from the courtyards rather than from the street. The rooms in the House of the Menander are very open, usually having curtains or wooden screens rather than doors, and there is very little furniture. The overhanging roofs of the *atrium* and peristyle would have made the rooms cool and dark, which was very suitable for the heat of a Mediterranean summer, but was less comfortable in winter. The disadvantages of such an open plan were particularly acute in the houses in the Roman towns of a remote, colder province such as Britain.

Houses in Herculaneum are very much like those in Pompeii. The town was small and nearer Vesuvius on the coast of the Bay of Naples. It suffered a similar fate to Pompeii during the eruption of AD 79, but with one important difference – the houses were buried under a mud flow rather than ashes, and the resulting solidified mass has hermetically sealed all the remains within the houses. In addition the mud was up to 60 feet deep in places, thereby ensuring the survival of roofs and the upper parts of houses. Despite the smaller area excavated, Herculaneum is important to the archaeologist because of the wealth of detail discovered in the houses. Wooden doors, curtains, roof beams,

trellises, tables and beds have all survived in remarkable condition, as have loaves of bread, fruit and even papyri with writing on them.

For housing of a different sort we must turn to Ostia, where much of the town was apartment blocks rather than spacious town houses. Ostia was the port of Rome at the mouth of the Tiber, and it became buried in flood silt after the river ceased to be maintained following the fall of the Roman Empire. The *insulae* (apartment-blocks) were the cramped homes of shopkeepers, workmen and dockers, as well as providing accommodation for the many sailors from all over the Mediterranean. Individual flats had one or two rooms only, with no cooking or washing facilities. Water was fetched from fountains and baths taken at the public baths, and cooking was probably carried out on portable braziers, which also provided a small amount of heat in the winter. Unlike Pompeii, whose poorer inhabitants probably ate at bars, in Ostia there are very few such bars because of Imperial decrees against them. The emperors obviously feared that trouble would occur if men gathered at the bars of a cosmopolitan town like Ostia. Small light wells in the centers of the *insulae* provided the only source of light for the inward-facing flats, and they must have been extremely dim at the lower levels, compounded by their lack of decoration.

Life in an apartment-block flat could be noisy, noisome and even dangerous, as the satirist Juvenal records:

'Here we inhabit a city supported for the most part by slender poles, for that is how the bailiff patches up the cracks in the old walls, telling the inmates to sleep at ease under a roof ready to tumble about their ears. No, no, I must live where there are no fires, no nightly alarms. Ucalegon below is already calling out for water and moving his possessions – smoke is pouring out of the third floor garrett above, but you know nothing about it – if the alarm begins on the ground floor, the last man to burn will be he who is sheltered from the rain by nothing but the tiles.'

Despite such disadvantages, towns and cities were highly desirable places to live, since they were more secure than the countryside, and offered easier employment than the hard drudge of farm work.

RIGHT A remarkably preserved wooden screen-door in a house in Herculaneum.

BELOW A street and apartment block in Ostia.

ROMAN ROADS

In the forum at Rome was the Golden Milestone. On it was inscribed the distances in Roman miles to the principal cities of the empire. Set up in 20 BC by Emperor Augustus, it marks the hub of the road network. Quite literally, all roads led to Rome, and it was one of the great achievements of the road builders that they were able to bind the empire together in a comprehensive network that provided easy access between all places of importance. For strategic reasons alone, the leaders of the Roman Republic and later the emperors decided that proper provision must be made to ensure that the army and its supplies could be transported from place to place quickly and efficiently. This was the motivation for the setting up of roads, and it is possible to trace the advance of armies into new areas through the remains of Roman roads.

As a result of the army, then, the major roads were constructed throughout the empire. They were laid out by *gromatici* (professional surveyors), who used simple instruments such as the *groma* which was made up of two pairs of plumb lines. This and levelling instruments were used to construct a series of straight lines between the places to be connected by the roads. For instance, on the road between London and Chichester (Stane Street), there are three major alignments of road. Originally, the surveyors appear to have planned a direct, straight line between the two towns, for the first 12½ miles out of London are aligned almost directly on Chichester, 55 miles away. In laying out the road, however, it was decided to make some major deviations to cope with the terrain. As many of the roads were not primarily for wheeled traffic but for the army, some quite steep slopes were used on occasions when the surveyors did not think it worthwhile changing their main alignment.

The roads were made of a variety of materials, usually local in origin. Foundations were well dug with rubble pitched in; sometimes oak piles were used if the ground was marshy. The top surface was of finer material, tamped down. There was a camber, and side ditches to drain off rainwater. In towns and on important roads, a durable pavement of shaped stone slabs was laid down to cut down on maintenance.

Although the military built most of the major Roman roads, their subsequent upkeep was the responsibility of the local populace. In addition individual towns and settlements had to provide themselves with branch roads if one of the main routes did not go through them. Their need for roads was, of course, commercial, an aspect that became increasingly important as the provincial towns became more prosperous. In the east of the empire, where there were many cities already in existence at the time of the Roman in-

RIGHT A paved road over Wheeldale Moor, Yorkshire.

BELOW LEFT A *groma*, used for surveying roads and buildings.

BELOW RIGHT The straight track of a Roman road, the Fosseway, still preserved in the British countryside.

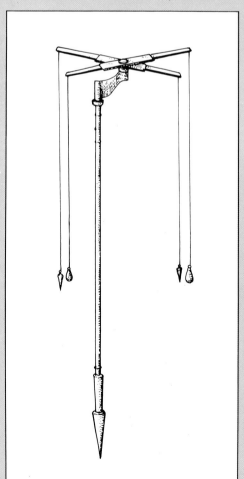

ABOVE A typical Roman bridge, built in AD 22 near Rimini, Italy.

BELOW The handsomely paved road leading from Ephesus to the town.

vasions, roads had been built in earlier times, often purely for commercial needs. Although in nearly all cases these also suited Roman needs, the army continued to construct new roads to link up their forts and garrisons.

Roads greatly eased the problem of communications that had existed in many places before the Romans came. Inns and horse-changing stations were provided for official messengers, and an efficient postal system was established. It has been estimated that a fast horse messenger could travel about 40 to 50 miles a day. Another result of having good roads was that the army could get to far-flung trouble spots in a remarkably short time – Caesar took only 27 days to get from Rome to the further parts of Spain, marching his army by road all the way. The two capitals of the later Roman Empire, Rome and Constantinople, were 25 days apart. However, for ordinary travellers, land transport was often slow and difficult. It was also expensive, being up to 40 times more costly per mile than going by sea. Doubtless, long-distance travel was only for the rich or those on official business. Few others would have travelled beyond their provincial boundaries, if indeed they needed to go even that far.

CHAPTER V
VILLAS AND THE COUNTRYSIDE

In some respects the Roman landscape was very similar to today's. Most areas of the empire were extensively farmed, and the visitor could travel through mile upon mile of well-managed olive plantations in North Africa, for instance, or through the vast wheatlands of the Somme valley or the prairie-like sheep pastures of Sicily. Woodland was controlled, marshes drained and roads constructed to link towns in the most economical way. However, development of the countryside was not universal, and there were wide variations in the level of rural exploitation. For instance, in northern France present evidence shows that the high level of agriculture attained in the Somme valley was not equalled elsewhere, especially to the west, in Normandy and Brittany. In these areas there were far fewer Roman villas and much woodland remained uncleared. Buildings in the local native style were more common, and from all points of view, there was less 'Romanization.'

The concept of Romanization of the countryside is the theme of this chapter. First, the highly developed areas of Italy and the Mediterranean lands will be discussed and then how the Romans' agricultural methods and life-styles were transplanted to the newer provinces in Germany, Gaul and Britain.

Roman villas were the usual centers of rural life. Nearly all areas had them, although in places such as the eastern empire and southern Italy everybody lived in towns, going out from them to the fields each day rather than actually staying in the countryside all the time.

Nearly every villa so far excavated was both a farm and a country house, very few having only living quarters and being for pleasure only. A typical villa would have had a well-appointed set of rooms for the owner and his family, with quarters adjacent to these for the bailiff and the slaves. The farm buildings would also have been nearby, either attached to the bailiff's quarters or placed around a courtyard in which the main building formed a part. It was not common for the farm itself to be completely detached from the house, and most villas were laid out on very compact functional lines.

An example from Italy illustrates these generalizations. At Sette Finestre in southern Etruria, a large villa has been excavated recently that is, in many respects, typical of the sort of rural establishment of the richer agricultural lands in the Mediterranean basin. It is situated near the Roman colony of Cosa, not far from the coast and the main road from Rome north to Gaul, about 75 miles from the capital. In the surrounding area is a flat plain, bordered on one side by the sea and on the other by

relatively inhospitable hills. The plain has the only fertile ground in the region, and for this reason has attracted settlements like villas, which are very common here and much rarer further inland.

The villa itself is built on artificial terraces in the side of a small hill in the middle of the plain. The lowest terrace was a private garden where the owners could walk undisturbed, in which there would have been shrubs and herbs arranged in formal patterns. The front wall of the garden was built in the form of a miniature town wall, with watchtowers at intervals along it. This was no doubt an affectation on the part of the owner, but the towers are a most interesting feature, as very few contemporary town walls still survive, and so Sette Finestre provides a valuable insight into the way in which Italian towns were fortified in the second and first centuries BC.

The rear wall of the garden was also the base of the next terrace, upon which the residential quarters of the villa were built. This was the main part of the villa and would have been occupied by the owner when he was there. He probably would have spent some time in Rome, as the villa is sufficiently richly appointed to have been occupied by a man of equestrian or senatorial rank. Unfortunately there is no inscription surviving to give his name. In design, this part of the villa is very similar to some of the town houses described in the previous chapter. It has a central peristyle off which most of the rooms open, with the other main parts of the building ranged along the main axis running through the peristyle. On the garden side was a verandah that overlooked the garden and the valley beyond. Bedrooms opened onto the verandah, and this must have been the most private and secluded part of the villa. The rooms were decorated with painted wall plaster in the *trompe l'oeil* (false perspective) style, and there were mosaic and marble inlay floors.

Further up the hill on the far side of the peristyle was the *atrium* and the entrance to the residential quarters. This completed the part of the villa set aside for the owner, which was known as the *villa urbana* since it was like a town house; the other parts were the farm proper, known as the *villa rustica*. The farm was not laid out on such a standardized pattern as the *villa urbana*, but was, all the same, well-built and regularly planned, so that there were specific areas devoted to different aspects such as the slave quarters, the pig sties and the grape presses. These last are of some interest as there are at least three of them and they must represent one of the mainstays of this particular villa's prosperity – vine growing. The presses operated by using large stone weights mounted on wooden beams to press out gradually the juices from sacks full of grapes. The liquid ran into a large fermentation tank or *lacus* where the sediment was allowed to settle out. The

LEFT The stylized portrayal on a wall-painting of a small Roman villa.

ABOVE Le Mura di Santo Stephano, Anguillara, an unusual three-storey villa near Rome.
BELOW Axonometric drawing of the villa at Sette Finestre, Italy.
BELOW RIGHT Plan of the villa at Brixworth, Northamptonshire, Britain.

wine was then poured into *amphorae* for transport elsewhere. It was a drink that would be thought very heavy and bitter today, and since it continued to ferment in the *amphora*, must have become vinegary quite quickly. However, wine from Sette Finestre and other villas around Cosa was shipped to many places in the empire, particularly Gaul, and it no doubt had a good reputation in Roman times.

The area around the villa probably belonged to the villa, yet the discovery of other villas in this area has posed a problem, for there does not appear to be enough land for all the villas to be self-supporting. Were Sette Finestre and its neighbors built with wealth that was made elsewhere, or was the land in fact rich enough to allow the owner to build such a sumptuous villa from the profits of farming? This is a question that cannot be answered easily, but there are clues in the landscape itself that surrounds the villa.

Part of the program of research connected with the excavation is the intensive surveying of the region for other archaeological remains. The results of this have given a fascinating insight into the development of this particular corner of Italy during the Roman period.

The first occupation of the area came with the setting up of the colony of Cosa in the third century BC. At this time the land was parcelled up into square plots allocated to each of the colonists – this is the centuriation referred to in the previous chapter. The land must have been managed on egalitarian lines, with each plot being roughly equal. However, after a century or so, it appears that some of the colonists were more successful than others and had acquired part of their neighbors' plots, resulting in the building of moderate-sized villas on the centuriated land. This

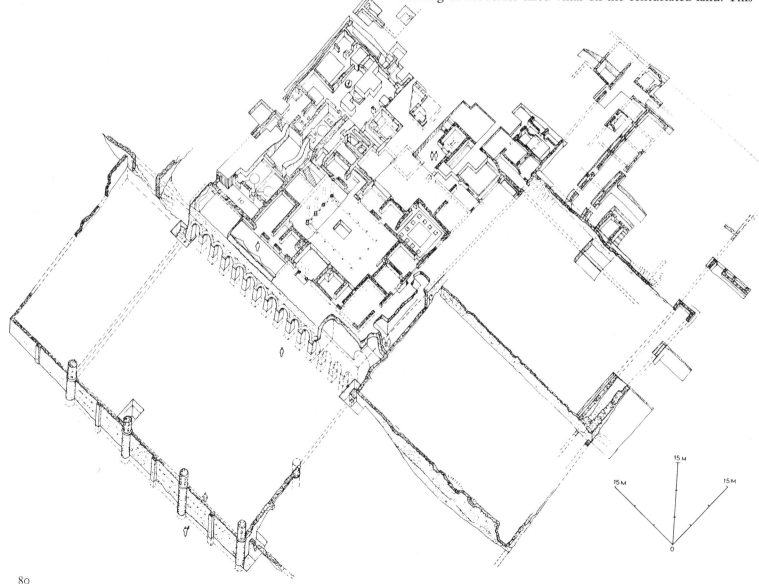

change in the pattern of land holding would have continued but for the political events of the early first century BC. The seizing of power by the dictator Sulla seems to have meant that the land surrounding Cosa was confiscated by him, for we know that the townsfolk supported one of his opponents. This had two major consequences: the town never recovered from the removal of its agricultural land and was abandoned not long afterward and, secondly, this event coincides with the building of the villa at Sette Finestre and its neighbors on the old centuriated land. It appears that the confiscated land was given out to men who rapidly developed the villas in the area, completely transforming the economy of the area in the process. Large estates were formed, and the villas were built by the *nouveaux riches* who were supporters of Sulla and who had made their money through acquiring the vast tracts of land throughout Italy taken from his opponents. Most of the large villas near Sette Finestre were built at this time, many it seems by the same architect, as several have the same decorative towers that adorned the front terrace of the villa.

This influx of wealth and capital transformed the agriculture of the region, shown by the evidence of wine export and the large-scale growing of vines and olives for profit. The first century BC marked the high point in the development of this particular area following the building of these large villas and the introduction of slave-run agriculture on a large scale. This also seems to have been the case elsewhere, for ancient literary sources such as Cato and Columella, both writing on agriculture, offer advice on the best way to run an efficient, profit-making farming establishment, by means of a carefully controlled estate managed by slaves. Their typical farm is not much different from the one

just described at Sette Finestre, although a man devoted to simple living, as Cato was, would not have cared for the sophistication of its *villa urbana*. This type of villa is found in many other parts of Italy, especially near Rome and further south in Campania. Examples can also be seen in other provinces bordering the Mediterranean, especially North Africa, Spain and southern Gaul. In Greece and the east they were less common, since large tracts of good agricultural land were few and far between. Where rich land did exist, it tended to be settled with towns, since the population was much denser, and the landowners were much more inclined to live in the towns rather than on their rural estates.

This concrete evidence can shed some light on that nebulous process of 'Romanization,' one of the main methods by which *pax Romana* (Roman peace) was imposed on the provinces. It has been shown that villas were nearly always farms, and that in the second century BC the tradition developed in Italy for wealthy land owners to live on their estates, rather than staying in Rome or other cities all the time. As a result the typical form of large town house, deriving ultimately from Greek prototypes, was transplanted to the countryside to become the living accommodation of the villa, in addition to the working farm which was already the typical rural building. Many of the fully developed villas were established in Italy during the second and first centuries BC, and it is not surprising that they were also built in the provinces from the first century BC onward.

The architectural style of villas varied from province to province, due to a combination of the local heritage of rural building and the different Roman styles in fashion at the various times that the provinces were conquered. The way in which

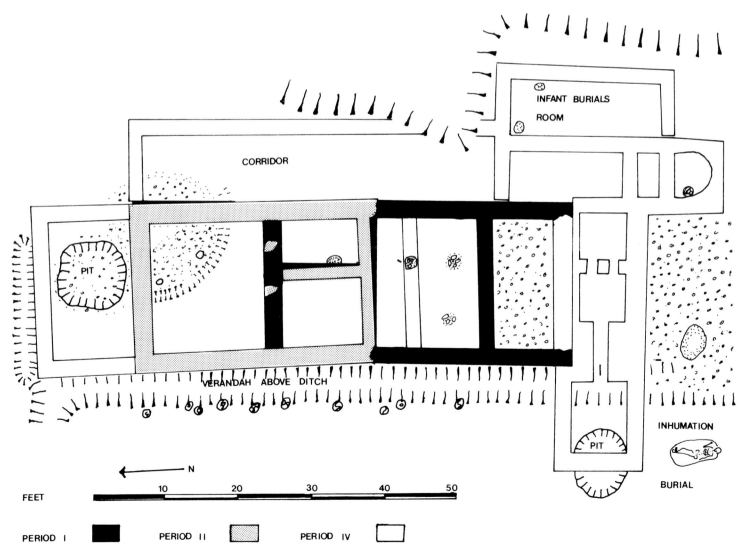

INFANT BURIALS ROOM

CORRIDOR

PIT

VERANDAH ABOVE DITCH

INHUMATION

PIT

BURIAL

FEET

N

10   20   30   40   50

PERIOD I   PERIOD II   PERIOD IV

Roman villas were introduced to a new province is well illustrated in Britain, where the most intensive recent archaeological work has been done.

Britain before the Roman conquest was very rural, heavily dependent on agriculture. The typical farm was a cluster of round huts built of timber, thatch and daub, whose inhabitants lived very simply with relatively few material comforts. No doubt the Romans regarded the local 'architecture' with contempt and they soon set about educating local notables and their sons in the Roman way of life. As a result, Roman customs such as wearing the toga, speaking Latin and building towns and villas became fashionable and widespread, particularly among the British aristocracy. 'The Britons spoke of such novelties as civilization, when in reality they were only part of their enslavement,' was the perceptive comment of Tacitus, a historian writing a generation or so later.

Villas started to be built in Britain within a couple of decades of the conquest of the province. On the south coast in Sussex, and in the area to the north of London around St Albans, several large villas were set up, including the palace at Fishbourne. After that, villas became popular throughout the lower-lying parts of Britain, although the hill peoples in Wales and the north never accepted Roman architectural ideas. Very few of the villas were as sumptuously decorated as those in Italy or the other Mediterranean provinces. Elaborate mosaics and wall paintings were never very common, and it was more usual for early villas to consist of three or four rooms only, with beaten earth or plain mosaic (tessellated) pavements. Excavations under these villas often reveal traces of the round huts that preceded them, and it is fair to say that in many cases it is the outward form of Romanization that was adopted by the builder of the villa rather than any deep-seated change of culture. In other words, the way of life for the Britons probably continued essentially unchanged at first, and in many of the more humble villas the change was simply the conversion of one large round room into several smaller

square rooms. A typical example is Brixworth in Northamptonshire, which starts out as a round hut, to be replaced by the simplest form of villa, in this case four squarish rooms placed end to end with a wooden verandah along the west side. This humble beginning was embellished by the addition of more rooms and a corridor on the eastern side to link the main rooms together. A bathhouse was also added on one end in the fourth century.

Compared with an Italian villa like Sette Finestre, Brixworth is extremely unpretentious. However, it does reflect the level of wealth in the provinces, for Brixworth is a typical expression of Roman culture in the countryside – a small farm with one or two creature comforts, that was the center of a modest estate, probably practicing mixed pastoral and arable agriculture. The occupants of such villas worked the land themselves – slaves probably being few and far between in such a relatively poor province as Britain.

The gradual improvement of Brixworth seems to indicate that its owners made a profit, which is an important factor in the Roman occupation of Britain and the other north European provinces. Before the Roman period much of the population was living at subsistence level, and very little produce was sold for a profit. With the coming of the Romans, two things happened: first, taxes were imposed (or if they already existed, were increased) which stimulated the farmers into producing surplus goods in order to raise money. Second, the notion of producing a surplus was gradually developed into a general commercial sense and, after a hundred years or so, Britain was a full contributor to the trading activity of the Roman Empire. The final development of Brixworth, and the more magnificent third and fourth century villas such as Woodchester and Bignor, was the end result of this process of commercialization, as much a part of 'Romanization' as the introduction of the toga and Latin.

There was quite a difference in the level of Romanization within the different provinces. For instance in Britain, the area of

LEFT The foundations of the grape-presses at Sette Finestre villa. Wine was one of the mainstays of the villa's economy.

RIGHT A hypocaust in Fishbourne palace. This type of underfloor heating was common in villas in the colder northern provinces.

BELOW Drawing of the small villa at Mayen, Germany. Most of the farms in the empire would have been as unpretentious as this.

BELOW A pre-Roman house reconstructed at Butser Ancient Farm, Hampshire, England. Many people continued to live in buildings such as this after the Roman conquest of Britain.

Cranbourne Chase in Dorset had very few villas, but instead a large number of villages of round huts of the sort that were in existence before the Roman invasion. In this area these villages continued unchanged and there is little evidence of any lasting cultural influence from the Romans. On each side of Cranbourne Chase there are areas with villas in them, and the suggestion has been put forward that the Chase was an imperial estate. This means that any profit from the land went to the imperial purse rather than to the tenants, thus discouraging the building of villas. Alternatively it may have been an enclave that resisted the imposition of Roman ideas. This seems to have been the case elsewhere, both in Britain (as in Wales, Devon and Cornwall) and in other provinces (as in the northwest corner of Spain, the area of the Rhine mouth). Generally speaking, these undeveloped areas were not on favored agricultural land, which was nearly always farmed on Roman lines. This is not to say, however, that the local population of a province was pushed out to make way for Roman villa owners in all the best areas. Very few of the people living in villas in the provinces were Romans or even Italians – the vast majority were local people who had adopted the Roman way of life rather than sticking to their own customs. In other words the Roman provinces were not like the colonies of a modern empire. There was no mass immigration to newly opened territory, as happened in America or Australia. Nor was there such a wide ethnic and cultural difference between the conquered and the conquerors as to make it difficult for the Romans to have their way of life accepted, except perhaps in the areas that remained un-Romanized mentioned above. There is no evidence of such things as native reservations in the Roman Empire. From this point of view, it is possible to say that there was a genuine desire on the part of the Romans to give their newly acquired provinces the benefits of their civilization, and they felt it was a duty to 'Romanize' their conquered peoples. This is a very different attitude from that of many modern empires, often much more interested in commercial exploitation than anything else. Not, of course, that the Romans annexed

new territory without an eye to the agricultural and mineral resources of the area. For instance, the geographer Strabo attempted to discourage an invasion of Britain by writing:

'No advantages would arise by taking over the country. At present we gain more from customs duties on their commerce than direct taxation could give us, if the cost of maintaining an army in the island and collecting the taxes is deducted. The unprofitableness of an occupation would be even greater in the case of the other islands near Britain (that is, Ireland).'

Despite his comments, Claudius was not deterred from sending in the legions in AD 43.

As well as the wide variation in architectural style in the villas of different provinces, there were also great differences in the type of agriculture practiced. This was largely the result of the climate, which, for example, prevented olives from being grown in the north or oats in the south. The climate in Roman times was very much as it is today, with rainy temperate weather in the areas closest to the Atlantic, wet winters and hot dry summers in the Mediterranean, and more extreme temperatures in Central Europe. Rome's empire was confined to the Mediterranean area at first, with the result that much of its agriculture and trade was geared to the crops usually grown there.

Since agriculture was overwhelmingly the most important activity and source of employment in the empire, there is a wealth of evidence surviving to show how it was practiced. Our main sources are the archaeological remains themselves, and the writings on agriculture in the literary sources. However, because of the Mediterranean bias of much of the literary evidence, we know more about Roman agriculture in Italy and geographically similar areas than we do of any other part of the empire. Even in provinces such as Britain and Germany, where archaeological investigation of villas and countryside has gone on for many decades, there is little information on such matters as the yearly agricultural cycle, which are so well documented in books such as Columella's *De Re Rustica* (On Agriculture). Only in Italy is it possible to combine the written and the archaeological information to gain a rounded picture of country life.

The outstanding impression gained from a reading of the ancient agricultural writers is one of the desire to make as great a profit from the land as possible. Advice is given on such diverse matters as how to choose a farm bailiff that is trustworthy and efficient, how to plant vines for the maximum return on the capital investment, or which cash crops are best for a market garden near to a large city. A remarkable amount of detail has survived in these sources; for instance Columella even tells us how many man days it should take for working an *iugerum* ($\frac{2}{3}$ acre) during the agricultural year. From ploughing to harvesting, the total is 9.5–10.5 per *iugerum*, or 14.5–15.7 man days per acre. This can be compared with modern figures: in England at the end of the eighteenth century, 12 man days per acre was considered average; in the Cordoba region of Spain, where manual agriculture on startlingly similar lines to those described in the Roman agricultural works was practiced until recently, 20 to 24 man days is the figure quoted; and lastly, in the highly mechanized area of Kansas, USA, 0.4 to 0.8 man days is now usual. It is interesting to see that the figures compare favorably with those from Spain, which is the closest comparison in terms of the farming techniques used. Was Columella idealizing his figures to give a favorable impression, or were the slave-run villas of the Sette Finestre type, which is what he was describing, actually as efficiently organized as he claims? Whatever the answer, the most important point to emerge is the fact that Columella even bothered to calculate these figures. In the Roman world, such precision was very rare, and other writers seem unconcerned with matters like efficiency and economic management. However, it appears that in agriculture at least, there was some attempt at organization along rational or 'scientific' lines.

LEFT A hunting lunch, on a mosaic from the Piazza Armerina villa, Sicily. In the center a large chicken is being roasted. Hunting was a popular pastime among the aristocracy.

BELOW Mosaic of a villa with lookout towers, from Tabarka.

ABOVE A wall-painting of a large *villa maritima* (seaside retreat). Such villas were common in the Bay of Naples and near Rome. Senators and other wealthy citizens would use them in the summer months when it was too hot in the cities.

RIGHT A goat herd milking. Goat's milk was popular in Roman times, and provided the bulk of cheese and butter. However, the goats themselves were voracious eaters, and it has been suggested that they were partly responsible for the ruination of farmland in some parts of the empire due to overgrazing.

PREVIOUS PAGE A bullock cart carrying a wild animal in a cage, the aftermath of a hunting expedition, from the Piazza Armerina villa.

The same rational approach can also be seen when the agricultural writers turn to subjects such as the treatment of the soil or crop husbandry. For instance, Columella gives a detailed account of field drains, specifying which soils are most suited to open drains and which to covered or hidden ones. His recommendations are exactly the same as those followed until the beginning of this century, when contour draining was widely introduced.

All the agricultural writers say a great deal about vine growing, since viticulture brought a high return for the money invested, yet the vines required careful handling to produce that return. Advice is given on the types of vine suitable for different soils, for there were apparently a large number of varieties of grape that had been developed over the centuries. This is not to say that the Romans knew about or consciously practiced selective breeding so as to improve the fruit, but it is clear that the likes and dislikes of the different varieties were appreciated and that new types were introduced experimentally from other areas. The vineyard required a great deal of preparation, including the complete turning over of the soil to a depth of three feet or so. This was usually done by contract labor, as the slaves concerned with the day-to-day running of the villa would be occupied with other tasks. Archaeological evidence of this trenching comes from southern Italy where Roman fields with deep rock-cut furrows in them have been found. Contract labor was also used for harvesting and treading the grapes.

The overall impression of these passages from the literary sources and from the remains of villas such as Sette Finestre is of a bustling, but labor-intensive efficiency, and an interest on the part of villa-owners to improve their farming methods, and plant new crops. However, efficiency and innovation should not be stressed unduly, for we have no evidence of anything like labor-saving machinery or of selective breeding for genetic improvements. That the Romans were capable of the former cannot be doubted (*see* chapter six), but there seem to have been social constraints on many technical developments that prevented them being introduced. The only known exception to this in farming was the *vallus* (mechanical harvester) which was used in the spacious wheat-fields of northern Gaul. In this region, the weather was unpredictable enough to necessitate rapid harvesting during the time available, and it is possible that there was a labor shortage. These problems would have encouraged the development of the *vallus* as a suitable solution. However, this is exceptional, and in other areas the harvest was brought in by slaves and hired laborers using sickles or reaping combs.

Animals on the Roman farm were probably not as common as they are today. The diet was much more vegetarian and the average Republican smallholding was too small to allow any space for grazing. For most people, meat was a luxury, to be enjoyed on holidays when sacrificial animals were slaughtered and the meat handed out, and occasionally at other times. In Italy and Rome the most common meat was pork, with mutton following it in popularity. Beef was rare, since cows were not usually kept except as draft animals. In the northern provinces these preferences were reversed, with beef and mutton being more popular than pork. These differences must be due to the variations in culture between the peoples of the north and the Mediterranean, variations that were not eradicated by the Roman invasions. However, it is not yet possible to say exactly why particular animals were preferred as their main source of meat by different groups within the empire.

It is known, however, what the animals looked like, for large numbers of their bones have been found in the rubbish dumps excavated in Roman towns, villas and forts. There were two major breeds of cow, a small short-horned type that was common in the north, and a larger type that may have resembled the

ABOVE A cowherd and his dog look over the stock. To his right is a Priapus figure and a brazier, representing fertility and purification.

BELOW Hadrian's villa, Tivoli, a famous Imperial retreat near Rome.

large white Tuscan cattle of present-day Italy. After the Roman invasions of Gaul, Germany and Britain, the larger cow was introduced in the north and the two types were interbred, to produce the ancestor of the cow breeds that are familiar today. There were also a number of breeds of sheep, according to whether they were needed for meat, wool or milk. Goats were kept for their hair and their milk.

An interesting problem is presented by the remains of pig bones, for their general shape suggests that they were simply a smaller version of a wild boar, and it is possible that most pigs were simply left to roam semiwild in the woods and hill pastures.

Hunting certainly had a major place in the Romans' use of the countryside. There are many references to boar or deer hunting, as for instance on the exuberant inscription from Bollihope in County Durham: 'To the unconquerable Silvanus (god of the woods), Gaius Tetius Veturius Micanus, prefect of the Sebosian cavalry unit . . . set up this (altar) for capturing a wild boar of remarkable fineness which many of his predecessors had been unable to bag.' There were more exotic beasts to be found in the wild woods and scrubland of the empire too. Lions still prowled in Syria and bears in Germany. There were wolves, wild goats and a wealth of other game in many of the hilly areas that were generally little exploited by the Romans except for sport.

VILLAS AND THE COUNTRYSIDE

The countryside was also used for leisure. The country house was the retreat of many an overworked senator or knight escaping from the heat of Rome or his home town. For most, the country house was also the villa, but for the richer Roman there was the true country retreat, which tended to have few or no facilities for farming, and was often by the seaside. Houses of this type situated just outside the town limits were called *villae suburbanae*, of which the most famous is Emperor Hadrian's retreat at Tivoli near Rome. Seaside villas were called *villae maritimae* and were usually positioned with a portico or verandah overlooking the sea. A large concentration of them lay along the shores of the Bay of Naples and neighboring islands, an area in many ways regarded as the playground of Rome, very much as it is today. One of the most famous of these villas was the villa Iovis built by the Emperor Tiberius at the top of a 1000-foot cliff on the island of Capri. It consists almost solely of the emperor's private apartments, together with a sun terrace and a grotto at the foot of the cliff.

For rich and powerful men such as the emperor, the countryside was a place of retreat from the cares of day-to-day affairs. For the majority of country dwellers, however, the drudgery of farming work made them leave for the pleasures of the city in droves. As shall be seen in the final chapter, by the end of the imperial period this had led to the problem of deserted farmland, and the emperors felt forced to bind peasants legally to their native soil. Such was the lot of probably the most misused class of people in the Roman empire, and their dissatisfaction was an indirect cause of the decline of Roman power.

ABOVE LEFT A fractious mule refuses its food, a mosaic from the Imperial Palace, Constantinople, *circa* AD 567–8.

ABOVE Ox cart bringing in the grape harvest. On the right the grapes are being trodden. From Santa Costanza church, Rome, fourth century AD.

LEFT A captured boar being taken back to the villa. From Piazza Armerina villa, Sicily.

RIGHT The portico of a second century AD villa near Utica, Tunisia, surviving in a remarkable state of preservation.

FISHBOURNE PALACE

In the Roman countryside just outside the town of Noviomagus (Chichester, England) stood one of the most remarkable buildings to be erected in the northern provinces. From the 60s AD, just over 20 years after the invasion of Britain, building activity went on that was to culminate some twenty years later in a vast palace. It was not really a villa in the normal sense, for it had reception rooms and audience chambers for official functions, but it did have many of the characteristics of the *villa maritima* (seaside retreat).

The palace was arranged around a large courtyard, within which were the re-remains of carefully laid-out bedding trenches for an ornamental garden. The east wing, facing Noviomagus, was the entrance, made up of an imposing colonnaded hall that gave onto the garden. Rooms led off on the north side, arranged around small porticoed courtyards. Perhaps these were rooms for guests, or for members of the owner's family and entourage. There were similar sets of rooms and small courtyards in the north wing, probably for the same purpose. In the corner between the two wings was a large aisled hall, of the same dimensions as the entrance hall. This was probably for assemblies of some sort, and perhaps court cases were held here, or speeches made.

The west wing was probably the most important in the whole palace. Directly opposite the entrance hall in the east wing was a set of steps leading up to an audience chamber. The owner of the palace would have sat here in state, able to observe all who came across the garden to seek his judgment or advice. The other rooms served as reception rooms and offices, possibly also for providing guests with

meals. Behind the west wing was a long corridor linking the rooms together. It was 18 feet wide with semicircular ends, and is very similar to the exercise corridors that were provided in many Mediterranean villas. Doubtless the owner would have been crowded with supplicants and petitioners if he went out for exercise, so he built himself a covered private area in which to walk or run. The south side of

the palace is the least well-known today, since it lies under a modern road, but it is very likely to have been the residential quarter for the owner, facing onto a private garden with the sea beyond. In the southeast corner was his private bath suite, and perhaps also the slaves' quarters.

Ownership of the palace has not been established beyond doubt. Its early date and sumptuous appearance must indicate official subsidy for the construction of the building, as it is unlikely that any of the native leaders would have been wealthy enough to erect the building from their own resources. We know that the king of the local tribe, Cogidubnus of the Regnenses, was a staunch ally of the Romans, both during the invasion of the country and at the time of a major rebellion in AD 60. The palace may have been a reward for his support. Alternatively, but less probably, it may have served as the seaside residence for the provincial governor.

About 30 years after it was put up, alterations were made which resulted in the division of the palace into smaller units. It is thought that this change followed the death of the king and constitutes the division of the palace among his heirs. Building work continued until the palace was ruined by fire in the mid-third century. Pirates raiding from the sea may have caused the final conflagration, as we know that the Roman authorities were having difficulty patrolling the seas at this time.

ABOVE LEFT The garden, after replanting.

LEFT Reconstruction of Fishbourne palace at its fullest extent.

TOP RIGHT One of the early geometric black-and-white mosaics, seen during the excavation.

RIGHT Mosaic of a boy riding a dolphin, laid not long before the palace burned down in the third century AD.

BELOW Marble bust of a youth, from the palace.

The Tower of the Winds,
Athens, late first century BC.
Inside was an elaborate 24-hour
clock and possibly a
planetarium.

CHAPTER VI
TECHNOLOGY, INDUSTRY AND TRADE

In matters of science and technology the Romans owed nearly everything to the Greeks. It was from the philosophical investigations of Plato's Academy and the Lyceum of Aristotle that ancient (and ultimately, of course, present-day) scientific ideas were developed. The Romans took over these ideas for their own use, for they had no scientific tradition of their own and they were strongly influenced by Greek culture in all walks of life.

When the Romans started to take an interest in the eastern Mediterranean in the third century BC, the center for scientific study was Alexandria. Here, in the Museum, which was not a place filled with exhibits as we are accustomed to think of a museum today, but much more like a teaching university, about a hundred professors taught a wide variety of subjects. There were facilities such as observatories, botanical gardens, dissecting rooms and, the most important part of the institution, its famous library, which was the largest in the ancient world, holding about half a million papyrus rolls.

The work done at the Museum laid the foundations for all the main subjects that are studied today, and the professors produced text books for their students that have often remained in use up until recent times. The most famous and most highly developed of these was the *Elements of Geometry* by Euclid. Mathematics had always been one of the most respected branches of ancient philosophy, and it attracted men of the highest intellectual power. Pythagoras, for instance, was one of the founders of the subject and established many fundamental theorems, such as that of proportionals. He based his theorems on the philosophy that problems could be investigated by the intellect alone, without reference to material things. This was an influential school of thought in classical Greece and without it abstract ideas and the theoretical basis of such subjects as mathematics and physics could not have developed. Euclid was responsible for establishing a system for the study of geometry along logically constructed lines, based on a few definitions and common notions. His work has stood the test of time so well that it was the standard geometry textbook for English schoolchildren until very recently, and still forms the basis of the subject.

Archimedes was one of Euclid's immediate successors. He too was a mathematician, with books such as *On Spirals* and *On Conoids and Spheroids* to his credit, but he is best known as an inventor. The Archimedes screw was, and still is, used for lifting water from the Nile to irrigate the fields, and his siege machines for the defense of Syracuse are regarded as the finest developments in their field. This practical side to ancient science was apparently of most interest to the Romans, although the scientists themselves derided it. Plutarch says of Archimedes, 'He looked

upon the work of an engineer and everything that caters for everyday needs as ignoble and vulgar.' A typical product of Greek engineering science is the steam engine of Hero. Steam pressure was used to make a sphere rotate, an invention that startlingly precedes the development of steam power in the seventeenth century by many hundreds of years. Sadly, it was never put to practical use, because the engineers were not interested in the applications of their subject.

However, Roman science was essentially the development of these applications. Men such as Vitruvius and Frontinus wrote treatises on architecture and aqueducts respectively, which give every detail of construction techniques, water flow, foundation depths, proportions of columns and so on. Apart from these important contributions, only Greeks practiced science in its true sense in the Roman Empire. Ptolemy the geographer, for instance, constructed a map of the world based on longitude and latitude, and wrote a book on astronomy.

If one takes science to have the wider meaning of an ordered intellectual analysis, however, there were several fields in which Romans made notable contributions. Varro, well-known for his book on agriculture, also wrote a treatise on the Latin language which is one of the first coherent analyses of Latin grammar. He undertook this task partly because of the need to translate large numbers of books from Greek into Latin. Varro's grammar was intended to be part of an encyclopaedia covering the subjects of logic, rhetoric, maths, astronomy, music, medicine and architecture. Although none of this project survives apart from the grammar, it set the style for other encyclopaedias of the Roman and Middle Ages. The most famous and the most idiosyncratic is Pliny's *Natural History* which is a long, rambling discussion of man's use of natural objects.

Greeks also held the forefront of the field of medicine. Scientific study of human anatomy had developed in classical Greece under the same enlightened conditions as other branches of science. By the time of the Roman dominance of the east, there were detailed text books on subjects such as the eyes, and much debate centered on the results of dissections, for instance on the purpose of the arteries. In the first century BC this knowledge was transported to Rome by the influential doctor Asclepiades, who achieved widespread popularity through his recommendation of exercise, baths and massage as one of the best cures for minor illnesses. He also made more serious contributions to medicine, such as isolating malaria from other diseases, and distinguishing pleurisy from pneumonia. Surgery developed at the same time, and there are records of doctors performing eye operations to remove cataracts, and removing gallstones.

TECHNOLOGY, INDUSTRY AND TRADE

Surgical instruments have been found at many sites in the empire, over 200 being recovered from Pompeii alone. Some of the instruments such as those for obstetrics, are very much the same as those used today.

Of course, the services of a doctor were not available to everybody in the empire. They had to be paid for, and it is likely that only rich citizens and their households were given adequate medical treatment. However, the wide distribution of surgical tools throughout the empire does suggest that most people had the possibility of obtaining medical help, provided that they could afford it. The army was certainly well provided for, with hospitals at all the major forts, and soldiers with first-aid training being on hand in the field.

The general state of health of the population is very difficult to assess, since the literary sources say little, apart from the physician Galen's references to malnutrition among country dwellers in the second century AD. However, we can glean some facts from the archaeological remains of skeletons in cemeteries. Diseases such as leprosy and syphilis affect the bones, and conditions like arthritis and fractures are also easy to detect. Leprosy was

Steam power used to open the doors of a temple.

BELOW Part of Ptolemy's map of the world.

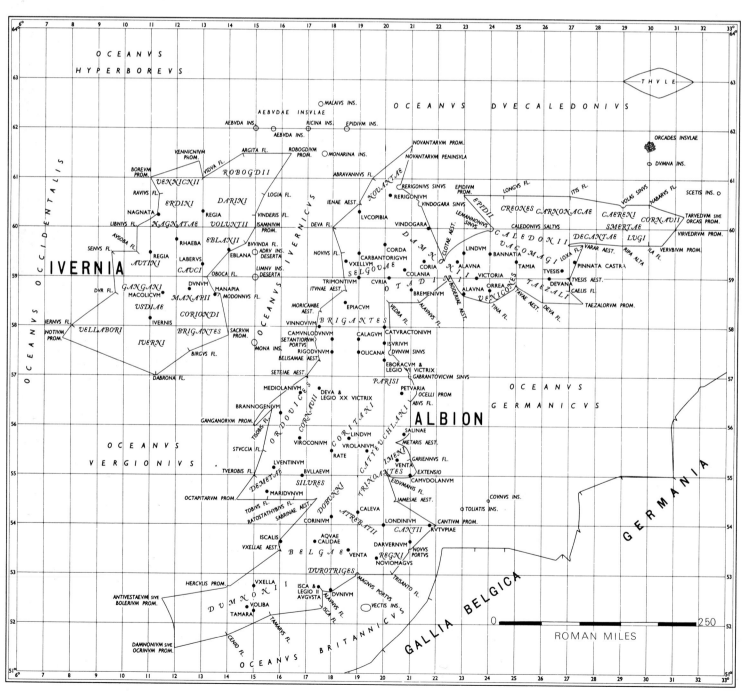

thought to have been brought to Europe after the demise of the Roman Empire, but recent finds of skeletons have confirmed its presence in fourth-century Britain, and presumably it must have spread there from elsewhere in the empire. Other studies have discovered that in Roman towns with lead piping skeletons in their cemeteries have higher lead levels than would be expected. Lead poisoning thus seems to have played a part in making the life expectancy only 30 for women and 45 for men in some areas, if the statistics from tombstones can be relied upon. Work has also been done on tooth decay, suggesting that it was less prevalent than it is now, owing to the lack of sweet foods and the grinding effect of grit from millstones in bread.

In the later empire epidemics swept across Europe from the east, starting with the plague that Marcus Aurelius' army caught and spread to the west in AD 166–67. It is difficult to decide which disease is being referred to when the epidemics are described, since only rarely are symptoms given. The doctor Dioscurides wrote of bubonic plague in Egypt in the first century BC. This is a disease that still provokes fear, but many of the epidemics in the empire may have been of diseases that are relatively innocuous today, such as chickenpox and German measles. However, in a population with poor health, and without any immunity to a new disease, these ailments could have had a disastrous and fatal effect.

Turning from medicine back to engineering and technology, it is worth considering the archaeological evidence for the technological achievements of the Romans. The aqueducts that supplied most Roman towns and, in a different sphere of activity, the mechanical wheat harvester used in northern Gaul, have already been discussed. The Romans developed other mechanical aids like the crane operated by a treadmill, which used pulleys to raise stone blocks for buildings. Cranes had been used by the Greeks for erecting their temples and monuments, so they cannot be regarded as a Roman invention, but their use only became widespread in the Roman period. Watermills were also probably Greek in origin, but they only became common through Roman interest.

Waterwheels were used for two different purposes – grinding and raising water. Grinding corn and crushing olives were the most common uses, with the power of the water driving a large millstone via a set of cogs, much as a modern mill does. Corn was also ground by hand, using a quern, or by a donkey-driven mill; windmills had not been invented at this time. When waterwheels were used to raise water the action was reversed from an ordinary watermill so that an animal such as a donkey drove the wheel round and round and each blade lifted some water the height of the wheel. The water was usually used to irrigate fields, but occasionally more sophisticated wheels are found, such as those in the copper mines at Rio Tinto in southern Spain which were used for draining the mine shafts and galleries.

The main point to be made about Roman technology is that it was not particularly inventive. Nearly every mechanical aid that the Romans took advantage of had been invented or developed at an earlier period. The Roman contribution was to refine the technology and spread engineering knowledge throughout the empire. The impact this made on the more backward provinces must have been enormous. For instance, in Britain, the number of iron tools found on excavated sites increases dramatically with the Roman invasion, indicating the more widespread use of a metal that is extremely useful but is difficult of manufacture. Apart from tools and machines, crafts such as road building, architecture and pottery making were all brought to a high level of development by the Romans and they laid the foundations, both literally and metaphorically, for the accomplishments of later peoples.

One craft about which there is a great deal of detailed information is potting, since many kilns have been excavated, and pottery

ABOVE A treadmill crane being used to construct a temple, shows typical Roman ingenuity.

BELOW A soldier's wounds being dressed during a battle, from Trajan's Column.

itself survives in the soil very well. Pots were used for all sorts of different purposes in Roman times – for cooking, serving, eating and drinking, as well as for the bulk transportation of goods such as wine or honey, and storage. Clay was fired in kilns to make roof-tiles, lamps and statuettes. As a result there were kilns in virtually every district of the empire. Some were built to a very low standard and were designed simply for the cruder cooking pots, others were refined and sophisticated enough to produce high-quality decorated and glazed pottery.

A typical Roman kiln was a domed chamber of clay, which could hold several hundred pots, under which was a firing chamber and a stoke hole. A fire was lit in the stoke hole, its heat and smoke passed through the pottery chamber and out through a vent. For the finer pottery a kiln was used which kept the pottery in a separate compartment from the smoke. This allowed greater control of the color and finish of the vessels, and prevented large numbers of vessels from cracking, which was a common problem. Firing usually took about two days, with a further week or so for cooling. Nearly all the ordinary Roman pottery was plain, without any form of decoration or glaze. This meant that only four colors of pot were possible – gray, black, white or red – depending on the type of clay and the precise way in which the pottery was fired. The Roman kitchen and dining table must have been rather somber as a result. More-colorful effects were achieved by coating the pot in a slip or glaze, and by adding decoration.

LEFT The Lycurgus Cup. The design is carved from a single piece of glass.

RIGHT A glazed molded flagon, dated the first century AD.

BELOW Cupids making up medical preparations, from a wall painting in the House of the Vettii, Pompeii.

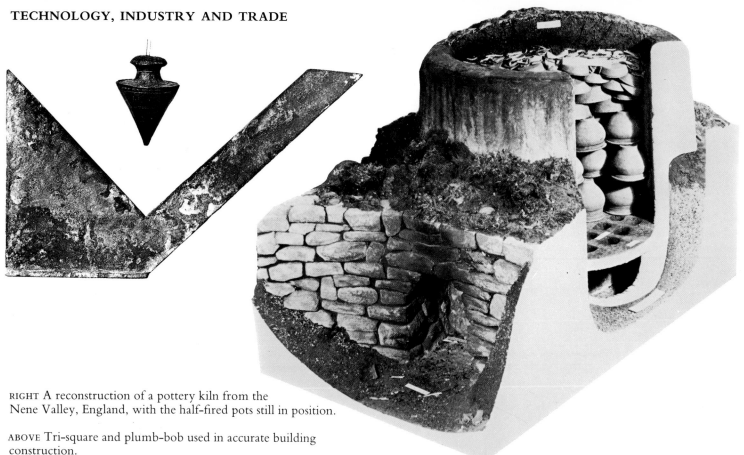

RIGHT A reconstruction of a pottery kiln from the
Nene Valley, England, with the half-fired pots still in position.

ABOVE Tri-square and plumb-bob used in accurate building
construction.

One of the most common types of decorated pottery was
samian ware, a bright-red table service decorated with small
figures around the bodies of the vessels. This pottery provides a
good illustration of the expertise that Roman potters were
capable of. The vessels were made in molds on a potter's wheel,
a method which allowed standardized shapes to be made, and
also eased the design of the decoration. Since the molds were of
clay, they could be impressed with punches of the individual
elements in the design. In this way, the designer did not need to
make up a new pattern for each pot, and identical vessels could
be made in an ancient form of mass production. Also, the punches
would be used in different combinations when a new design was
wanted, which meant that the time and effort of making a design
was reduced. The reason for attempting to save labor through
mass production was probably that the potters were slaves, who
farmed when they were not potting. Since the main time of year
for potting was the summer, because the clay was most easy to
handle then, savings of time may have been needed in order to
cope with farming activity too.

The other specialized processes in the making of samian ware
were the preparing of the surface finish – the slip or gloss – and
the firing. The shiny red slip was made of the same clay as the
matt body of the pot, made shiny by using a chemical such as
natron to make the clay form a very fine suspension in water.
After evaporation the syrupy slip was coated on the pot. This
method is very much the same as modern ways of preparing a
slip, but it is interesting that attempts to reproduce the shiny
effect were unsuccessful until very recently, when experiments
were done that repeated the probable ancient techniques, using
the same type of clay. Apart from the esthetic appearance of the
shiny slip, it was also waterproof, a distinct advantage over
nearly all other types of ancient pottery, which required greasing
or coating in pitch before they could hold water. The firing of
samian vessels was done in a closed kiln which kept the smoke and
the pottery separate, thus preventing discoloration and ensuring
an even heat.

Another important type of pottery was coated in the familiar
vitrified glaze that is now universal. The Romans were the first
to use glazes at all widely, but it was an expensive and difficult
process, and only small drinking cups and small bottles could be
made in this way. The technique of glazing seems to have been
lost after the end of the Roman Empire, and it was not until the
twelfth century that glazed pottery starts to be found again.

Archaeologists are also interested in pottery apart from the
light it sheds upon ancient technology. Because it survives so
well, and because of the possibility of tracing virtually every
sherd to its place of manufacture, pottery is of great importance
in understanding ancient trade. Individual kilns and workshops
produced distinctive shapes and decorative styles. In addition,
chemical analysis of pot sherds can often reveal which geological
deposit the clay came from. In general, the larger and coarser
vessels, used for storage and cooking, were not transported very
far. There were kilns just outside most towns; they were not
permitted inside the walls because of the fire risk. Usually a
number of kilns were built together, so that fairly continuous
production could be carried out. These kilns supplied the local
needs of the district and, if the potters were commercially
minded, they set their sights higher by also making some
speciality, such as lamps or fine table pottery. If it was of good
quality and achieved widespread recognition, the speciality
often came to be traded over vast distances. Many of the different
varieties of glazed and slipped wares became popular, brought
fame to the pottery and started a fashion which others followed.
The potteries at Cologne (Köln) were typical of this pattern, for
they started as suppliers of the colonists of the town, but after a
hundred years or so began to make a series of fine drinking cups
with lively scenes of dogs chasing wild animals on them. These
became well-known in the whole of the northern provinces and
were widely exported.

Samian ware was traded in a slightly different way from other
sorts of pottery. The workshops and kilns were usually in the
countryside, grouped together in large cooperative ventures.
The kilns tended to be used only for samian ware and a few other,
similar types of pottery. Large quantities of the same pottery
were produced, sometimes identical plates by the thousand, as
inscriptions found at the kilns record. The pots must have been

exported on a large scale, since this type of pottery is found in virtually every corner of the empire. Boat loads must have been shipped down the rivers of Gaul, where it was produced, and thence across the Mediterranean or to the frontier districts, where it was very popular with the troops. In fact, samian ware was produced on such a large scale and was so popular that it swamped all its rivals and became the universal standard of ceramic taste in the Early Empire. It is one of the only ancient industries which is known to approach modern systems of production and distribution.

Pottery has been discussed at some length because it provides a good example of the way in which the Romans produced and traded commodities. Other materials do not survive nearly so well, or else are not capable of being referred back to their place of manufacture. The literary sources are also silent on such mundane activities, as it was felt beneath a Roman gentleman's consideration. People who engaged in trade were looked down on by the aristocracy, who regarded agriculture, politics or the professions as the only respectable pursuits. As a result, we have to rely on the mute, and often contradictory material evidence from the archaeological sites themselves.

Another commodity, wine, is well-documented from Roman excavations, by virtue of being traded in pottery containers known as *amphorae*. Wine was made in all the Mediterranean countries that now produce it, and the discarded containers have been found throughout the empire and indeed beyond, such was the demand for some of the wines. Different wine-producing areas used *amphorae* of distinctive shapes, allowing us to assess the size of their market in Roman times. Naturally enough, Italian wine (and olive oil, which was shipped in similar containers) had the highest reputation, at least in the Republic and the Early Empire. It has already been shown that the villa at Sette Finestre was involved in wine production, and the *amphorae*, made near the villa, with the mark of Sestius stamped on the rims, were distributed up the coast of Italy, into the South of France, and up the Rhône Valley which at that time was beyond the boundaries of Roman rule. Evidently the Celtic Gauls had a taste for Mediterranean forms of refreshment, as opposed to their native beer.

The information about trade available from the study of *amphorae* can be used to show how trading patterns between different parts of the empire develop and change through the centuries. For instance, a study of the *amphorae* from Ostia, the port of Rome, reveals a startling alteration in the balance of trade of Italy during the second century AD. Up to that time Rome was supplied by local and Italian producers for the great majority of goods like wine and oil. However, by the late first century the provinces were developing their own industries in these products. Spain and Gaul were soon displacing the Italian trade with their own products, a trend which is confirmed by the large numbers of new or enlarged villas in those countries that date from this period. These provinces, too, were supplanted in the Roman market place by the end of the second century by the rapid growth of the North African oil industry, which successfully competed for the lucrative free oil rations given to the citizens of Rome. By the third century, African products dominated commerce in Rome, especially after the time of the African Emperor Septimius Severus (193–211), who favored his country of origin. Local Italian products were distinctly uncommon, and it seems that the original territory of the Roman Empire was suffering an economic collapse at the hands of the more efficient and now wealthier provinces. This has a number of wider consequences for the later history of the empire, which will be discussed more fully in chapter ten.

The transport of these goods, especially anything that was produced and consumed in large quantities, was nearly always by ship. Roman merchant ships were not large – on average about

ABOVE Molded and red-slipped samian ware drinking cup. Such vessels were common in most of the Roman world during the early empire.

BELOW A water-filter made from reused *amphorae*, Ampurias, Spain.

BOTTOM A Roman aqueduct leading to a waterwheel (the present wheel is modern), Hama, Syria.

LEFT A man transferring an *amphora* of wine or oil from a sea-going vessel in Ostia Harbor to a river barge for the journey up the Tiber to Rome. The mosaic is in the Piazzale delle Corporazione, Ostia.

RIGHT Large bread-oven from Pompeii, part of an establishment that also had several donkey-driven corn mills, and which must have supplied bread to much of the town.

BELOW *Amphorae* in a wooden rack preserved in position in a shop in Herculaneum. Just visible on the shoulder of the middle *amphora* on the bottom rack is the painted label giving details of manufacturer and contents.

50 tons. Large ships were rare, although we do hear occasionally of the craft like the grain-ship *Isis*, which was 180 × 45 feet and capable of carrying 1200 tons. They relied on sails for motive power, unlike warships which were rowed. At first a single large square sail was the norm, which did not make it easy for ships to sail against the wind. Later smaller square sails were added fore and aft which eased this problem. Merchantmen were very slow, averaging only 3 or 4 knots, which meant that all perishable goods had to be laboriously preserved before a voyage. The record for a voyage from Italy to Egypt was eight days. It was not possible to sail all the year round, particularly in the smaller boats, for Mediterranean winter storms were fierce and, as the shipwreck of St Paul graphically demonstrates, the threat of loss of life and goods was high. The lack of navigational aids also tended to prevent winter sailings, for steering was done by the sun or the stars, which was not, of course, possible during cloudy weather.

Although transport by ship was slow, it was very cheap compared with other methods. It has been calculated that land transport was 35–40 times more expensive per mile than shipping by sea, and that river barges were five times the cost per mile of sea vessels. This, of course, made the sea lanes the preferred route for transporting both goods and people. Despite the excellent quality of many Roman roads, the lack of means of transporting large quantities of goods by land, except on mule trains or by ox cart, kept costs high.

The high cost of moving anything a long distance in the ancient world meant that all bulky or low-cost goods tended to be produced and consumed locally. This meant that the provinces of the empire had different products available to them, with the result that day-to-day living was probably quite different depending on where one was born – some places having a good range of products on sale, others suffering shortages and high prices. A notable exception to the rule of not moving bulky items long distances was the transport of grain from Egypt to Rome

RIGHT An excavation of a wooden river barge at Pommeroeul, Belgium. Most bulk goods would have been carried by water, since costs were much less than by land.

BELOW A sculpture of an oared ship carrying barrels of wine, from a tomb at Neumagen near Trier, Germany.

for the free bread ration. This was because of the special needs of Rome itself, and the availability of funds from the emperors to meet the vast expenses involved.

In general, only luxuries came long distances. The best example of this is silk, which came from China, at first through the hands of a large number of middlemen, but eventually via Greek and Roman trading posts in India. In the second century AD a certain Alexander sailed to South China, reaching the town of 'Cattigara' which may be either Hanoi or Canton. Roman objects have been found in the area of the Mekong delta, and in quite large numbers in India. It is very likely that there was direct trading between India and Egypt or Asia Minor by sea. Some of the Roman finds in India, especially at Arikamedu near Pondicherry, may be the remains of trading posts manned by Romans and Greeks. Certainly the amount and variety of goods imported to India (pottery, wine, linen, coral, glass) and exported to Rome (pearls, ivory, spices, and perfumes), would justify such a trading post.

Although the general opinion is that the Romans were not particularly inventive or technically minded, from studying their trade and industry it seems that they were very industrious and strove to introduce existing techniques everywhere they went. They were very willing to adopt other peoples' discoveries, particularly the Greeks', and by doing this gained many advantages over more self-contained nations. However, by spreading the fruits of the empire throughout the vast lands that they controlled, they inadvertently sowed the seeds of decay in Italy itself, which led ultimately to a decline in the country which was not overcome until the later Middle Ages.

ROMAN COINAGE

The first Roman coins were large bars and cakes of bronze each weighing about 5 pounds. They were introduced in about 300 BC to assist in making purchases within the relatively restricted area of central Italy. A few years later a set of more convenient circular bronze coins was issued, which were still extremely weighty compared to modern coins; the standard being the *as* (one-pound weight of bronze). For external trade with such people as the Greeks, silver coins of Greek type were used (*didrachms*) as the silver coins were much smaller, and silver was the normal metal used for exchange in the Mediterranean. The expansion of Roman territory during the third century BC led to increasing strains in the use of this cumbersome dual system, so in about 211 BC it was decided to alter the currency so

that it conformed more to the system prevalent elsewhere. A silver *denarius*, worth 10 *asses*, was issued, together with halves and quarters. Bronze coins remained in circulation, although their weights were no longer one pound per *as*, since the relative value of bronze had increased during the Hannibalic Wars. The silver and bronze coins were supplemented by occasional issues of gold, which at first appear to have had no fixed relationship to the other coins because they were used for bullion only, and

therefore were weighed and valued anew each time they were bought or sold. Later on, their value was fixed at 60 *asses*. Gold coins were rare until the end of the Republic when Julius Caesar started issuing them in large quantities.

With slight modifications, this system of currency lasted until the end of the Republic. During this period, responsibility for manufacturing coins was in the hands of junior politicians at Rome, who eagerly used the opportunity to put their own designs on the coins, usually a reference to their own name or family, or commemorating a famous event or general. The use of coins in this way led to the more obvious propaganda of the Imperial coinage.

Augustus reformed the coinage, as he did so many other aspects of Roman life. He used as a basis the *denarius* which, with the gold *aureus*, 25 times the value of the *denarius*, formed the state coinage. In

ABOVE LEFT An early Roman bronze bar ($6\frac{1}{2} \times 3\frac{3}{4}$ inches), the original currency of the city.

LEFT The denominations in use during the reign of Nero, Left to right, top to bottom: *aureus, denarius, sestertius, dupondius, as, semis, quadrans.*

RIGHT Men being paid for piece work in the wool industry.

BELOW RIGHT A bronze arm-purse with 28 *denarii* from Birdoswald fort, Hadrian's Wall. The money represents about a tenth of a soldier's annual wage.

Republican *denarius* with head of Roma.

Claudian coin celebrating the conquest of Britain.

RIGHT AND ABOVE Both sides of the medallion of Constantius issued on the recapture of London from rebels, AD 296

other words, these coins alone were sufficient for the main spending of the government and army pay and official contracts. Local bronze coinages were issued to cope with day-to-day transactions. In Rome, the bronze was reformed into the coinage that ultimately came to predominate everywhere. There were *sestertii* (4 per *denarius*) and *dupondii* (2 per *sestertius*) in brass, and *asses* (2 per *dupondius*), *semisses* (2 per *as*) and *quadrantes* (2 per *semis*) in copper.

Roman coinage reached its finest development during the early Empire. The artistry was of a high standard, and is often considered to be at its best under Nero. There is a bewildering variety of coin types (Marcus Aurelius issued 1500 different designs), usually used for propaganda. For instance, Claudius issued coins showing a triumphal arch marked 'DE BRITAN' after his conquest of Britain and Vespasian issued coins with the legend 'JUDEA CAPTA' after the siege of Jerusalem. Sometimes the coins covered up the true state of affairs – an issue with a message such as 'PAX AUGUSTA' (the Imperial peace) may hide an intrigue in the Imperial court or a revolt in the provinces.

To judge from the finds of coins on archaeological sites, there was a gradual but not serious inflation throughout the Early Empire. At first the low-value coins were the most common in circulation, an *as* being used to purchase a loaf of bread, for instance. Examples of more expensive prices and costs are: a meal for 2 *denarii*, a laborer's annual pay of 60 *denarii*, a soldier's annual pay of 300 *denarii*, a slave's freedom for 1000 *denarii*, a statue erected in a public place for 1200 *denarii* and a large mausoleum for 20,000 *denarii*. It cost Hadrian about 5 *denarii* per foot to build a road in southern Italy, and anything up to a million was normal for a large public building. The fairly stable prices of the first and second centuries gave way to a sudden burst of inflation in the third century, during which prices increased by possibly a thousand times. However, this affected mainly those who were hoarding coins, and it has been shown that the ordinary wage earner was, if anything, slightly better off at this time than before. Diocletian attempted to stop the inflation by reforming the coinage toward the end of the third century. He issued revalued gold and silver coins, worth approximately 2000 and 100 *denarii* respectively, and gave out an edict of maximum prices. Neither measure really worked, for inflation continued and further coin revaluations were made subsequently, but the edict of prices remains one of our most important documents about the ancient economy. It regulated the cost of everything, from the sale of grass (six pounds per *denarius*) to the monthly fees for a student of architecture (100 *denarii*) and a 'British cape' (6000 *denarii*). A laborer now earned about 7000 *denarii* a year.

CHAPTER VII
LEISURE AND ENTERTAINMENT

Perhaps the most famous Roman building of all is the Colosseum, Rome's massive amphitheater at the south end of the forum. Visitors cannot fail to be impressed by its size, and those with an inkling of what went on there in Roman times usually pause to wonder at the cruel and often repulsive social values that allowed such inhumane activities to be glorified as a sport. The Colosseum was an arena for the games, the scene of innumerable contests between man and man, man and beast, or wild animals on their own. Together with horse racing in the *circus*, the games were the mainstay of popular entertainment in Roman times. Crowds would flock to fill the elliptical rows of stone seats – there was room for about 73,000 people – and displays would last for days at a time. We know that Emperor Titus opened the building in AD 80 with 100 days of games, during which 5000 wild animals were killed in a single day, according to his biographer, Suetonius.

Most of the entertainment provided was the spectacle of watching animals fighting one another, or attacking prisoners. This was cheaper to organize than gladiators, who were the top billing at most events. Many provincial arenas rarely saw shows with gladiators in them, and the poorest towns may have contented themselves with the relatively innocuous sports of cock fighting and bull or bear baiting. However, in Rome itself and in the other great cities, no expense was spared. Animals were brought from the remoter reaches of the empire and beyond – lions, tigers, leopards, bears – and their prey, possibly sheep, deer or something more exotic, like ostriches. The arrangements for organizing the animals were complicated, especially for the more ferocious animals. Underneath the arena was a maze of rooms and corridors which became a temporary menagerie during performances. Lions and such beasts, usually starved beforehand, were manhandled in iron cages from their underground pens to lifts operated by counterweights that raised them to the level of the arena. The Colosseum had 32 lifts, allowing a number of animals to appear simultaneously. Generally their opponents were huntsmen, known as *bestiarii*, and the spectacle often took on the appearance of a hunt or *venatio*, with a stage set of shrubbery and a pack of hounds to enhance the effect. Much of the show would have been similar to a modern bullfight. The *bestiarii* would display their skills, for instance by throwing a cloak over a lion's head, or waving the proverbial red rag at a charging bull. If they were threatened the men could retreat to shelter, either a screen at the side of the arena, or a spherical basket fitted with spikes, like a hedgehog, after which it was named.

There were many variations of this form of spectacle, ranging from the circus-turns of trained animals – panthers pulling chariots or elephants writing Latin words in the sand with their trunks – to the wanton butchery of scores of animals by shooting them down with arrows from the safety of the sidelines. One of the consequences of the wild-beast shows was that a huge demand existed for the capture of animals throughout the empire, to the extent that units of the army in Germany were seconded to duty as bear hunters. Ultimately, demand exceeded supply, and many of the larger carnivores ceased to exist within the confines of the empire, partly as a result of being overhunted. Lions disappeared from Mesopotamia, elephants from North Africa and hippopotamuses from the Nile.

In the Colosseum, *venationes* took place in the morning, as a prelude to the main event in the afternoon, the gladiatorial combat. In the same manner as the wild beast shows, there were many variations on the form of contest that took place. As a warm up, there were often mock battles using blunt weapons, and occasionally this formed the whole afternoon's entertainment. But what thrilled the crowd more than anything was the *munus* (fight to the death between pairs of gladiators). It was, in effect, a form of human sacrifice, since the games ultimately had religious connections, and they were staged, for example, as a thanksgiving by a successfully elected magistrate. The majority of gladiators were convicts, prisoners of war or slaves sent to the arena by their masters as a form of punishment. However, the highest reputation was accorded to those who volunteered to fight, since they were generally more proficient at arms.

There were several different types of gladiator. They were originally known as Samnites, after one of Rome's finest opponents from the south of Italy, who were possibly in the habit of holding contests of this sort when the Romans conquered them. There were also other national names for gladiators, particularly Thracians and Gauls, after two groups of people renowned for their fighting traditions. With slight variations, these groups wore a strong vizored helmet, a large shield, a dagger or short sword and a greave to protect the left shin. The armor together with the shield gave protection to the entire left side, which would have been exposed to blows from an opponent's sword. The only other clothes were a belt with a metal or leather band to protect the genitals, and leather straps wound round the right arm that held the weapon, and occasionally on other limbs. The *retiarius* was a different sort of gladiator, since he was not provided with any armor save a covering for his left arm, and used a net and trident as weapons. He was usually pitted against one of the other types of gladiator, and his only hope of winning was to keep an opponent at bay with the trident

ABOVE A stone lion that once adorned the parapet of Capua amphitheater.

LEFT *Bestiarii* killing leopards in the arena, on a third century AD mosaic from Moknine, Tunisia. Note the man holding a tray with bags of money for payment to the *bestiarii*. Also of note is that the leopard in the foreground is called Victor.

BELOW The arena of the amphitheater at Italica, Spain. The underground rooms for men and animals are clearly visible.

until a skillful throw of the net ensnared him. A thrust of the trident would then put an end to the fight.

Contests were usually fought to the death, but if the combatants were evenly matched and the fighting went on for a long time, a draw would be declared and both gladiators would be sent off to fight again another day. A wounded or cornered gladiator could submit, which he did by lying down on his back and raising his left arm. At this point the victor could take his opponent's life, but it was customary for him to give the power of decision to the sponsor of the games, usually the emperor. If the loser had fought well, or had lost through a stroke of ill-luck, the emperor would raise his thumb, which was the signal that his life had been spared. However, if the fight had been cowardly or weak, the emperor could simply put his thumb down, and the victor would cut the loser's throat. The crowd loudly signalled their opinions about the fight, either holding their thumbs up or down and shouting *Mitte!* (Let him go) or *Iugula!* (Kill him). It was an unwise emperor who disregarded the wishes of the spectators.

Going to see the gladiators was one of the great pleasures of Roman life. *Graffiti* on the walls of Pompeii record the 'sighs of the young girls' for a successful gladiator, and there was as much argument about swordplay and equipment as there is about tactics in a football match today. Indeed passions could spill over into fighting, of which the most famous example was the amphitheater riot at Pompeii in AD 59, between the people of that town and visitors from neighbouring Nuceria. As Tacitus records:

'It happened after a trifling incident at a gladiatorial contest given by a man expelled from the Roman Senate, Livineius Regulus. During an exchange of insults – typical of these rough country towns – abuse escalated to stone throwing and finally swords were drawn. The Pompeians fared best, many wounded and mutilated Nucerians being taken to the capital (Rome). There were also many bereaved parents and children.

The emperor ordered a senatorial inquiry, which was held by the consuls. After they had reported, the Senate banned shows in Pompeii for 10 years, dissolved illegal association in the town, and exiled Livineius and his fellow-instigators.'

Perhaps the best description of the strong feelings that the arena could inspire comes, ironically, from the writings of a man bitterly opposed to the amphitheater and all its associations, Saint Augustine:

'Alypius had gone to Rome before me to study law, and unbelievably had been swept off his feet with an incredible passion for the gladiatorial shows. He opposed and detested such things, but chanced to meet some friends, who by comradely pressure and persuasion, forced him to go along to the amphitheater to see one of those cruel and bloody shows. He said to them on his way there, 'You can drag my body in, but don't think that you can make me move my eyes, or yield my mind to the spectacle. Even though I am there, I shall be absent, and have the better of you and the show.' After this his friends were even keener to take him, to see if he could really do this or not.

RIGHT Model of the Colosseum.

BELOW Interior of the Colosseum, showing the foundations of the banks of seats on each side, and the extensive underground rooms below the arena floor. Lifts raised the animals to arena level.

BOTTOM Exterior of the amphitheater of Nîmes, France.

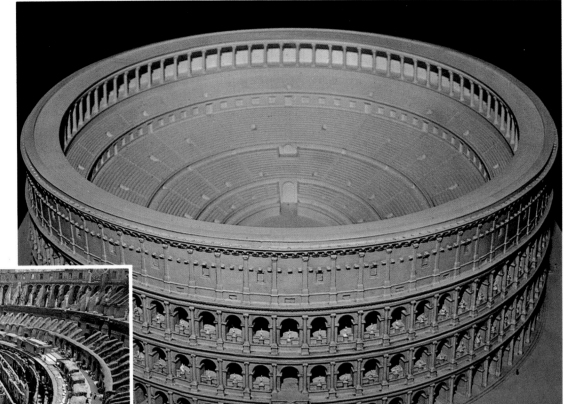

LEISURE AND ENTERTAINMENT

They arrived at the arena and took some empty seats. The crowd was alight with savage enthusiasm, but Alypius shut his eyes and forbad his soul to accept such an evil scene. But he should have blocked his ears, too! A man fell during one of the fights, and a great roar came up from the crowd. His curiosity overcame him, and he opened his eyes, feeling capable of ignoring whatever he might see and rising above it. His soul then suffered a worse wound than the gladiator had in his body. His fall was in fact more wretched than that of the man in the arena, for his soul had been reckless rather than strong by placing its trust in itself rather than in God. He saw the blood and drank in the savagery – far from turning away, he stared fixedly. Without knowing why, he was delighted by the guilty contest and drunk with bloodlust. He was no longer the individual who had gone there, but one of the crowd, a true companion of his friends.

There is little more to be said. He looked, he shouted and cheered with enthusiasm. Leaving with an addiction that would force him to return, he not only went again with his companions but would drag others with him.'

Christian writers condemned the amphitheater not only because it was considered cruel and inhumane to enjoy such sport, but also due to the large number of Christian martyrs who died in the arena. It was the fate of the lowest classes in Roman society to be condemned to the wild beasts (*ad bestias*) for certain offenses. Christians who refused to take the oath of loyalty to the emperor were included in this category because they were considered to be seditious and no longer worthy of citizenship. In this way many prominent and worthy townsfolk met a grisly and agonizing end, such as Blandina and her fellow citizens at Lyon in AD 177. She was bound in a net and left to the attentions of a maddened bull, and her companions met a similar fate, after which their corpses were left for six days for the crowd to abuse. To us, these abominations are hardly conceivable, especially in such a public manner. But, sad to relate, similar but more sophisticated atrocities are still committed today in many countries, but behind the walls of state prisons so as to reduce public opposition. We cannot condemn Roman attitudes without remembering that modern moral standards are scarcely better.

What is most appalling about these spectacles, however, is that many Romans derived a great deal of enjoyment from watching them. Emperor Claudius forced condemned and defenseless men to attack each other in order to enliven his midday meal, and he was so keen on the shows that he did not leave the amphitheater

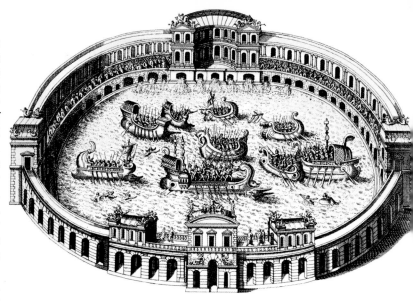

ABOVE A *naumachia* (mock sea-battle). Although fanciful, this engraving gives an idea of a less common entertainment.

BELOW Wall-painting of the riot in the Pompeii amphiteater in AD 59, that led to its closure for 10 years.

all day. Indeed, the scenes of mass butchery which these public executions entailed soon began to bore the crowds, and so they were enlivened by the addition of elaborate mechanical stage sets and simple plots of a mythological nature that always ended with animals being released onto the victims. For instance Daedalus flies across the arena, never to reach the other side: he falls to the ground into the clutches of a waiting bear. At the top of a miniature Mount Etna, a condemned man is chained, when suddenly the mountain collapses, throwing him into a cage of animals.

In explanation of such enjoyment of these scenes, all that can really be said is that fighting and combat were imbued in Roman ideals of success, and where personal participation was not feasible, as it was not for the vast majority of Romans, the excitement, without the dire consequences of actual involvement, could be had by being a spectator. The games fulfilled the fantasies of the average Roman, brought up in bad social conditions with little other chance of venting his frustrations and relieving his boredom. Life was cheap in Roman society; slaves and, at one time, women, could be killed without reference to the courts. Prisoners of war and criminals were without rights at all, and were felt to be suitable victims in what was in origin a

form of human sacrifice; to Roman eyes, an extension of the kind of death meted out to animals at the altar. But none of this condones the pleasure of the crowd while it watched the protracted agonies of a man or woman being mauled by an inept wild animal.

For a less cruel but more exciting form of entertainment, Romans went to the *circus* or horse-racing track. This sport was much more ancient than swordfights in the arena, for according to tradition the religious celebrations that went with the races dated back to the time of Romulus. Initially races were of horses and riders alone, the addition of a chariot probably being an Etruscan innovation. The original track was immediately to the south of the Palatine hill, in the small valley of the Murcia stream. The slopes of the Palatine and Aventine hills provided space for the spectators, who could look down on the races taking place along the banks of the stream. The horses would probably have gone up one bank and down the other, crossing at the top and bottom ends where the shrines to Consus and Ceres stood. In time this track was formalized by the addition of permanent seating and enclosure of the stream and bank. Eventually, there were tiers of stone and wood seating sufficient for something like 200–250,000 spectators, which by any standards is an

LEFT A charioteer in a *quadriga* (four-horse chariot). His sponsor is depicted larger than the others on the left. The cones and pyramids mark the *spina* that ran down the center of the circus. The dolphins on a pedestal in the background are part of the apparatus for indicating the number of laps left. On the right are the starting gates.

BELOW AND BELOW LEFT Two scenes of gladiators fighting in the arena, from a fourth century AD mosaic.

enormous crowd. The overall size of the circus was 1969 by 656 feet, with a length for each lap of about 1870 feet. A race consisted of seven laps, with four chariots as a rule, but sometimes up to 12, taking part. In Imperial times a day's racing was 24 individual events, plus the opening parade through the streets and a dinner for the spectators afterward. Races lasted for seven, nine or 15 days depending on the nature of the celebrations.

The race itself was dominated by the *factiones* (colors) into which the chariot teams were divided. There were four – the Whites, Greens, Blues and Reds – each with their own stables and private sponsors for, unlike the arena, horse racing was not dominated by the emperor's own team but was run along more commercial lines. A team from each faction would draw lots for positions in the starting-gates or *carceres* (prisons). This was done by placing four balls of the appropriate colors in an urn which could be swung on a pivot. It was then swung upside-down and the balls released into four cups. The placing of the different balls in the cups determined the order of the charioteers in the

carceres. Their chariots were either drawn by two horses (*bigae*) or by four (*quadrigae*), and occasionally by up to 10 (*decemiuges*). The most popular was the *quadriga* because it was both maneuverable and powerful. On this type of chariot, two mares were usually yoked to the central pole, with two stallions on either side attached by traces to the chariot's frame. The stallions were the most important, for the left-hand one had to act as a pivot at the turns, while the other pulled the chariot round.

The start was signalled by the sponsor of the race, splendidly attired on a platform above the starting-gates, dropping a white handkerchief into the stadium. The rope holding the gates shut was then raised and chariots, each dressed in one of the four colors, rushed out. It was the negotiation of the bends that decided the outcome of the race, since they turned 180 degrees and only the chariots on the inside stood any hope of gaining ground along the next straight. There was a great deal of jostling near the turns, especially toward the end of a race, with those on the outside trying to force the chariots on the inside to touch the

ABOVE The stadium for athletics at Aphrodisias, Turkey, probably the best-preserved Roman example.

LEFT A charioteer of the Red faction with one of his horses. He wears a leather helmet and leather straps around his torso for protection. First–second century AD mosaic.

BELOW The starting gates and towers of the Circus of Maxentius, just outside Rome on the Via Appia. Part of the stand for spectators can also be seen.

stone *spina* that divided the course in half and crash. Such a crash, called a shipwreck, was often fatal for the charioteer, especially if he could not cut himself free from the reins that were wound round his waist. Another tactic was for a following chariot to edge up to the one in front so that the horses pushed into the back of the fragile chariot frame. This could also cause a shipwreck, but had the drawback of also being risky for the aggressor.

Both charioteers and horses enjoyed immense prestige and honor if they performed well. There were star charioteers, who had won more than 1000 prizes, and several of them accumulated large fortunes, such as Diocles, who retired after 4257 races in which he had won 1462 times and had earned 35,000,000 sesterces. Large sums changed hands among the spectators as well, for feverish betting took place, resulting in impassioned scenes in the final stages of every race. As a precaution against rioting among the dissatisfied betters the emperors handed out food and threw gifts to the crowd, such as purses or 'raffle tickets' for something more substantial, like a house or even a ship, at the end of the day's racing.

An aspect of the circus that is made much of by Ovid in his book, *The Art of Love*, was the opportunity that it offered for members of the opposite sex to meet each other. Unlike the amphitheater, which tended to be a male preserve, men and women mixed freely on the seats of the stadium. As Ovid says, the intervals between races allowed conversation, and the excitement of the occasion made the audience less inhibited: 'The fair one has smiled and her sparkling eyes give a promise – that is enough – the rest is up to you.'

Such was the public interest in the circus that the four factions or colors eventually began to assume a greater importance than simply racing teams. The Blues and Greens became the most important of the four, and Blue began to be identified with the

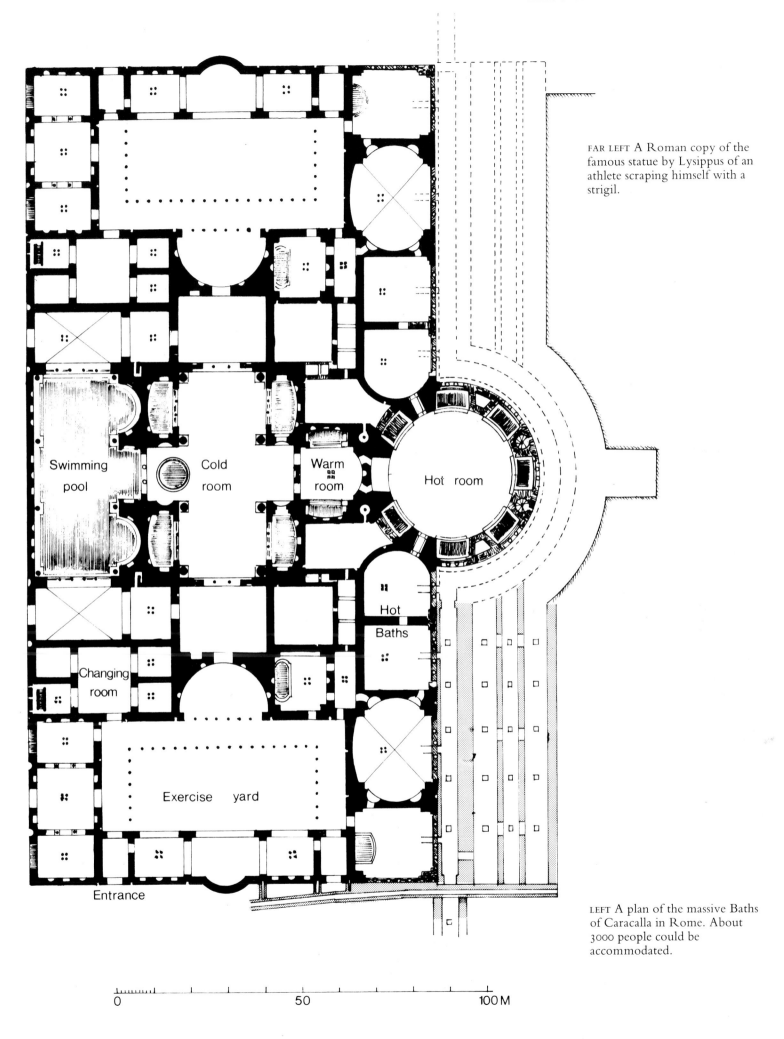

FAR LEFT A Roman copy of the famous statue by Lysippus of an athlete scraping himself with a strigil.

Swimming pool

Cold room

Warm room

Hot room

Hot Baths

Changing room

Exercise yard

Entrance

LEFT A plan of the massive Baths of Caracalla in Rome. About 3000 people could be accommodated.

0   50   100 M

ABOVE The Great Bath at Bath, England. Swimming pools such as this were rare, but at Bath they were used for healing purposes, being filled with hot water from the sacred spring nearby.

ABOVE LEFT The Baths of Diocletian as incorporated into more recent buildings in the sixteenth century. Excavations of part of the baths are going on in the foreground. From an engraving by du Pérac, 1575.

LEFT The small, private Hunting Baths at Leptis Magna, Libya. Apart from minor restoration of the vaults, the baths survive almost entire as they were covered by a sand dune.

RIGHT The Romans were much less inhibited about nudity than we are today. In fact, the phallus was a powerful symbol used to ward off evil, as on this amulet.

aristocracy and the Greens with the populace. This politicization of the circus culminated in the Byzantine era with the so-called Nika riots of AD 532. The factions had been allowed to push their weight around indiscriminately until Emperor Justinian decided to clamp down on them. This caused protests at the next race meeting, and the Blues and Greens refused to participate. Rioting broke out soon after that and only ended after much of the city of Byzantium had been burned and 30,000 people killed; such were the dangers of provoking the factions.

The circus below the Palatine Hill, known as the Great Circus or Circus Maximus, was not the only such structure in Rome despite its vast seating capacity. There were four others in the outskirts of the town, which gives some idea of the popular demand for racing. Many other towns also had circuses, which were called hippodromes in the east. However, it was an expensive form of entertainment, and only the richer towns could afford to build a permanent circus. Most of the surviving examples are in cities skirting the Mediterranean, such as Nîmes, Leptis Magna or Perge in Syria. Very few towns in the northern provinces constructed race tracks, however, and even in places where they were built, these massive monuments have not survived very well for they occupy large areas of ground and are not really suitable for conversion to any other use. Many were also made of perishable materials, such as wood. Only rarely, such as at the Circus of Maximian just outside Rome, can we gain a good impression of the atmosphere of the race track.

Horse racing in the circus was ultimately derived from Greece, where the most famous hippodrome was at Olympia, used for the four-yearly Olympic games. The games associated with the ancient Olympics also included many other events, such as

BELOW The *frigidarium* of the Baths of Caracalla.

running, wrestling and discus throwing. All of these sports were adopted by the Romans, who were happy to see the Olympics continue (up to AD 395). Other games were established elsewhere in the Roman world. Nero is credited with setting up a new series at Rome, to the approval of most people, but with many reservations on the part of the aristocracy, who regarded Greek games as effeminate and not a proper training for war (which was the original justification for most forms of sport). Archaeological evidence for these games is almost entirely absent, except for four stadia in Greece – at Olympia itself, Athens, Delphi and Epidaurus – and the stadium at Aphrodisias in Turkey and that of Domitian at Rome, now under the Piazza Navona. In other parts of the empire, stadia were often not permanent and the main evidence for an interest in games and exercise is the *palaestra* (exercise yard). This took the form of a sand-covered courtyard, surrounded by a portico and some rooms. Often, schoolmasters owned the yards and the young men of the town were taught wrestling and athletics there. One of the best examples is at Pompeii, where the *palaestra* was a large square space of about three acres with a swimming pool in the center next to the amphitheater; doubtless this was also the place where the gladiators practiced, and where men of all ages and states of health could keep fit. Physical health was always regarded as of great importance in the ancient world, as it was the main way of staving off disease. Even men in sedentary activities took exercise, such as the poet Seneca, who used to run foot-races in his old age against a young man that he kept on his staff for the purpose.

Allied with the desire to keep fit, the average Roman went to great lengths to keep clean. Every town had its set of public baths, to which everyone would go several times a week, for a wash, a chat with friends and a little exercise in the *palaestra* that was usually attached to the baths. For people living in tenement blocks in the big cities, the public baths were essential, for their apartments had neither water nor toilet facilities. However, bathing was not a chore in Roman times, since it was one of the main meeting places in any town and, apart from the sports mentioned earlier, was the main form of relaxation for the townsfolk. This was because a good bath took a long time, and there were many opportunities while there for conversation or activities such as board games.

Although the baths are thought of as a typically Roman institution, they are in fact Greek in origin. Early examples have been found at Olympia where the athletes used them after taking part in the events. Originally they were simply cold baths, but hot baths were developed by the fifth century BC, heated by a raised floor under which hot air from a furnace circulated. In Roman times the raised floors were known as *hypocausts*, and were also used to heat the living rooms of buildings in the colder provinces. The Romans adopted the baths in the late Republic, and gradually it became customary for everyone to bath, once a day by Hadrian's time. Richer citizens had private baths attached to their houses and villas, while others either joined a private bathing club or went to the municipal public baths. From the time of Augustus, the public baths were free and they rapidly became the main venues for taking a bath for rich and poor alike. Hadrian is known to have gone to the public baths, mingling with all who chanced to be there at the same time, and Commodus is reputed to have taken up to eight baths a day.

The main public baths of Rome were put up by Agrippa (Augustus' right-hand man), Nero, Titus, Trajan, Caracalla, Diocletian and Constantine. Each was in a different quarter of the city, and they catered both for the increasing population and for the upsurge in popularity of the baths. Those of Caracalla and Diocletian were the largest in the ancient world, each capable of holding up to 3000 people at once. Both are well preserved, Diocletian's being the larger (1247 by 1214 feet,

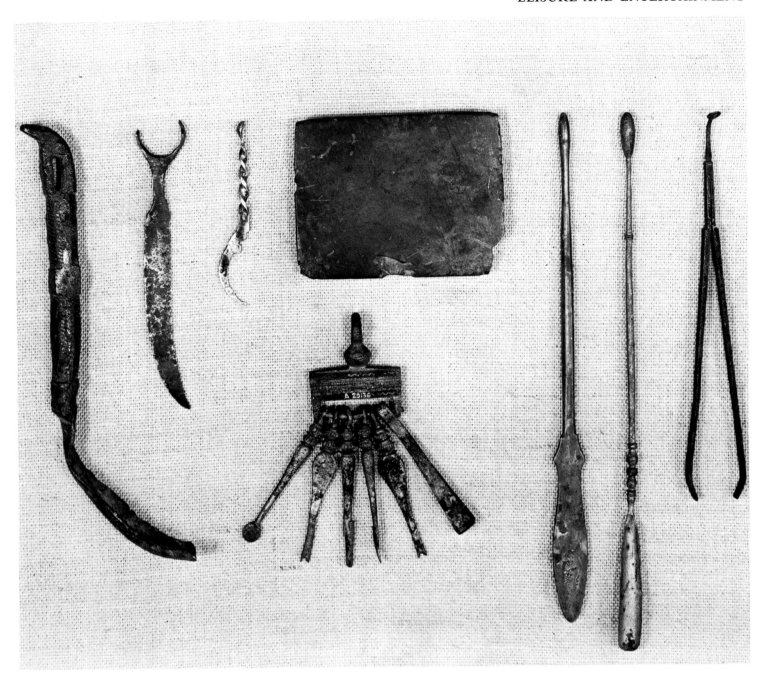

ABOVE Roman toilet instruments, including tweezers, nail and ear scoops, razors and a strigil.

across the courtyard; 820 by 590 feet for the baths block itself), but Caracalla's being the better preserved.

A bather entered the building through one of the left- or right-hand entrances, either to the central swimming pool, or to one of the two *palaestrae* to get some exercise. There was an *apodyterium* (changing room) in which clothes were left or changed for a simple tunic if games were going to be played. The bather now had a choice. Either he or she could go to the *palaestra*, and after some exercise there, repair to a *sudatorium* or *laconicum* which supplied dry heat on the lines of a Turkish bath in order to work up a sweat, or else go straight to the *caldarium* or hot, steamy room. This was the central part of the Roman bathing system. The bather got clean by applying olive oil instead of soap and using a strigil or scraping spoon to remove the mixture of oil and sweat. Although a metal or wooden strigil may seem to modern tastes rather a brutal method of removing dirt, it did in fact work very well, massaging the skin at the same time. In practice, it was not possible to clean oneself all over with these methods, and bathers went with the slaves to help rub them down, or hired an attendant to give assistance. After passing

through a slightly cooler room, the *tepidarium*, which helped to acclimatize bathers to the air temperature outside, a large hall was reached, used for relaxation and conversation before leaving. In this room was the *frigidarium*, where conscientious bathers would plunge into a cold bath before getting dressed.

Around the great public baths were gardens, equipped with kiosks, seats and shops. Here, bathers could stroll and talk before leaving for dinner, since the normal time for bathing was the afternoon, after the day's work was done. The emperors also tried to make the gardens edifying for the public, by supplying them with statues and libraries. In this way, the baths became major centers of popular culture, in which many people passed all their leisure hours.

The running of these vast complexes presented several problems to their designers. The large quantity of water used every day was supplied from branches off the main aqueducts. Water was stored in underground cisterns, on the same level as a warren of service corridors, down which slaves hurried with wood for the furnaces or towels for the bathers. The removal of all the services to a lower level helped to make the baths more compact and capable of handling large numbers of people without any holdups. Architecturally, this resulted in the most sophisticated buildings that the Romans ever produced, the different rooms interlocking with one another in a most effective way, and much use being made of concrete vaults to give enough space within the building.

Private baths copied their public counterparts in nearly all respects, except that most did not have the elaborate gardens and ornamentation. The best example is the Hunting Baths at Leptis Magna, which survived under a sand dune until being discovered in the 1930s. Everything except the tops of the vaults was preserved, and it has been possible to restore the building to its original appearance, giving us a unique insight into the arrangement and decoration of one of the smaller type of baths. They were probably owned by a guild or association of hunters, to judge from the scenes of a leopard-hunt in the amphitheater depicted on the walls of the *frigidarium*. Originally, most baths must have had wall decoration of stucco or marble, and mosaic or marble floors.

A variation on the normal type of baths were those connected to medicinal springs. Most of the mineral sources that are known today were first exploited by the Romans, both for drinking and for bathing in. They were ardent believers in the efficacy of the water from certain springs for curing diseases. The waters were endowed with religious qualities, and large temples with associated baths were set up over spring sites. This was the case at Bath in southwest Britain, where medicinal water of hot bath temperature was run into large swimming pools where bathers could soak aches and pains away.

In the evenings, most Romans retired to bed after their evening meal, since the day began at dawn for most people, and lighting was difficult, expensive and carried the risk of fire. However, entertainment was available, mostly in street-corner taverns and bars where the proverbial delights of 'wine, women and song' could be indulged in. Many taverns were the haunt of drinking clubs, which convened under largely spurious titles such as 'the association of carpenters of the IX region.' These were ostensibly craft guilds providing a certain amount of professional protection for their members, but many met simply in order to enjoy an evening's entertainment. The bars supplied wine, ale, hot or cold snacks and, in many cases, prostitutes as well. A relatively small town such as Pompeii had far more prostitutes than would be tolerated in any modern western town of a comparable size. Roman attitudes to sex were much freer than today's, little stigma being attached to men who sought casual sex with women or other men. As a result, many bars doubled as brothels, and there were larger, specially organized establishments (*lupanaria*) as well. The women were slaves, and lived in extraordinarily bad conditions, to judge from the arrangements in the 'Lupanar' at Pompeii. Their poor living conditions reflect the double standards that the Romans held, for although male desires could be freely indulged, women who became prostitutes were ineligible for marriage, had to be registered by the magistrates, and had to wear the toga as a sign that they were no longer true women.

LEFT Bawdy mosaic from Ostia, second century AD.

RIGHT Men hunting, on a mosaic from Apamea, Syria.

BELOW A footprint showing the way to a brothel in Ephesus, Turkey.

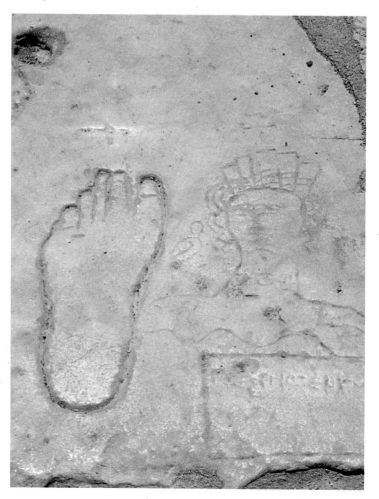

ANIMALS IN ROMAN LIFE

Roman poetry about nature and the countryside is one of the most important classes of ancient literature. There was a deep respect for the creatures of the countryside, especially those exploited in some way by the Romans. It was man's relationship with the animals that counted most, for only those that came into direct contact with man were written about or depicted in detail. The reasons for contact with the animal world were varied: they were used for food; for transport; in agriculture; for products such as feathers for personal adornment; and were important in the less practical pursuits of hunting, sport and simple observation of nature.

The scientific interest in animals was provided for by the zoos kept by wealthy people. *Leporaria* or *vivaria* contained a large variety of different species, often in parkland conditions. Besides scientific observation, many animals were kept for pleasure in these parks, so that guests at a meal could watch them while dining, for instance. Beasts such as deer, boars, wild goats and perhaps the more exotic lions or tigers were kept.

Of course, another reason for the *vivaria* was the provision of animals for the wild beast shows in the amphitheater. For most Romans the spectacles in the arena were their only opportunity to see these animals alive. Naturally, the course of events in the amphitheater meant that the beasts were not alive for very long, and the circumstances were not ideal for a calm appreciation of each animal's normal behavior, but it did mean that unusual species came to the attention of the Roman public. Giraffes, rhinoceroses, leopards, lions, tigers, hippopotamuses, hyenas, elks, elephants and even seals all met their fate in the arena. There were also menageries

ABOVE RIGHT The wolf and twins.
RIGHT CAVE CANEM, 'Beware of the dog,' at the entrance to a house in Pompeii.
BELOW A wild cat with bird, and two ducks.

ABOVE A mosaic from Zliten, North Africa.

BELOW Ostrich, from Piazza Armerina villa.

attached to the great amphitheaters, which admitted visitors on occasion.

To the ecologist, such slaughter is wanton destruction, but fear of the extinction of endangered species was completely absent in the Roman mind. In fact, hunting for the amphitheater probably drove many of the larger species beyond the confines of the empire. Expeditions to capture the animals were big business, and a highly skilled job. The large villa at Piazza Armerina in Sicily was quite probably the property of a man who had made his fortune capturing animals in North Africa and transporting them to Rome, for the mosaics show scenes of ostriches, antelopes and other creatures being loaded onto boats.

The predominance of the larger, more spectacular animals on Roman mosaics and wall paintings should not blind us to the depiction of the more humble species. Small birds, such as thrushes, can be seen perched on the decorative scroll work of mosaic borders. There are mosaics of mice and cats, or dogs on thresholds of houses, with the legend 'CAVE CANEM' (Beware of the dog!). Sea scenes are common, with an exuberant variety of fish, squids, octopus and so on, many of which can be accurately identified. Fish, too, were kept for show in *piscinae* (pools), although breeding them for the table was the main purpose of the pool.

In sum, Roman interest in wild life was largely a predatory one. Accurate drawings and descriptions of the animals were a by-product of the large-scale trade in animals, birds and fish for food or entertainment. However, pets were cherished – an epitaph for 'Patrice,' a lap dog, tells how her master carried her corpse to a special marble tomb in floods of tears, remembering what joy she had brought in her 15 long years.

BELOW Nilotic mosaic with a crocodile and a hippopotamus, first century AD.

CHAPTER VIII
THE VISUAL ARTS

The Roman attitude to the arts was curiously ambivalent. They worshipped the Muses as enthusiastically as the Greeks, yet they regarded many of the more artistic pursuits as effeminate and not really suitable for a warlike nation. The Greek passions for theater, sculpture and so on were not so powerful in their appeal in the Roman world, and in many fields the Romans did not develop the Greek forms they had inherited. However, even quite humble villa owners attempted to embellish their homes with a painted wall or mosaic floor, and popular types of art, such as musical plays, flourished.

The one form of entertainment not mentioned in the previous chapter was the theater. Plays in the ancient world usually aspired to a higher cultural level than that of the arena or race-track, on occasion being comparable to the most lofty writings in prose and poetry. Despite this, many plays achieved great popularity, being staged continually throughout the period of the Roman empire down to its last days. Another measure of the apparent appeal of the theater is the size of the surviving auditoria.

The Roman theater's architecture was copied from theaters built by the Greeks, from whom the custom of staging plays also came. The main part was a semicircular bank of stone or wooden benches on which the audience sat. The number of people that these benches could accommodate was extraordinarily large when compared with modern theaters – in Rome, the three theaters of Pompey, Balbus and Marcellus could hold about 27,000, 7700 and 14,000 people respectively, as against a capacity of 2–5000 for the largest modern theaters and opera houses.

Such large crowds were not only there to be uplifted by the performance, they were also there to be entertained. In fact, the size of the auditorium in a theater such as Pompey's tended to swamp any subtleties that a play might have had, leading to a very strong trend in Imperial times away from the staging of classical plays toward a style that included music and virtuoso performances by solo actors. These came to be known as pantomimes and, although they included all the main elements of the tragedies from which they were derived, were far removed from them in grace and artistry. To keep the theater audiences, these types of plays became increasingly common during the first century AD, and they effectively killed off the performance of serious new plays after that time. Classical comedies were also swamped by the rise of mime. The theater was transformed to such an extent by its mass popularity that Domitian permitted criminals to be substituted for actors in death scenes, so that they could actually be killed. In this way, the theater attempted to compete with the rising appeal of the amphitheater.

Serious plays were still written during the empire, but they were seldom put on in the large theaters, where producers tended to go for the traditional classical drama if a serious tragedy or comedy was called for. However, it was still possible to stage new works, not only plays but also musical performances, poetry and prose readings, in the smaller *odea* (singular *odeum*) which were much like theaters in plan, but with a capacity of about 1500 or less. Such performances were usually private recitals for the author's friends, and they became a popular form of upper-class entertainment.

Apart from the seating for the audience, a theater was made up of three other parts. Immediately in front of the seats was an open flat area known as the *orchestra*. In Greek theaters this was the place where the plays themselves were performed, but in Roman times the space was usually taken up with seating for the local magistrates around its edge, and with musical players if they were needed for a performance. The play itself was moved back onto a platform at the back of the *orchestra*, called the *pulpitum*. Here, a wooden planked stage formed the area where the action took place. Immediately in front of it was a stone stage front, which was often embellished with carvings or colored marbles. Between the stone and wooden parts of the platform was a gap where the curtain was housed. While the play was on the curtain was folded into the gap, to be raised by means of ropes and wooden struts during intervals and at the end. Behind the stage was the most eye-catching part of the theater as far as the audience was concerned. This was the permanent stage set or *scaenae frons*. Originally, Greek theaters had no such masonry back-drop for their plays, making use instead of the superb natural settings surrounding their theaters. However, a *skene* (tent or hut) eventually came to be placed behind the *orchestra*, for the use of the actors, and the gradual development of this feature and the area just in front of it resulted in the increasing use of the *skene* as a convenient prop in the plays, especially those later Greek ones, by playwrights such as Aristophanes, that were set in Athens or other cities. However, Greek stage sets were always small affairs, capable of some adaptation for different plots, whereas the Roman *scaenae frons* rose to the full height of the theater's seating, often 75 feet or more, and was decorated with an imposing but permanent architectural façade of columns, arches, pediments and statues. Doubtless this splendor enhanced the feeling of pride that the townsfolk had about their civic amenities, but it did tend to dominate the play and draw attention away from the actors on stage.

Many impressive remains of theaters survive in virtually every

LEFT Two identical copies of a Greek statue. The use of plaster casts made copying easy and widespread in Roman times.

LEFT Dressing for a satyr play. The masks for the performance can be seen in a box and on the table to the right.

BELOW RIGHT Ivory plaque of a player in the pantomime, with a multiple mask to represent different characters.

BELOW View from the rear of the auditorium toward the stage of the theater at Djemila, Algeria.

province of the empire. All self-respecting towns possessed one, often in a position of prominence in the center. Good examples exist at Arles and Orange in France, Sabratha in Libya, and Athens in Greece, and Pompeii. Probably the best preserved is at Aspendos on the south coast of Turkey, where virtually the entire structure still stands. It held about 7000 on its stone seats, and had a stage 160 × 23 feet. There were five doors in the wall of the stage set which served as entrances, together with a further entrance from each side of the stage. It was also possible to use the two upper storeys of the splendid façade of the stage-set as ancillary entrances for the actors, allowing them to call down as if from a balcony or some similar effect. To complete the stage was a wooden roof that gave some protection to the players in the event of a sudden downpour.

The audience was not so lucky if the weather turned to rain during a performance, despite the awnings that were suspended between poles above the stage and behind the uppermost row of seats. It became common for theaters to be provided with a covered colonnade or portico for the audience to use if it rained or during intervals. One of the best examples of such a portico is behind the large theater at Pompeii which together with the *odeum* (small theater) beside it, forms one of the most compact and best preserved theater complexes in the Roman world. The *odeum* is of particular interest, for it is the earliest known Roman theater, pre-dating the first one in Rome by about 30 years. By contrast with the larger theaters, *odea* tended to be roofed, usually with a rectangular set of beams, as the problems of making a large circular or semicircular flat roof were never overcome by the Romans. The *odeum* at Pompeii is no exception to this, the semicircular seating being crammed into the rectangular walls by cutting off the seats on either side. The stage is much simpler than in a larger theater, with a backdrop painted on the wall rather than made of real columns and pieces of marble.

Many towns found it too expensive to build and maintain both a theater and amphitheater, so in the poorer northwestern

provinces, or in the east where games in the arena were unpopular, theaters tended to be erected that could be adapted for use as an amphitheater if necessary. This happened at Corinth where a high wall was built around the *orchestra* to form a semicircular arena for wild-beast shows. Such theater/amphitheaters were especially common in Britain, where present evidence suggests that no town had both amenities in separate buildings. A good example of the combined type has been excavated at St Albans, near London, where there is a circular amphitheater with a segment removed on one side for the insertion of a small stage. The *orchestra* has a high wall all round it, with entrances more like those of an arena than of a theater. The stage is also very small: more of a concession to the town's play lovers than a dominant part of the auditorium. Another interesting facet of the St Albans theater is the presence of a temple immediately outside the auditorium, in a position that suggests that the theater and the temple were closely connected. Such a link would not be surprising, for the origins of drama lay in religious festivities, and in Roman times plays were only put on during official religious holidays. It is also quite possible that many theaters were used as the venues for large-scale religious rituals and gatherings.

Religion had a much stronger influence on the other arts, particularly in the Republican period. Many early statues were images of the gods housed in temples, or votive offerings of some sort. This, to a certain extent, dictated that the statues should be of an idealized person – the perfect shape of an Apollo or a Venus. Greek values in sculpture were also dominant throughout the Republic, as the Romans had no strong tradition of sculpture of their own, and even in later times the work of Greek artists tended to receive higher praise from Roman writers than products by their own craftsmen.

During the late Republic, the religious ties in sculpture began to be loosened, with the result that the Romans adopted two new fashions that had begun a little earlier in Hellenistic Greece. Copies were now made of famous works of classical Greece, allowing art collections to be built up for the first time, but at the same time removing the works of art from the religious context of the originals. This had the secondary effect of freeing new work from the old idealism, leading to the fashion of having individual portraits and private sculptures. Another consequence was that sculptures increasingly came to be regarded as works of art to be admired, since their religious meaning and context were slowly disappearing. Statues were moved from their original positions so that they could be displayed better, their sculptors became well-known figures, and their works were more and more used for decorative purposes. Statues were placed in niches in ornamental façades of buildings, and special building types such as *nymphaea* or fountain buildings, were developed to allow statues to be displayed to the public to best advantage. Sculpture in the round also became less common, being replaced on many buildings by high reliefs, a form that combined the advantages of the solid structure and coherence of free-standing statues with a neat and disciplined method of display that did not detract from the architectural lines of the building. Reliefs were also a good medium for telling narrative stories, which the Romans eagerly adopted in order to relate historical events. The best examples date from Imperial times, such as the history of the Dacian Wars unfolding in a spiral up the column in Trajan's Forum.

The wealth pouring into Italy during the late Republic and early Empire was, among other things, spent on embellishing private houses, and public buildings put up by private finance. Patronage of the arts by the rich became the major source of employment for many artists, accentuating the trend toward private, secular art. Portraits became common, executed in a style that marks a distinct break with earlier traditions. The idealized depiction of a person, that strove to give an idea of personality and character through, for instance, the expression

ABOVE The *odeion*, or small covered theater, at Pompeii. It would have been used for musical performances, readings and private shows.

LEFT The *scaenae frons* (stage backdrop) at Aspendos, Turkey, still survives to its full height. Such a large elaborate backdrop would probably have dominated the players completely. Second century AD.

RIGHT Merida theater, Spain, showing a partial reconstruction of the columns of the *scaenae frons* as they probably appeared. The seating in marble at the front of the auditorium was for the local councillors.

ABOVE The *nymphaeum* (fountain building) at Miletus, Turkey, built in the second century AD.

RIGHT Statue of a senator holding the busts of two of his ancestors. Although the head of the senator is restored from another ancient statue, all three heads show formal Roman portrait sculpture.

on the face or the gestures of the hands, was supplanted by a much purer realism – a 'warts and all' likeness that gave great emphasis to the physical features. At its best this type of sculpture also revealed a great deal of the sitter's character, but many of the portraits tended to be sentimental pieces simply meant to preserve a person's features for posterity. An aspect of life that accentuated this trend was the practice of taking death-masks, and using them as the basis of a portrait. Sculptures produced in this way were often formal, carefully produced exact likenesses, made for display in the family's shrine to its ancestors.

A form of sculpture that fell halfway between the individual portrait sculpture and the idealized human figure was the portrayal of emperors and other prominent men. Usually these were works placed in a public area, such as a forum, which meant that the person depicted was carved in a less intimate and more formal style. Gestures and expressions implying leadership, oratorical ability or military prowess were combined with sufficient realistic portraiture to allow the public to recognize the man easily. The emperors often enhanced their authority and claim to supreme power by having statues put up throughout the provinces. Sometimes these statues assumed the persona of a god, leading to depictions of Claudius as the all-powerful Jupiter, or Commodus as his favorite hero, Hercules.

Evidence from statues recovered from waterlogged or very dry burial spots shows that the plain marble finish that we are familiar with today was often embellished with paint to pick out details. Complicated costume, such as chain mail, was painted onto a plain surface, and objects such as spears or swords were often cast in bronze and attached to the statue.

The use of color was not, of course, confined to statues. Interior decoration was often a riot of bright, even gaudy, color

schemes. Walls, floors and ceilings were all embellished with patterned and figured frescoes, mosaics and stuccos, which gave the average, rather small Roman domestic room a very cluttered and sometimes claustrophobic air. The designs were often exceedingly complicated, characterized by a desire to fill all the available space with a pattern of some sort. This is especially so at Pompeii, where the total effect of Roman interior decoration of the Early Empire can be appreciated best.

Wall paintings were prepared as frescos, that is by applying pigments to the damp plaster. The chemical changes brought about by the drying of the plaster resulted in a remarkably durable and colour-fast finish. Details were painted over plain-colored backgrounds, sometimes after the plaster had dried, which unfortunately makes them liable to fall off. The styles of the paintings were very varied, and can be divided into four major groups.

The first style was in vogue in the second and first centuries BC, and is characterized by the predominance of plaster imitating other materials, such as marble. This was doubtless an attempt to substitute the much cheaper plaster for the real thing, but by doing this, the wall painters were able to free themselves from the restrictions that faced those who worked in marble. Gradually the plain imitation marbles were augmented by plaster columns and pilasters. Blue was added in the upper parts

LEFT Wall-painting in the fourth style, in vogue at Pompeii just before the destruction of the town in AD 79 from the House of the Vettii, Pompeii. The scene at the bottom probably shows the myth of Apollo and Daphne.

RIGHT The wall-painting, known as 'The Music Lesson,' in the third style, early first century AD, from Herculaneum.

BELOW In Gaul and Britain, amphitheaters and theaters were often combined into one building, as in this reconstruction of Verulamium theater, Hertfordshire. When it was wanted for use as an amphitheater, the arena would be cleared of seating as a space for the gladiators and beasts.

ABOVE Restoration of a *cubiculum* (bedroom) at Boscoreale villa, near Pompeii, with late first century BC wall-paintings in second style, and a mosaic of the second century AD.

LEFT Bust of Commodus attired in the costume of his favorite mythological hero, Hercules. The emperors often portrayed themselves in such a glamorous light.

BELOW Stucco work on the ceiling of the Stabian Baths, Pompeii.

of the walls as a hint of sky between the columns. This trend reached its full development in the second style, which was a fully fledged *trompe l'oeil* style. Rows of columns, walls and buildings were painted in true perspective to create the illusion of a world beyond the wall. Usually there were no people, and it has been suggested that the recurring motifs in some of the compositions, such as doors, masks and rotundas, together with certain symbolic detail, represents the doorway to the world of the dead. Such macabre symbolism, especially in domestic rooms, may be thought odd in modern times, but for the Romans it was merely a manifestation of the ancestor cult worshipped in every house. Ghosts of the ancestors were supposed to have dwelt in the houses of the living members of the family, so the existence of an illusory doorway to their world would have been perfectly acceptable. Of course, a practical result of the false perspectives and imaginary rooms was the feeling of a much greater space inside what were, on occasions, rather small and dark rooms.

The second style culminates in the reign of Augustus, the emperor's own apartments being decorated with frescos in this style. About 15 BC, however, there is a distinct and swift change: the perspective form is lost and a plain but highly inventive classicism replaces it. This third style coincides with a remarkable resurgence of Greek artistic ideals in the Augustan period, in which the forms of sculpture, painting and decoration prevalent in the fifth and fourth centuries BC Athens were used as the inspiration for new works. For painting this meant a reaction against the large-scale compositions occupying entire walls in favor of a panelled division of a wall with areas of single colors. The panels were divided by elaborate borders of, for instance, chains of very realistic flowers and leaves. Thin lines

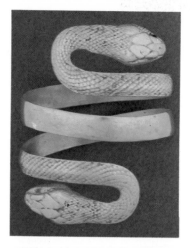

ABOVE Gold earrings in filigree work, from Granada, Spain, second or third century AD.

TOP A gold snake bracelet, a popular design since snakes were associated with death, and so were thought to delay death if worn in this way.

also served to divide up the panels, and to connect the central painting to the edges of each area of the design. The paintings were usually fairly small, but carefully executed mythological scenes. Famous Greek and Hellenistic compositions were copied, such as Pan and Nymphs in the 'House of the Fatal Loves' in Pompeii.

The severe and rather intellectual classicism of the early third style gives way in the softer artistic climate of the reigns of Tiberius, Caligula and Claudius to a more romantic style. The paintings are more visually expressive, with less emphasis on the composition and symbolism to tell the story. In addition, the latest compositions in this style see the return, in a subdued way, of the architectural features of the second style. The resurgence of *trompe l'oeil* is fully apparent with the advent of the fourth style during the reign of Nero. Here is seen the combination of the two preceding phases of wall-painting in a fantastic manner. The architecture of the 'rooms beyond the wall' are no longer credible structures, but spindly colonnades and pergolas give an impression of depth. The pictures hung in the panels of the third style remain, but now seem to be floating in space, or at best part of a curtain or tapestry suspended between two buildings. Fine

early examples of the style are by the painter Fabullus in Nero's Golden House in Rome. His paintings have an impressionistic quality about them, especially the landscapes of villas by the seashore. In Pompeii, of course, fourth-style paintings are most common of all, as they were in fashion at the time of the eruption of Vesuvius that destroyed the town in AD 79. One of the best groups of paintings there is in the House of the Vettii, which was entirely redecorated in the new style not long before the final disaster. Apart from the architectural panelled style, some rooms are decorated with panels that have winged figures flying across the plain background, bordered by narrow bands at top and bottom, some of which carry detailed vignettes of everyday activities (goldsmithing, fulling cloth) being carried out by cupids.

The fourth style marks the culmination of Roman wall-painting fashions, for after the late first century AD, no significant developments occur. There was a period of very rapid change between the end of the first century BC and the mid-first century AD, during which the architectural *trompe l'oeil* style was replaced by classical, but then achieved something of a comeback in a synthesis with the classical style. However, after

this wall painting settles down. Later developments are associated with such buildings as the Christian catacombs and churches, where the representational nature of the fourth style at Pompeii is abandoned in favor of elaborate symbolism.

An interesting aspect of wall painting given by the excavations at Pompeii is that many walls were decorated with first-style paintings at the time of the eruption. In other words, fashions of a hundred years earlier were still accepted, perhaps owing to the difficulties of making changes to such a permanent form of wall-covering as fresco. The same applies to mosaic; some mosaic floors lasted for up to 200 years before being replaced. The owner of a house obviously had to choose the designs he wanted carefully if he intended them to be in position for that length of time!

Since walls are less durable than floors, only when exceptional circumstances preserve the walls (such as at Pompeii) is detailed information about the layout of wall-paintings available, whereas floor decorations such as mosaics are widely preserved throughout the empire. Mosaics were laid with small cubes or *tesserae* of durable material, such as red brick or white limestone. Colored marble was used in the more expensive mosaics, either as *tesserae* or as shapes cut to fit the pattern, known as *opus sectile*.

The first mosaics were made of colored pebbles, laid in geometric patterns in Greek houses. Later, figures are included, such as in the famous lion-hunting scene from Pella in northern Greece. This technique was introduced to Republican Rome, and the newly developed method of cutting the stones into small cubes also came into fashion. Cutting meant that very small patterns could be produced, with details such as faces made up of stones as small as one millimeter across.

By the first century BC mosaics were common in villas and town houses of the wealthy, but in contrast to the brightly colored wall paintings of the period, they were often subdued, even monochrome. Black-and-white designs, such as the Neptune and sea creatures mosaic from Ostia, came to form the most common style in the region of Rome and Central Italy. Elsewhere, colored mosaics were more common, sometimes reproducing famous paintings, as in the mosaic from the House of the Faun at Pompeii that reproduces the battle of Issus between Alexander the Great and Darius in 333 BC. Only the rich could afford mosaics with figured designs and patterns, other people being content with at best a decorated panel set in a plain background or plain floors of red cubes (tessellated pavements). A particular feature of mosaic patterns was the use of Greek borders, such as the Greek key, the wave design, or various types of woven rope (guilloches). The brighter colors in a design were

ABOVE *Opus sectile* (cut marble-work) showing the fourth century AD consul Junius Bassus in a procession at the circus with charioteers of the four factions.

RIGHT Second century AD mosaic in the black-and-white style popular in central Italy, showing Neptune and sea-beasts. From the Baths of Neptune, Ostia.

sometimes laid with glass cubes specially made for the purpose. This meant that they were more delicate, contributing in part to the gradual change in position of fine figured mosaics from the floor to the wall over the centuries. By the fourth century nearly all the highly decorated mosaics produced in Rome were laid on walls, often in a Christian context. From these derived the beautiful and vibrant wall and vault mosaics of the Byzantine churches.

Roman houses of the Imperial age had little interior decoration other than frescos on the walls and ceilings, and mosaics on the floors. Tapestries and carpets only became common at a later date, and curtains or screens were generally plain. However, furniture was often richly carved, as the surviving pieces from Pompeii and dry areas such as Egypt or Syria indicate. Tripod tables were a popular embellishment to a reception room, with legs of animals like lions or deer. Couches had lathe-turned legs, with highly elaborate carvings of lions' heads, for instance. In Britain, an interesting local variation on the wooden lion-legged table was one made of shale, a soft stone mined from the Dorset coast. Generally speaking, furniture was sparse in a Roman house.

Smaller objects were also carefully made. Practical items, such as flagons in bronze, silver and gold, or gems with which to make a personal seal, were artistically formed. Metal ware was the preferred type of table service in rich households, many of the items being elaborately chased with designs in low relief. Large collections were common, even provoking legislation against them to deter ostentation and decadence. The hoard found at Pompeii in the House of the Menander consisted of 118 pieces and was typical for a fairly wealthy man, but by no means as

ABOVE A perspective wall-painting in the second style, *circa* 60 BC, from Boscoreale, showing the doorway to the other world.

large as the richest in Rome might possess. As with so many other aspects of Roman life, Greek influence was very strong, for the Romans enthusiastically took to silverware after the conquest of the East in the second century BC. Drinking cups were among the most popular types of silver vessel used, as they could be used for show in a cabinet or handed round during a meal. They were usually covered with elaborate designs, sometimes mythological scenes, sometimes exceedingly life-like flowers, leaves and berries. Mirrors, too, were common, one side being polished to form the reflecting surface, the other having roundels with busts of the gods or emperors. Religious plate was often silver, and jugs and saucepan-like ladles formed part of the paraphernalia of a sacrifice. Obviously with these objects, decoration that had a religious connotation was most common, many vessels being richly covered with figures of gods and goddesses.

For the poor man, or the diehard conservative, pottery was the principal substitute for silver and gold. Consequently pottery fashions followed those of metalware, and in some cases there was virtually direct imitation of the scenes and designs on silver vessels. This was particularly the case with the best-produced pottery of the Early Empire, Arretine ware. Later on, the pottery became less dependent on metal vessels for its artistic inspiration, allowing the designs to be more suited to the material in which they were being made. Flowing designs of leaves, tendrils and running animals proliferated on the pottery of the second century AD, and later more abstract painted designs came into vogue.

Much the same happened with glassware, which also started out as an attempt to imitate metal vessels. However, glass was not common during the Early Empire, only becoming very popular from the end of the second century. After this, very fine glass was produced, with cut-glass and embossed designs. It gradually supplanted pottery as the usual table ware in more humble households.

Turning from household objects to more personal items such as jewellery, it is possible to see the same sources of influence as for silver and gold plate. At first expensive jewellery was rare and frowned upon to the extent that legislation restricted gold rings to the upper classes only, but after the conquest of the east, jewellery became more and more common. Women wore diadems, gold hair pins, earrings, necklaces, bracelets, rings and brooches. Gold, silver and bronze were the usual materials for jewellery, although iron rings are sometimes found in the provinces. Many pieces had the settings for gems, which were normally uncut semiprecious stones or glass paste. Roman (and Greek) gems often had a motif cut into the surface of the stone.

Intaglio-cutting, as it is known, reached its finest state of development in Greek times, but after the practice was introduced to Rome in the late Republic, there was a major revival, mainly at the hands of Imperial gem-cutters such as Dioskourides. Cameos were also produced, using a method that resulted in the motif standing out from a different colored background.

By contrast, the clothing that formed a backcloth for the jewellery was often not very elaborate. Colored cloth without decoration except along the hems was usual for women, and a plain white toga, sometimes with a border stripe was the male costume. Both men and women wore the same type of clothing, made up of some sort of tunic undergarment, covered with a long fairly narrow length of cloth, either wound around the body (for men) or held in place with brooches (for women). Methods of putting on the toga varied at different periods, and they had a tendency to become increasingly complicated as time went on. The art of putting one on properly was only acquired

BELOW Members of Augustus' family, on the *ara pacis* (altar of peace) in Rome, late first century BC. Aristocratic dress is very clearly shown on this frieze.

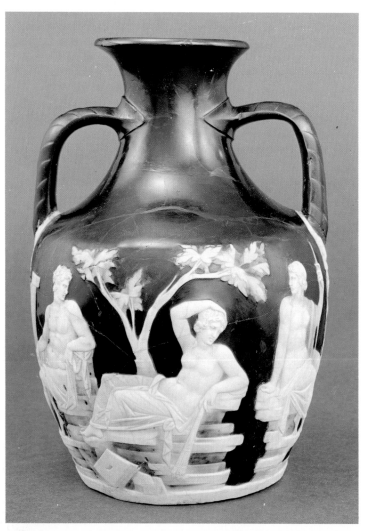

after long practice, and usually needed the assistance of another person. Eventually, togas, despite their distinctiveness as a national dress, were worn less and less, being reserved for ceremonial occasions only. The emperors vainly tried to stem this trend by legislation. Domitian made it compulsory for the theater, and Commodus for the amphitheater. By the late Empire, sleeved tunics, and poncho-like cloaks and mantles were in fashion; similar in fact to the costumes of the Greek Orthodox and western churches.

For many, the art of classical Greece during the fifth and fourth centuries BC marks the high point of ancient artistic achievement. For the Romans also, Greek art was the subject of great admiration, and had a profound influence on all Roman endeavors in the arts. However, some features were Roman in their final development – narrative historical sculpture, for instance, or portrait statues. It must also be to Rome's credit that her empire was the main vehicle for the spread of Greek and Roman artistic ideas, with the consequence that modern interest in and revivals of the ancient arts owe an enormous debt to Roman, as well as Greek, artists.

LEFT The Portland Vase, one of the most famous pieces of glasswork from the ancient world. Produced for the court of Augustus in the late first century BC, it was made by carving away the upper white glass layer to achieve a cameo effect.

RIGHT A silver *phiale* (shallow dish) from Eze, southern France, showing the journey to Olympus in chariots of Hercules, Minerva, Mars and Dionysus. It is of Greek workmanship, fifth to third century BC, but the style was popular and influential in the Roman world.

BELOW Late Roman jewellery, fourth century AD.

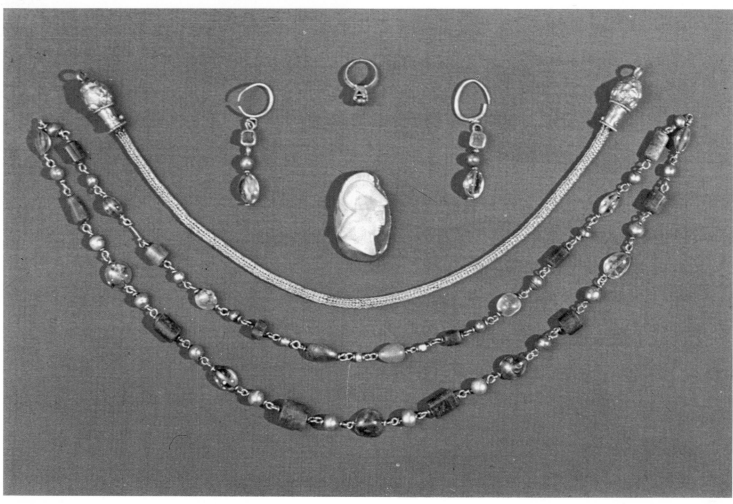

LAYING OUT A ROMAN MOSAIC

Early Greek mosaics were made of small pebbles carefully selected from Mediterranean beaches. However, the laborious and time-consuming gathering of the pebbles ended when techniques for cutting stone into *tesserae* (cubes) were developed. It was then possible to use a wide variety of stone and other materials, from many different sources. As a result mosaics became more common, spreading to all Roman lands. With the expansion of the empire, mosaic-laying techniques became common knowledge, every province having its schools of mosaicists who travelled out from the larger towns to lay mosaics in villas, baths, houses and gardens. Archaeologists can now identify the different mosaic schools by analyzing the detail of the design, for each school had distinctive patterns of such things as leaves or rosettes.

Ancient mosaicists used local materials whenever possible, white limestone, gray shale and red tile being very common. The burning of stones helped increase the variety of colors. For more exotic colors, marbles were used, often picked up as scraps from marble-masons' yards. Glass provided blue and green highlights, but was rarely used in floor mosaics because of its fragility. Later, when wall mosaics became more common, glass was used for

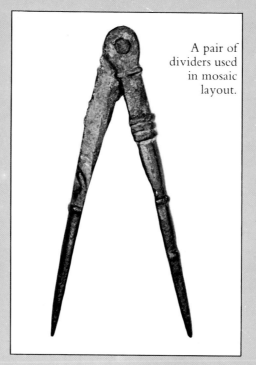

A pair of dividers used in mosaic layout.

larger areas, eventually forming the major part of the design. The *tesserae* were probably prepared in the workshop, but finished on the spot, since different parts of the mosaic required cubes of different sizes. Faces, for instance, were composed of small *tesserae* in order to give the features a realistic gradation of color. In contrast, the filling in of the background could be done with much larger stones. A small anvil and chisel were probably used for splitting stones into the cubes, although the surviving evidence is not definite.

The first stage in actually laying the mosaic was to prepare the foundations. The architect Vitruvius proposed a carefully graded series of layers of pebbles and crushed brick bonded together with mortar, the total thickness being two feet or more. In practice, most mosaicists were content with shallower foundations, which were usually entirely satisfactory, but there were occasionally unforeseen

RIGHT Layout lines in plaster under a mosaic, from Masada, Israel.

BELOW Second century AD mosaic overlying one of the first century.

results, such as the mosaic cracking as the foundations settled over a buried wall.

Next, the main outlines of the design were either scored into the mortar surface of the foundations, or painted onto them. This provided the working guidelines as the mosaicist worked on the details of the pattern. The cubes themselves were laid onto a thin bed of fresh mortar, and squeezed down so that the mortar rose up to fill all the spaces.

Three main methods of laying out the design were used. In the direct method the pattern was laid, cube by cube, on the spot. Awkward floor areas and unique designs would have provided suitable opportunities for using this rather time-consuming technique. A more convenient method was to assemble parts of the design in the mosaicist's workshop, and then lay complete sections of the final pattern at once. The cubes could be laid out in a sand tray, lifted with the aid of glue and sheets of cloth, relaid in mortar in the right position on the floor, and the cloth facing soaked off. An alternative to this was to glue the cubes onto a cloth or sheet of papyrus which had the design drawn on it. This could then be turned

over and mortared into position, which meant that after the cloth or paper had been removed, the design would be reversed. Very rarely, a third method was used: that of laying the design in mortar in a tray, which was in its turn mortared in place on the floor. All these 'indirect' methods were used either for the *emblemata* (panels) which carried the artistic centerpieces, or for complicated but standardized parts of the surround, such as the *guilloche* (rope pattern). One result of

this method was that the patterns occasionally did not meet up properly when the indirect sections were joined up. Also the central *emblemata* were often of much finer quality than the surrounds, presumably because the latter were not laid by the master mosaicist but by his apprentices.

After the cubes had been laid in the mortar, the finished mosaic would have been grouted to fill any remaining cracks, sanded to a flat surface and polished ready for the owner to admire.

BELOW An *emblema* (center panel) showing a horse and dog.

RIGHT Compass-designed first century AD mosaic.

CHAPTER IX
MYTH AND RELIGION

Religion permeated every sphere of Roman life. The gods were consulted before any major decision was taken, whether in affairs of state or simply in the home. A vast army of gods and goddesses presided over every facet of existence, from birth to death, from peace to war, and from the personal to the national.

The most striking aspect of Roman religion is the variety of deities worshipped. This is because of Rome's long period of development, and a sense of religion that allowed and welcomed new cults into the city. The earliest rituals appeased gods that were local and Etruscan in origin. However, with the Etruscan deities came Greek ideas of religion, since the former were strongly influenced by Greek culture. Greek gods also came to Rome via the colonies in southern Italy, resulting in the setting up of cults of the familiar Olympian gods in Rome in the early years of the Republic. Later, the oriental mystery religions began to be introduced to Rome, from the time of the Punic wars onward. These included the Imperial age introductions of Mithraism and Christianity, which will be considered in more detail at the end of the chapter.

The local gods were the most primitive in the Roman pantheon, for they were originally spirits that resided in particular objects or places, such as Jupiter Feretrius who was the god of an oak tree on the Capitoline hill. They had no human form, being simply intangible spiritual forces that were either good or evil. The task of mortal Romans in this religious world was to persuade the deities to be good to them, usually by making sacrifices. Sacrifice was the major ritual in Roman religion and was, in effect, a bargain between the god and the person or people performing the rite. Usually, a plant or animal held to be sacred to the god was burned or killed on an altar beside the place where the spirit lived. Most sacrifices were performed on fixed sacred days, by representatives of the whole community – the priests of the cult – and were designed to keep a particular deity happy and favorably disposed toward the Roman people. Sacrifices were made for more personal reasons too. For instance, a merchant might make a vow to present an altar and a sacrifice if he safely journeyed across the ocean. This brought the protection of the god or goddess during the voyage, since they would receive a sacrifice if no mishaps occurred. Of course, if the merchant did not reach his destination safely, no sacrifice would be made, and since the deity had not fulfilled its part of the bargain, it would be held in less regard by the worshippers, and might ultimately be considered weak and ineffectual, unworthy of worship at all. In this way, some cults were built up to national and international

proportions because they were thought to be successful and powerful. Others fell by the wayside, only worshipped at a single local shrine, if at all. In addition, the weaker gods might be absorbed by a more successful cult of a similar nature. This meant that the worship of the god was physically transferred to the place where the more powerful deity resided, often resulting in a mass of small shrines around the major temples.

In order to ensure that the Roman gods were appeased at the most appropriate time, a series of divine laws were formulated which regulated the worship of all the gods and goddesses held to be important for the well-being of the community as a whole. Priests were chosen or elected from the most important families of the city to be the officials who interceded between the gods and the people. They often had special training and knowledge of such matters as divination, and they performed special rituals at certain times for the benefit of everyone in the city. Two of these rituals will illustrate the way in which the priesthood worked. The Salii, the warrior priests of Mars, performed a ceremony in March that involved wild, leaping dances while carrying the *ancilia* (shields) of the god. Mars, besides being a god of war, was also one of the most ancient agricultural deities in Rome, and it is thought that the leaping was a form of sympathetic magic to make the crops sprout from the ground. In fact, during the reign of Marcus Aurelius, the aged Salian priests were apparently replaced by younger men because they were not leaping high enough! The second ritual was a more general one, that of the lustrum or purification, in which a procession went around the thing to be purified, whether it was a farm, an army or a city. The priests stopped at predetermined points to offer sacrifices and prayers, some of these spots being permanent positions of altars or shrines. There was a fixed route for the lustrum of the Palatine hill, the original settlement of Rome, around which the procession went on the day of the Lupercalia. At a humbler level, Cato describes the purification of a farm by the leading of a calf, a lamb and a piglet (*suovetaurilia*) round the boundaries of the land before sacrificing them. He gives the prayer formula to be used during the ceremony:

'Father Mars, I pray and beg you to be gracious and merciful to me, my house and my household, in which matter I have ordered this *suovetaurilia* to be led around my land, my ground and my farm. I beg you to keep away, ward off and remove sickness, visible and invisible, infertility, destruction, ruin and unseasonable events; that you let my harvests, my grain, my vineyards and my plantations flourish and be fruitful, preserve my shepherds and my flocks in good health, and give good health and strength to me, my house and my household. To this end of purifying my farm, my land and my ground, and

LEFT Interior of the Temple of Bacchus, late second century AD. At the top of the steps is the plinth for the cult-statue.

BELOW The *lares* (gods of the household) and a snake (symbol of death) from a small shrine in the House of the Vettii, Pompeii, *circa* AD 60.

of making a lustration, as I have said, deign to accept the sacrifice of this suckling *suovetaurilia*. Father Mars, to this end deign to accept the sacrifice of this suckling *suovetaurilia*.'

In this ritual the head of the household was the priest, as he was in all sacrifices involving the well-being of the house and its contents. In effect, the state priesthoods were the household priests writ large, since the city of Rome was regarded in some ways as one enormous household, with its own hearth (the temple of Vesta in the forum) and its own boundaries around which the lustral *suovetaurilida* was led. Some of the priesthoods became very sought-after positions, because of the legal and political power that they conferred. The *pontifex maximus* (chief priest) and the augurs who made divinations before decisions were taken, tended to be important posts.

An aspect of state religion that had a widespread impact on everyday life was the calendar. Unlike the modern seven-day week, with every seventh day a religious holiday, the Roman system was much more variable. Some months had virtually no days when business could be conducted, for example, February, since all the days were devoted to religious rituals, and other months, such as March, were suitable for business all the time. This meant that everyone had to have close contact with the priests in order to ascertain whether it was a holy or a secular day, and the large number of holy days often impinged on day-to-day life.

The practice of augury was inherited from the Etruscans, for whom it appears to have been one of the major aspects of religion. Essentially, augury was the foretelling of the future by observing natural signs, the meaning of which required specialized training to interpret. Rome had a college of augurs, known as haruspices or 'gut-gazers,' who looked at the entrails of sacrificial victims before they were dedicated at the altar to make sure that they were perfect and pleasing to the god. A bronze model sheep's liver found at Piacenza in northern Italy gives the divisions that the augurs made of this particular organ, and the deities who should be appeased if any area of the liver was damaged or an abnormal shape. Another task of the haruspices was divining from lightning, which was especially ominous if it took place during a sacrifice or lustration. The area of the sky that it came from was significant, as was the spot where it struck the ground. These spots were held sacred and altars dedicated there – one such was on the Palatine Hill next to the house of Romulus (the Puteal). Other prodigies were interpreted by the augurs, possibly inexplicable noises such as underground rumblings, or the more mundane explanation of the flight of birds in particular directions during a sacrifice.

The introduction of Greek gods during the early years of the

Republic caused the gradual personification of the gods. Greek religious ideas were rather more advanced that the simple spirit world of early Rome, as they believed in a group or pantheon of universal gods and goddesses who presided over man's affairs. They were likened to immortal humans with special powers, with the result that a great mythology grew up about the deeds (and misdeeds) of the gods, unlike in Rome where little mythology could be built up about the exploits of intangible spirits. These differences between Greek and Roman religion were not so great as to prevent the Roman deities from acquiring the characteristics of their Greek equivalents, with the result that Rome's most important early god, Jupiter, was identified with Greek Zeus and was endowed with Zeus' personality. Similar changes occurred with the other gods until almost the entire Greek pantheon of gods could be freely worshipped in the Roman heartland.

With the Greek gods came Greek temples and temple architecture. Purely Greek buildings were confined to the Greek colonies, but in Etruria there was already a tradition of building temples in a local version of the Greek style and it was from this area that the main influence came for the design of temples. Early examples are known to have details of architecture that would look quite in place on a classical Greek temple, and they continued to be put up until the end of the Roman Empire in a style that an ancient Greek would recognize.

The best examples of temples date from the late Republic and from imperial times. At Nîmes, the Maison Carrée is perhaps the most well-preserved temple built in the Augustan style. It shows

ABOVE A circular temple in the *forum Boarium*, Rome. It is the earliest surviving marble building in Rome, late second century BC, and was probably dedicated to Hercules Victor by the rich oil merchant M Octavius Herrenus. Hercules was a patron of oil merchants.

RIGHT The *apotheosis* (transformation into a god) of Sabina, wife of Emperor Hadrian. Members of the Imperial household were usually deified after their deaths, unless they had offended the public.

well the similarities with Greek temples – the columns in the porch, the pediment with room for a sculptured frieze, the large, deep room inside to house the image of the god, and the open area round about that was the sacred area of the temple precinct. It also exemplifies the differences between Roman and Greek styles – the high podium or platform with steps at the front rather than all round, the lack of a colonnade all round the building, despite the vestigial attached columns that give the appearance of a walkway round the temple, and the comparatively large size of the interior. This particular temple was in the forum of Nîmes (ancient Nemausus, a colony set up by Augustus), which was the favored siting for the major temples of any town, often being the place where the imperial cult was worshipped.

The imperial cult was a peculiarity of Roman religion, since it was not allowed in Rome, but was actively spread in the provinces. Worship of the emperor, particularly the spirits of dead emperors, was a practice that the Greeks and other eastern civilizations had carried out for a long time before the Romans adopted it, since it was simply an extension of the Greek notion that the gods were immortals with human forms. As the Greek cults spread to Rome, emperor worship came too, although Rome never accepted that the living emperor was divine. However, it was thought to be a good way of keeping the peoples of the newly conquered provinces loyal, hence the presence of the cult in so many Roman towns. The goddess Roma, deity of the mother city, was also widely venerated outside Rome itself.

Another shrine that shows clearly the architecture of Roman temples is sited at Baalbek, in Lebanon. The temple dedicated to Jupiter is one of the largest in the empire, its gable being 130 feet

above ground level, and its neighboring temple of Bacchus has an interior that survives well enough to give a good impression of decoration and lay-out. The latter is dated late second century AD, and has the richly carved ornament of that period around the doors, the ceilings and the walls of the interior. Pilasters flank the inside walls and the cult statue was housed under an ornate canopy at the top of a flight of stairs at the far end. The effect, apart from the statue of course, was probably much like that of a Baroque church, a seventeenth- and eighteenth-century architectural style that owed much to the Roman architecture of this period. In contrast to the typical form of a Roman temple, the columns run all round the outside of the building in Greek fashion, which is perhaps a local variation due to its position firmly within the eastern, Greek, part of the Roman Empire.

Apart from the usual rectangular classical temples, other shapes were used for shrines, most commonly circular. In Rome the most famous example is the Pantheon. Another is preserved in the *forum Boarium* near the river, a small circular building with columns all round it, forming a continuous portico. The roof as it exists now is not like the original appearance, for it may have been hidden behind an architrave running around the building above the colonnade.

Circular temples were common, in fact possibly the usual form of temple, in western France, where Celtic religion had previously held sway. In the old Celtic areas, later the provinces of Gaul and Britain, the traditional Roman religion was not practiced, but instead an amalgam of Celtic and Roman developed. This was consistent with Roman religious views, which were very tolerant of local cults because these were held to be the authentic manifestation of the spirit world in much the same way as the

The Temple of Bacchus,
Baalbek, Lebanon, late second
century AD, one of the best–
preserved and largest temples in
the Roman world.

ABOVE A circular Romano-Celtic temple on Hayling Island, Hampshire, England, seen from the air as stunted growth in a wheat-field because of the wall foundations surviving underground.

ABOVE RIGHT Romano-Celtic temple at Autun, France, a tall tower-like structure which was a distinctive feature of Roman temples in the Celtic lands.

LEFT Cult-statue of Aion, god of time. One of the divinities of the Mithraic cult, second or third century AD.

RIGHT Trajan's Kiosk, Philae, Egypt. A Graeco-Roman temple with strong Egyptian influence, now under the waters of the Aswan Dam.

early Roman cults worshipped their own particular local gods. In political terms too, Rome saw that it stood to gain from combining local with Roman deities, since the local people would happily continue to venerate the gods in places known to the Romans. No secret cults would grow up and, in addition, Roman values could be introduced gradually by way of the new mixed religion.

Celtic religion was very similar to that of the Romans in many ways – the range of gods and goddesses was the same, the practice of sacrifice and divination similar, as was the powerful position of the priests. However, there were also major differences, principally because Celtic cults were more barbarous and primitive in

Roman eyes. Human sacrifice was practiced, and severed heads were commonly venerated as cult objects. The shrines were often very flimsy affairs, sometimes simply clearings in woods with few if any man-made structures. Roman changes were designed to humanize and civilize Celtic rituals. Human sacrifice was banned, as were the priests who practiced it, the druids. This was designed to make the religion more humane and to reduce resistance to Roman rule, which the priests were suspected of fomenting. Temples were built to house the new Romano-Celtic cults, of a type that was architecturally distinctive, probably derived mainly from the layout of the Celtic shrines but with the embellishment of columns and Roman architectural

details. A typical Romano-Celtic temple was a small square, tower-like building with windows high up in the walls to let a little light in. The cult image was either a statue, in the more Roman-style temples, or something more symbolic such as a stone or a pool of water in those temples that adhered more to the old Celtic practices. Around the temple was a covered walkway used for processions, and the whole shrine was set in a *nemeton* (sacred courtyard) in which public sacrifices and other festivals were held. The size of most Romano-Celtic temples means that they can have been little more than buildings to house the gods, unlike many Mediterranean temples that had space within for ceremonies and rituals. This was the result of Celtic religion being much more outdoor in its nature than Roman cults.

Other regions of the empire also had distinctive local cults that were combined with Roman religious ideas. Punic cults in North Africa, Egyptian and Semitic cults in the east were all allowed to continue under Roman domination, but were transformed by the introduction of Romanized versions of their original rituals.

A major defect of ancient religion in modern eyes is the lack of any moral teaching. Rituals were concerned with appeasing and bargaining with the gods to the exclusion of virtually every other consideration. This is seen best in the curse tablets that are occasionally found on temple sites, on which an aggrieved person would scratch a curse inflicting pain or even death on a suspected wrong-doer:

'A memorandum to the god Mercury from Saturnina, a woman, concerning the linen cloth she has lost. Let him who stole it not have rest until he brings the aforesaid things to the aforesaid temple, whether he is man or woman, slave or free. She give a third part to the aforesaid god on condition that he exact those things which have been mentioned above . . .'

For moral and ethical exhortation, the Roman had to turn to philosophy. Two major schools of philosophy existed in Republican and early Imperial Rome, the Stoics and the Epicurians. Their differences were in basic attitudes, Stoics believing in 'life according to nature' and the survival of the spirit after death, the Epicureans holding that nothing existed beyond the grave, freeing man to pursue 'true pleasure' during

ABOVE Mithraeum under San Clemente church, Rome.

BELOW Temple leaf to Jupiter Dolichenus.

ABOVE The Maison Carrée, Nîmes, an Augustan temple.

the one life that he had. However, despite such seemingly enormous differences of belief, both taught a philosophy of life that conformed to the highest standards of morality.

Beliefs in complicated and sometimes unremitting codes such as these tended to be an upper-class preserve; Cato and Marcus Aurelius were Stoics, for instance. For many other people eastern religions provided the moral teachings of the philosophies combined with a comforting creed of life after death. Yearnings for a religion of salvation were not fulfilled by official Roman cults, with the result that many people turned to the newly introduced cults of such gods as Cybele, Dionysus, Isis and Mithras. Judaism and Christianity were, of course, part of this movement from the east.

One of the major innovations of the eastern religions was that they had 'entry qualifications.' Faith in the power of the deity was professed at a ritual in which the novice would forswear his previous life and vow to lead a good and upright existence. Many of the cults had grades, the highest of which was most perfect and the best guarantee of future salvation. Typical of the 'entry qualifications' is this early example from a shrine of Dionysus

and Agdistis in Lydia (East Turkey):

'Worshippers must swear by all the gods that they harbor no evil intention toward anyone, man or woman; that they do no poisoning or evil magic; that they do not use or encourage love charms, abortion, contraception, rape or murder; that they do not steal, but are correctly behaved in this Community. If anyone carries out or plans such a misdeed, they will not allow or keep silent about it, but give information about it and punish it. A man will lie only with his wife, not with any other free woman or married slave woman, and he will not corrupt any boy or young girl. No man or woman who offends against any of these rules may be admitted to the Community.'

Despite such moral strictures, the Roman authorities were suspicious of the eastern cults because of their closed congregations and also because some of the rituals were orgiastic.

Mithraism was one of the most popular of the eastern religions, spreading among merchants and army officers, to whom its creeds appealed most. There were seven grades of membership, each with an initiation rite, that sometimes involved being drenched with blood from a sacrificed bull (the *taurobolium*). The moral code of the religion involved absolute courage, asceticism and chastity, which no doubt accounted for its appeal to such men as army officers. Mithraic shrines were small, semisubterranean rooms, with benches along the walls and an image of Mithras slaying the bull at one end. This representation was the creation myth of Mithraism, and was always carved or painted in the same way, with elaborate and arcane symbolism. Some of the associated altars had their backs hollowed out and holes pierced through the eyes and halo of the god. It would seem that the god's eyes were lit up with an oil-lamp or candle to create an air of mystery during the ceremonies. Incense was also burned in the form of pine-cones. In several respects Mithraism and Christianity were similar, certain aspects of their beliefs so angering the Christians in the fourth century that many Mithraic temples were deliberately destroyed because they were thought to be a parody of their own religion.

Although the Jewish and Christian religions came to Rome in the same movement of eastern cults as Mithraism and the others, they caught the attention of the authorities for a different reason. Both were exclusive, allowing no other gods to be worshipped at the same time, unlike all other ancient religions. This brought them into conflict with the requirements of emperor worship, and their refusal to participate in celebrations of such things as the emperor's birthday led to accusations of disloyalty and persecutions. Jews tended not to be persecuted, perhaps because of the strength and antiquity of their religion, whereas Christians, believers of the newest religion in the Roman Empire, were more fanatical in their beliefs, more secretive and isolated in their communities, and hence more liable to be denounced and prosecuted.

Despite the possible danger of execution, Christianity was an

attractive creed. Unlike many of the other 'mystery' religions, the final and absolute redemption of believers was preached, and the concept of the afterlife was much more concrete, promising virtually the physical resurrection of the body. Their moral code was not so concerned with obscure ethical principles so much as the doctrine of love between all mankind. This doctrine also brought conflicts with authority to Christians in the army or in official positions, for it was not possible to reconcile the belief in love with killing an enemy or ordering an execution.

The monuments associated with the early Christians were not churches, for permanent places of worship would have been dangerous in times of persecution, but catacombs, where they were buried. They followed the Jewish custom of burial in family groups; in other words, all the members of one congregation tended to be buried together. Large plots of land were needed for this purpose, and in a city like Rome where land was expensive and underground tunnelling easy, it became standard practice for long underground passages and chambers to be dug, with slots and niches for the bodies. The most famous catacombs were on the via Appia, to the south of Rome, initially dug on land given by rich pagan patrons, but later on the church's own ground. There were eventually 350 miles of passages. The most striking thing about the catacombs is the practice of painting the walls. The style was that of contemporary pagan paintings, but the subjects were drawn principally from the Old Testament. Some, however, were New Testament or even pagan (for instance, the labors of Hercules), and it is interesting to see the use of, for instance, winged Victory goddesses as angels.

After Christianity was tolerated and finally made the official religion in the fourth century, churches started to be built. Their

LEFT Mithras slaying the bull, one of the central parts of Mithraic belief, and the centerpiece of all Mithraic temples. Each depiction of this scene is the same, the snake, the dog and the scorpion nearly always being present.

architectural origins are the subject of much debate, but most scholars tend to agree that the official basilica or town court house is the most likely predecessor. For both spiritual and practical reasons, early churches consciously avoided any resemblance to a pagan temple, and the need to accommodate the congregation inside resulted in the building of large aisled halls. A good example is the Church of the Nativity in Bethlehem, first established by Emperor Constantine in AD 333. There is a nave and four aisles covering roughly a square of 93 by 95 feet, at the east end of which is an octagon with an opening in the center into the grotto where Christ was traditionally said to have been born. This octagon is more elaborate than the usual shallow apse because of the importance of the site. At the west end there was a colonnaded courtyard for nonbelievers and applicants to the faith. Some churches were enormous, being among the most impressive new structures of their day. The nave of the Lateran basilica in Rome, for instance, built *circa* AD 320, was 250 by 180 feet, and capable of holding a congregation of several thousand, such was the upsurge in popularity of the Christian faith after toleration. The basilica of St Peter in Rome, built in AD 329, drew the largest crowds, for it was built over the early Christian cemetery in which St Peter was buried, and was thus both an object of pilgrimage and the site of the principal church in Rome. It was 391 by 208 feet in total size, serving the needs of the popes and the congregations of Rome until the present building was erected in the sixteenth century.

The prominent position given to burial in early Christian belief was derived in great part from pagan practices. Funeral meals, celebrated by the living over the grave or in the mausoleum, were common to both streams of religion. In many pagan

LEFT The tomb of Cinq-Mars-la-Pile, central France.

BELOW Head of Christ from Hinton St Mary villa, Dorset.

RIGHT The ed-Deir tomb, Petra, second century AD, is 125 feet high.

cemeteries of the Early Empire, pipes were provided, down which offerings and sustenance could be poured for the dead. Tombs were often very elaborate affairs, with local variations throughout the empire that catered for different tastes or religions. There were also fashions at different periods, with cremation being popular at first, but gradually being superseded by inhumation in the second century. The change seems to have been initially upper class in inspiration, perhaps because coffins gave a larger surface for carving and ostentation than the small ash chests and urns associated with cremation. The rich also had large mausoleums, frequently put up by a prominent member of the family during their lifetime and subsequently used by the whole family. The emperors, of course, had the most imposing tombs, the mausoleum of Hadrian, for instance, being a large cylinder 210 feet in diameter, in which later emperors were buried up to the time of Caracalla. (It was subsequently used as a castle by the Popes, the Castel Saint'Angelo). Mausoleums were often of individual and quite striking design, such as the pyramid of Cestius by the Ostia gate in Rome, or the tomb in the form of a baker's oven put up by Eurysaces at the Porta Maggiore, also in Rome. Provincial tombs were very impressive too, such as those outside Petra in Jordan, a caravan city on the fringe of the empire. As a rule burials were made outside the city walls, both for religious and sanitary reasons, with the result that many of the roads leading to a town, such as the via Appia just south of Rome, were lined with tombs and mausoleums. They would have been the first monuments that a visitor came across as he approached, so to the townsfolk they became the ideal type of building for the display of personal and civic pride.

Roman religion, as we have seen, was rich in its variety and appeal. For most, the official cults of the state continued to serve a vital religious need, and as such, the cults were important as one of the means by which members of the community found a common identity. Certainly the traditional Roman regarded official religion as the oldest and most noble part of the state, a sacrosanct area of daily life which must never come to an end, otherwise Rome itself would fall. Others had different opinions. The state religion for them was an empty barrel, its contents having long ago drained away. Something new was needed, that fulfilled deep-seated emotional needs. The answer was found in

the mystery cults imported from the east, of which one, Christianity, became rapidly the most persuasive and appealing. As belief in these new religions grew, Rome became a veritable battleground of religions. The old religion received a serious setback when Constantine was converted and made Christianity official. This started to undermine the basis of state religion, and despite a revival of paganism later on, accompanied by sometimes violent controversies and clashes between non-Christians and Christians, paganism started to decline, except in the Celtic regions, where it remained a fundamental part of religious life. Ultimately, Christianity was triumphant, and both the state religion and the other eastern cults withered and virtually died. They were not quite extinguished, however, for the Christians took over pagan ceremonial days for their own use, such as the birthday of the Sun on 25 December, thus ensuring that we still commemorate, in a small way, the old gods.

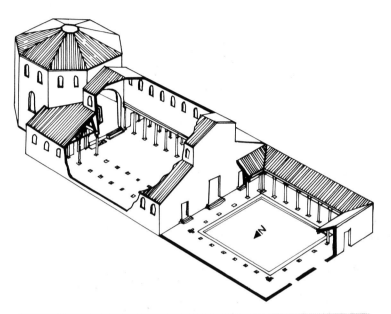

LEFT *Columbarium* (underground tomb for pagan cremation urns), via Appia, Rome, early first century AD.
ABOVE RIGHT Reconstruction of the original Church of the Nativity, Bethlehem, *circa* AD 333.
RIGHT The 12 Apostles, in the third century catacomb of the Aurelii, Rome.
BELOW An Italian ivory panel showing Judas Iscariot hanging and the Crucifixion, *circa* AD 400.

THE VILLA OF THE MYSTERIES

Just outside Pompeii on the road to Herculaneum were a number of imposing suburban villas. In one of them, excavated in 1929–30, was a remarkable series of wall paintings which are thought to portray the rites of the Dionysiac mysteries. The paintings were executed in about 60 BC as part of the redecoration of the villa at that time. Since other rooms in the house also have paintings of the Dionysac legends, it seems clear that the owner was connected in some way with the cult of Dionysus, either as a convert or as a patron. Followers of Dionysus were frowned upon by the Roman authorities, for the cult was of eastern origin, rather secretive and wild rumors circulated regarding its orgiastic rituals. Since it was a mystery cult and the initiates were forbidden to reveal what went on, the rituals are no longer entirely known.

The significance of each scene has provoked lively debate ever since the paintings were first uncovered. Either they show a ritual marriage of an initiate to the cult, which means that for the first time we have an idea of the mysteries that were revealed, or they show scenes from the mythological life of Dionysus. Taking the former interpretation first, since it is the most widely accepted, starting from the left is the entry of the bride to be. A young boy reads a sacred text and a woman is holding a plate with cakes on it. The seated women just to the right are preparing a sacrifice. The next few scenes are of the immortals. Silenus plays his lyre, while a satyr accompanies him on pan-pipes. A female satyr in front of him suckles a goat. Beside them stands a woman looking alarmed at the scenes occurring further along. She forms a clever linking piece between two walls, for at this point the main panel at the head of the room begins and she seems to be gazing upon it. In the main panel, the center is taken by Ariadne (now partly destroyed) who was the bride of Dionysus. Dionysus himself reclines in her lap, while to the left Silenus holds up a bowl to a young satyr. Behind him another satyr is holding up a grimacing mask, possibly so that it is reflected in the bowl. Gazing into bowls was a form of divination. On the other side of the throne, a kneeling woman is about to unveil an object, thought to be a huge ritual phallus – this possibly represents the final revelation of the mysteries. Standing over her is a winged demoness in the act of striking a half-naked woman in the next scene, who is being comforted by a seated woman. Again this is an ingenious linking composition across the angle of the room. After this the initiation is over, and the dancing naked woman celebrates by clashing her hand cymbals together. Behind her another woman produces a *thyrsus*, the ritual wand of Dionysus and

162

OPPOSITE A winged goddess strikes at a woman whose head is buried in a third woman's lap. The composition effectively moves the eye of the onlooker across the angle of the room.

BELOW Layout of the wall-painting of the Mysteries.

RIGHT The god Silenus holds up a bowl into which a youth stares. Behind another youth holds up a grimacing mask.

BELOW RIGHT The first scene of the painting. Possibly the entry of the sacred bride, or the education of the young Dionysus, depending on the interpretation accepted.

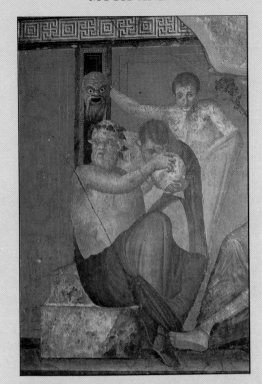

his followers. Following this scene there is a break in the composition for a window in the room. The final scenes are separate: first, the bride's toilet, assisted by winged cupids, and second the bride is seated on a marriage couch. This completes the sequence.

The alternative interpretation is that the scenes do not form a connected narrative at all, but show episodes from the various legends associated with Dionysus. Starting from the left again, we have the youthful Dionysus being taught by his mother Semele and aunt Ino. The woman with the plate is one of the seasons, bearing cakes to a table where the other three seasons are preparing the sacred cakes of Ceres. Silenus plays his lyre to signify the cosmic harmony of the seasons. The two satyrs with the goats are a male Pan trying to seduce his female counterpart. She is about to be transformed into a reed to

avoid his approaches, symbolized by the reed hanging from her neck. The frightened woman is Aura, one of the winds, who bore a child to Dionysus against her will. The central panels largely retain the same significance in this interpretation. Ariadne and Dionysus are positioned in the center, while to the left Silenus holds up the bowl to the young satyr. Possibly the bowl contains wine, the sacred drink introduced by Dionysus to the mortal world. On the right-hand side, a follower of Dionysus reveals the phallus, to the consternation of the winged figure, who is holding up her hand so as not to gaze upon it. She is Nemesis, sent by Juno, the wife of Jupiter, in vengeance for the birth of Dionysus to her rival, Semele (Jupiter in the guise of an ordinary man, had seduced Semele, daughter of King Cadmus of Thebes). The next scene is not so clear in this interpretation, but possibly alludes to the

birth of Dionysus, and to the celebrations by Dionysiac followers upon the consternation of Nemesis. The last two scenes show Venus at her toilet, watched by her jealous rival Juno, seated so as to gaze at her across the angle of the wall.

There are difficulties in accepting either alternative, for in both there are figures or scenes that are not satisfactorily explained. This is because of the rich variety of myths about Dionysus, and our ignorance of the exact significance of each part of the secret Dionysiac ritual. It is hard to believe that a Dionysiac ritual would be so openly displayed, which makes the second interpretation more acceptable, as these myths were well-known to those outside the cult as well as initiates. The different interpretations demonstrate that there is much still to be understood about Roman religion, and this equally applies to many other aspects of Roman archaeology.

The equestrian statue of Marcus
Aurelius in the Piazza del
Campidoglio, Rome.

IMP. CAESARI DIVI ANTONINI F. DIVI HADRIAN
NEPOTI DIVI TRAIANI PARTHICI PRONEPOTI DIVI
E. ABNEPOTI M. AVRELIO ANTONINO PIO

CHAPTER X
COLLAPSE OF THE EMPIRE

Different aspects of Roman life during the heyday of the empire have been examined, covering virtually all that was important to a Roman during his lifetime, with one or two exceptions beyond the scope of this book such as literature and law. A portrayal of the culture, particularly by means of the surviving archaeological remains, has been attempted, with the aim of explaining the successes and failures of Roman society. In this last chapter the themes explored earlier will be drawn together to assist in answering the most important question of all that remains; why did Roman civilization apparently decay and come to an end? The setting for answering this question is the history of the period from Augustus to the end of the empire in the west in AD 476. During this time all the causes responsible for the end of the empire emerged and began to have their effect.

Augustus' successors had distinctly less personal authority and capability to administer the vast territories under Roman control. Tiberius continued the policies of Augustus but lacked his flair for public relations. He was something of a recluse, spending the last 11 years of his reign in a pleasure palace on Capri without once setting foot in Rome. Sejanus, the prefect of the praetorian guard (the imperial bodyguard) became his trusted confidant and effectively managed the day-to-day running of the empire. The use of favorites such as Sejanus to help run affairs of state was repeated later by other emperors, but was one of the weak points of the imperial system. The favorites were resented by the Senate and aristocracy, as their advice was not so often sought, and their authority was diminished. Sejanus' position also emphasized the vital role the military played in keeping the emperor in power. Although Sejanus himself was accused of plotting against Caligula, Tiberius' heir, deposed from office and executed, his position set a precedent for other praetorians to follow.

Caligula succeeded to supreme power in AD 37 upon the death of Tiberius, but only ruled for four years. He was young, impetuous and completely irresponsible. He may even have been mentally unbalanced to judge from some of his actions, such as forcing disabled citizens to fight in the amphitheater, or considering the election of his horse Incitatus to the consulship. His judgment became increasingly cruel and arbitrary as time went on, ultimately causing the praetorian guard to turn against him and assassinate him. By doing this the guard proved itself to be the most powerful single group in Rome. As the Senate deliberated about the possibility of restoring the Republic, the guard took the initiative and elevated the only surviving male of the Julio-Claudian house, Claudius, to the emperorship.

Despite physical disabilities and a markedly suspicious and cruel streak, Claudius proved himself to be a capable ruler, organizing long-term projects such as the grain supply to Rome, and the draining of lakes and marshes for agricultural purposes. He also reversed Augustus' policy of not expanding the limits of the empire by invading Britain.

Owing to suspicions about the fidelity of the Senate, following its suggestion that the Republic should be restored, Claudius deliberately developed the practice of using members of his own household as advisors and executives. Some of his Greek freedmen, such as Narcissus, rose to great power, at the same time sowing the seeds of what was later to become the imperial civil service. In personal matters, Claudius fell increasingly under the influence of his fourth wife Agrippina the younger, who promoted her son by a previous marriage, Nero, as the next emperor. Claudius accepted him over his own son, Britannicus, and Nero duly became emperor after Claudius' death in AD 54. There were suspicious circumstances about the death which prompted the biographer Suetonius to accuse Agrippina of poisoning him with mushrooms. Poisoning also brought about the end of Britannicus.

Despite these intrigues, Nero's reign began well, mainly because he entrusted matters to his mother and to close associates while he himself developed his interest in the theater and the arts. However, he later took a more active part in affairs of state, especially after he had had Agrippina assassinated. Treason trials were revived, in order to dispose of senators whom he considered to be conspiring to kill him. This set the nobility against him, later to be joined by the common people as they were forced to pay higher taxes to cover the expense of his extravagances, such as the 'Golden House,' a palace set in a specially cleared park right in the middle of the city. Eventually, abandoned by the Senate, the people, the army and even his own entourage and the praetorian guard, he committed suicide.

This ended the Julio-Claudian dynasty, and the problem of the succession, which had always caused difficulty, now reached a crisis. Over the next two years, AD 68–70, various factions of the army, both on the frontiers and in Rome, put up their commanders as emperor, with the result that in AD 69, four emperors reigned – Galba, Otho, Vitellius and Vepasian – the first three of whom met violent ends. There was also a vicious and bloodthirsty civil war, showing clearly that the famous *pax Romana* merely covered up serious tensions only too ready to rise to the surface. Vespasian, the nominee of the legions stationed in the east and on the Danube, emerged victorious, and became the founder of the second major group of emperors, the Flavians. On the whole, their reigns were uneventful,

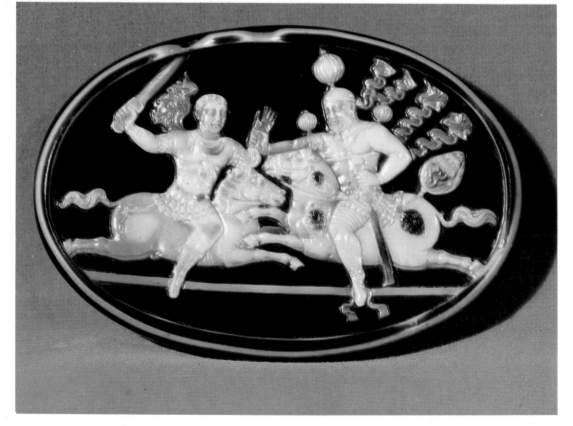

ABOVE Sacrifice of a bull, on an altar of the Imperial cult in the Temple of Vespasian, Pompeii.

LEFT Emperor Valerian fighting Sapor, king of the Persians, cameo gem, mid-third century AD.

RIGHT Hadrian's villa, Tivoli, built AD 125–35. The epistyle at the north end of the Canopus lake. The villa was Hadrian's suburban retreat near Rome, and contained architectural reminders of his travels around the empire. For instance, Canopus was the name of a canal in Egypt.

although they all pursued an aggressive foreign policy to conquer new lands in Britain, Germany and Rumania (Dacia). Much-needed stability was restored to the empire, especially under Vespasian, who regularized the depleted revenues, embarked on a policy of developing the provinces, and worked unceasingly to administer the affairs of state. Toward the end of the century, however, the third Flavian, Domitian, grew suspicious of the senators, since he had antagonized them by adopting an openly autocratic attitude. Treason trials were restarted, with paid informers causing terror among the aristocracy. More significant was his antagonism of the commanders of the praetorian guard who eventually had him assassinated in AD 96; another example of the power of the army to make or break emperors.

The successor was an elderly nominee of the assassins, Nerva, whose appointment was secure only after he had bowed to the wishes of the rank and file of the army and handed over the assassins for trial. He also curried favor with the troops by adopting a popular military governor, Trajan, as his heir to the throne. In doing this he in fact followed a precedent set by Galba some years earlier, but his choice of successor was much more careful, and he inaugurated a system of succession that was used for most of the next century. For the time being the temporary crises that accompanied the death of each emperor were over, and the empire entered a more tranquil phase.

Trajan was an active, progressive man. He introduced reforms such as the provision of *alimenta* (payments) for poor children in Italy, and he lightened the taxes imposed on the

LEFT The Aurelianic Wall of Rome near the San Sebastian gate.

BELOW A captured Parthian with characteristic head-dress, from the triumphal arch of Septimius Severus, Rome.

provinces. He started a vast building program in Rome, including his forum and basilica. Set in the forum was Trajan's Column, on which a spiral of carved reliefs told the story of the Dacian Wars, the emperor's greatest new conquest, which brought both military glory to Trajan and vast quantities of gold and silver to the imperial treasury. After Dacia, he fought a brilliant series of campaigns in the east, extending the empire to its limits, into Mesopotamia and to the shores of the Persian Gulf. However, in doing this he seems to have overestimated the capabilities of the army, for his communication lines were attacked and a retreat was forced. He died soon after, in AD 117, at a point when, militarily at least, Rome was at its greatest. For many, Trajan represented the ideal ruler, the *optimus princeps*, who was fair-minded at home and victorious abroad.

However, his eastern adventures had cost money, and it was left to his adopted successor, Hadrian, to sort out the imperial business that Trajan had left unfinished at his death. The new conquests in the east were abandoned and the frontiers consolidated, with the building of permanent barriers such as Hadrian's Wall a major feature of the new policy. Hadrian ended the expansion of the empire that had gone on more or less continuously up to his reign, thereby setting in train one of the problems that was to contribute ultimately to Roman decline. For Roman society was used to what we would now call a 'growth economy,' which could be achieved in two ways – booty captured by the army could contribute to the imperial coffers and at the same time pay for the army itself, thus relieving taxes, or the standard of living in the provinces could be raised by encouraging the provincials to buy Roman goods. The end of an expansionary policy meant that booty was no longer flowing in, with the result that the army became a fixed expense on the imperial balance-sheet. Hadrian attempted the second

option for growth as an alternative. He visited the provinces, encouraging the setting up of more Roman buildings, making the administration more efficient and putting forward the notion that the provinces were no longer conquered territory but proud members of a sort of provincial 'commonwealth.' It is no coincidence that Hadrian himself was a provincial, as was Trajan before him. They were Spaniards, and the most brilliant representatives of a newly important political force in Rome, the provincial senators, who increasingly made important contributions to the administration. This also applied to the army, in which Italians and Romans now played a minor part. Provincialization of the Roman administration, economy and army was one of the most significant underlying trends of the second century.

Hadrian appointed the elderly Antoninus Pius as his successor, whose long reign was peaceful and uneventful. There was little military activity apart from the expansion in Britain, where Hadrian's Wall was abandoned in favor of a new wall about 80 miles further north. Under the next ruler, however, the peace was shattered. Marcus Aurelius (161–80) was the first emperor to have to deal with a new and lasting threat to the empire – the Germans that bordered its northern frontier. The Marcomanni, based in the northern part of modern Czechoslovakia, were the most formidable of the peoples that pushed across the Roman frontier in the middle Danube area, pressing on over the Alps and attacking cities on the northern fringes of the Mediterranean. Aurelius spent 14 years in a more or less successful fight against them, ultimately dealing with the problem by allowing large numbers of Germans to settle within Roman territory near the frontiers in exchange for service as auxiliary soldiers. This move was a major step toward the takeover of effective control of the army by Germans, which happened in the fourth century.

After Marcus Aurelius came Commodus, who was a natural rather than an adopted heir, thus breaking the principle of succession which had been set by Nerva. Commodus was a vain man, given to self-glorification, especially in the guise of Hercules, whom he worshipped as a divinity, and equated himself with. He was suspicious of the Senate and conducted purges in the same manner as Domitian had done a century earlier. He met his end in the same way as Domitian too, for the commander of the praetorian guard had him assassinated. After this Rome slid rapidly toward civil war, in much the same fashion as after the end of the Julio-Claudians in AD 68. The praetorians controlled the elevation of different nominees to the throne, even to the extent of auctioning supreme power to the man who could give them the largest donative (a euphemism for a bribe). However, the armies in the provinces were also anxious to put forward their own candidates, of whom the most powerful was Septimius Severus, the man elevated by the Danube garrison. After several years of war he emerged victorious, and proceeded to consolidate his position by replacing the praetorian guard with his own Danubians, and by excluding senators from administrative posts.

The exclusion of senators marked a stride forward in the gradual removal of the aristocracy from effective power. This had the unforeseen result of eventually bringing about an unwillingness to serve in any sort of public office. Rich men withdrew from public life and retreated to their vast estates, which started to be used as country houses in the true sense, with large tracts of land and almost an absolute control of the estate workers. Town life, especially in the western provinces, became less attractive as ambitious men found their usual path to political office – via the municipal and provincial councils, and

BELOW Fortified road station or villa at Thesée, central France, built in the third century at a time of great rural insecurity.

RIGHT The emperor Severus Alexander hunting. Gold glass bowl, circa AD 235.

from there to the Senate – blocked. New town buildings became increasingly rare after the reign of Severus, since they were often put up during a local official's period of office in fulfillment of an election promise. It is possible to see in this trend one of the major changes that divides the earlier from the later Roman empire. Up to Severan times there was a public-spiritedness about service to the community. Officials were willing, and indeed vied with each other, to spend their wealth on the glorification of their home towns. In the third century and later this spirit was replaced by a more selfish one. Money was now spent on country houses, on rich furniture and fittings, on jewellery, leaving municipal projects to be funded by levies and taxes. This resulted in an increasing gap between rich and poor, since the rich were quite easily able to avoid paying taxes if they wanted to. The Christian writer Salvian deplored this attitude of the upper classes, which had become very clear by the end of the fourth century when he was writing. He felt that the higher a man's status, the greater his obligations. If these obligations were not carried out, a man betrayed the empire and contributed to its fall. Such a clear-sighted analysis was unfortunately too late to change the attitude of the landed aristocracy, who continued to think that their main obligations were to their estates and lands.

Emperor Severus campaigned actively in various parts of the empire, ending external threats to security for the time being. He also reformed the army by relaxing the rules that prevented soldiers from rising above centurion level. Pay was increased and marriage allowed. By doing this he created a privileged military class, paid for by increasingly large taxes, but intensely devoted to the emperor. On his death he is reputed to have advised his sons and heirs, 'Be friendly to each other, generous to the soldiers, and don't care about anyone else.' The emperor and his court had become, in the short period of Severus' reign, committed to the military at the expense of other classes in society.

The elevation of Severus' two sons, Caracalla and Geta, proved to be a mistake. Geta was soon murdered by his brother, and there followed a period of unstable rule by Caracalla. This came to an end with his assassination by the praetorian prefect, Macrinus, who was fearful for his own life and decided to forestall any plan of Caracalla's for his execution. Macrinus then became emperor, the first nonsenator to do so. His attempts to control financial affairs by revaluing the coinage and trying to avoid paying the now regular donative to the troops resulted in a rebellion organized by Julia Maesa, Severus' sister-in-law. Macrinus was defeated and killed, to be replaced by Elagabalus.

Elagabalus took his name from the Syrian sun god whose cult he was priest of, and it was to this cult that he devoted all his energies while emperor. He brought the exotic new cult to Rome, and demolished part of the Palatine to set up an enormous temple overlooking the Forum. However, the peculiarities of the rituals and Elagabalus' own unusual sexual proclivities alarmed Rome to such an extent that Julia Maesa induced the praetorians to murder the emperor and recognize her other

BELOW A model of the mausoleum of Diocletian, now the cathedral of Split, Yugoslavia.

RIGHT A porphyry bust, possibly Maximinus Daia, AD 307–13.

ABOVE The *porta Ostiensis* in the Aurelianic Wall, Rome.

LEFT The late Roman wall of Carcassonne, France, with Visigothic additions. Such walls were vital after the barbarian raids of the mid-third century AD.

grandson, Severus Alexander, instead. His rule was largely in the hands of his grandmother and his mother Julia Mamaea, since he was only 14 when first raised to supreme power. There were problems on the frontier, too, that ultimately proved the undoing of his reign, for while trying to end a German invasion by buying off the aggressors, he and Julia Mamaea were murdered during a mutiny of the troops.

This event marked the end of the rather undistinguished later representatives of the Severan dynasty. During their period in power the Severans had proved singularly incapable of being friendly to each other, as Severus had asked, but the rest of his advice was followed more closely, as the army became more and more clearly the élite of society while the empire started to collapse around them.

Collapse was sparked off in the early third century by a number of economic as well as political factors. Successive emperors, particularly Severus and Caracalla, had debased the coinage in order to pay the army. The result was inflation and a lack of coinage as the earlier, more-valuable coins were melted down. This hit traders hard and a recession set in that was to last until the closing years of the century and was to transform the economy of the empire. It became less and less possible to trade goods long distances, which meant that the provinces had to be more self-sufficient in such goods as food and pottery. The old trading networks, which had distributed goods over large regions of the empire and beyond, broke down, and local networks were built up in their place. The provinces furthest from

Rome no longer had that common bond which wide trading networks brought. They were free to drift along increasingly independent lines, with important political consequences, as will be seen. Another consequence was that Italy suffered more than other countries because it relied so heavily on imports. These were now drying up except from North Africa, which remained prosperous throughout the third century, and upon which Italy increasingly had to rely.

Inflation caused the virtual collapse of the money economy: by the end of the century prices had risen nearly a thousand-fold and the coinage was worthless. The emperors protected the troops from the effects of inflation on their wages by handing out bounties at frequent intervals in the form of gold coins and medallions. These kept their value throughout the century, and the troops were further protected by a change in their ordinary payment from coins to goods requisitioned from the civilian population. This depressed the money economy even further.

The politics of the third century after Severus Alexander became increasingly anarchic. It was the period of the soldier emperors, who came and went with alarming rapidity, more often than not at the hands of the troops. There were threats from both within and outside the empire, quite apart from the unstable nature of the army itself. Epidemics, first brought in by Marcus Aurelius' army from the east, spread through the empire. A new nation, Persia, had replaced the Parthians on Rome's eastern borders, and was much more aggressive than its predecessor. The Germans, particularly the Alemanni in south Germany, were raiding across the border regularly. One group, the Franks, passed right through Gaul and Spain and even raided North Africa. Two emperors were killed by the enemy – Decius (AD 249–51) who fell at the hands of Gothic invaders, and Valerian (AD 253–60) who was captured by

King Sapor of Persia and kept prisoner until his death, when he was reputedly stuffed as a trophy by the Persian king. The year AD 260 marks the low point of the third century, for it also saw the creation of an independent government within the empire in Gaul. The governor of Germany, Postumus, felt aggrieved that his troops were bearing the brunt of the fighting against the Germans, while the Danubian army had more troops, and seemed to be more successful at getting its nominees made emperor. He set up a Gallic Empire with its own government based in Trier and Cologne. Most of the western provinces joined him, including Britain, Gaul and Spain. Relations with the main empire were, of course, hostile, but Gallienus (AD 253–68) was so overwhelmed with problems elsewhere in the empire that he could not do anything about it.

During most of the next decade raids continued all along the northern frontier, culminating in the plundering of Greece and Asia Minor by the Goths and Heruls in AD 268. In the east, in AD 267 Queen Zenobia declared Palmyra an independent state, which covered the provinces of Syria, Mesopotamia, part of Asia Minor and Egypt. The empire was breaking up, and the writings of the period reflect the anxieties and tensions that people felt: 'The world is now falling into decay,' according to Saint Cyprian in the 250s. Later writers also saw these years as a crisis point in Roman history: 'It was almost the destruction of the Roman Empire,' wrote Eutropius. The *Historia Augusta*, written in the fourth century, saw the danger that 'the Empire built up in the venerable name of Rome would come to an end.'

However, despite all this, the imperial system proved remarkably resilient. The army recovered its fighting capabilities and started to repulse the raiders. Gallienus was partly responsible for this, as he made some reforms that went a long way to creating the rather different army of the later empire. All posts were now open to all ranks as the old link between the officers and the senatorial and equestrian classes was finally broken. A more-professional army was the result, as it now had officers that served for longer terms, who were more expert at their jobs. Gallienus also created a mobile task force, mainly of cavalry, that accompanied him to trouble spots. This acknowledged that pressure on the frontiers was so great that the legions could not be expected to cope on their own, and that a mobile reserve was needed. This force, however, became much more important than simply a reserve, as it was also, in effect, the emperor's personal army that went with him on campaign. It rapidly gained much more prestige than the legions, with the result that they started to decline in importance and became static peace-keeping forces on the frontiers. The change to cavalry was also significant, as it marked a general shift in military tactics away from infantry-dominated fighting.

The new army defeated the Goths as they returned to their homeland laden with plunder, killing 50,000 of them at Naissus in Yugoslavia. It went on to defeat the Alemanni and other German tribes in a series of battles that, for the time being at least, disposed of the problems of insecurity along the northern frontier. The mobile force also proved itself in other ways, for its commanders were in an extremely powerful position. Aurelian, its second commander, who later became emperor, organized a plot against Gallienus that overthrew the emperor and had him put to death in 268.

Aurelian (AD 270–75) was one of the most energetic emperors of the third century. Besides the repulse of German raids, he brought first Queen Zenobia's state and then the Gallic Empire back under Roman control. He abandoned Dacia (Rumania),

LEFT Porphyry statues of four tetrarchs now in the corner of St Mark's cathedral, Venice. Probably from Constantinople.

BELOW A collapsed tower in the town wall of Dura Europos, on the river Euphrates, Syria. The collapse is due to deliberate undermining by Persian besiegers in AD 256.

ABOVE The southwest side of the great dome of Haghia Sophia church, Constantinople, built sixth century AD, and the finest surviving building in the eastern capital set up by Constantine in AD 324–30.

LEFT The Basilica, an Imperial audience hall of Constantinian date in Trier, a town that became an Imperial capital in the fourth century AD.

RIGHT Colossal head of Constantine, *circa* AD 315.

ABOVE The triumphal arch of Constantine, built after his victory over Maxentius in AD 315. The ornamentation is partly original.

as it was too costly to defend any longer, and built a new defensive wall round Rome that was to serve it up to the Renaissance. New, strong defenses were built along the frontiers of the empire, with the result that by the death of Emperor Carus in AD 283, peace could be said to have returned to an exhausted Roman world. The change in Roman fortunes was swift and dramatic, achieved largely through the remodelled army under a series of brilliant and daring strategists. But the cost was heavy for the civilian population in terms of economic dislocation, heavy taxes and an increasingly militaristic and arbitrarily repressive government.

In AD 284 Diocletian came to power. He was a reformer who drastically altered the administrative face of the empire, in a way that could be regarded as a first step toward the creation of Medieval Europe. The empire was divided into smaller units, so that there were about a hundred provinces instead of fifty, in a move designed to prevent provincial governors acquiring too much power and making a bid for the throne. He also partitioned the empire into East and West, and appointed a second emperor to rule the western part while he took the east. In doing this he tried to make Imperial control of the provinces tighter, for the events of the third century had shown that a single person found

it difficult, if not impossible, to run the empire effectively without assistance. To spread the burden of responsibility further, and at the same time to cope with the ever-present problem of the succession, he appointed an assistant and heir to each emperor. His plan was that the emperors should both retire at the same time, allowing the assistants (who were called Caesars) to take power. They in turn appointed new Caesars, thus perpetuating the system, which became known as the Tetrarchy. Unfortunately, only under Diocletian himself and his co-emperor, Maximian, did the succession work as he intended. However, although the Caesars did eventually lose their power and rights of succession, the basic division of the empire into East and West became more and more clear-cut as time went on. There were major cultural differences: for instance, Latin was the main language in the West, and Greek in the East. The East was also much richer, more cohesive and able to withstand the barbarian onslaught of the fourth and fifth centuries. It was ultimately to form the basis of the Byzantine Empire.

Diocletian also reformed the army and the currency. The mobile task force created by Gallienus was vastly expanded so that each of the four leaders had his own field army that accompanied him to trouble spots. Frontier troops were demoted to patrolling strength only, and usually could not hold back attacks until the mobile armies had been sent for. This had the effect of turning some of the worst affected frontiers into battle zones, devastated both by the marauding barbarians and by the mobile armies trying to drive them out. Civilians moved away, leaving good agricultural land deserted and reducing the area available to pay taxes. Taxes, of course, were the source of income used to pay the army, which was by far the Roman government's largest expense. Diocletian created an efficient system of tax collection to ensure that the army was provided for. He also reformed the coinage, to prevent, admittedly rather unsuccessfully, the spiralling inflation of earlier years. This was accompanied by an edict that fixed the maximum prices for all goods and services – an ancient price and wages freeze. These measures went a long way to controlling the activities of the civilian population, and produced a tendency toward feudalism as people were increasingly tied to the land where they lived and to the profession they were engaged in. Agricultural workers on the large estates were kept almost as serfs, paying off debts by their labor. This meant that the poorest people in the empire, the ostensibly-free small landholders, were gradually absorbed by the great estates, whose owners became much richer as a result. Those who broke loose from this strait jacket found themselves dispossessed, and many sought a livelihood from brigandage. In fact, bands of brigands and revolts by agricultural workers (the *Baganudae*) were a major problem to the authorities in the fourth and fifth centuries. It is clear that the empire was no longer seen as the civilized saviour of the world by all sections of society.

Diocletian accompanied these measures with a patriotic propaganda campaign, using coins to spread the idea of the greatness of the Roman *genius* (guiding spirit). He also used religion as a medium for promoting loyalty to the state. This brought the Christians into conflict with him, for they did not worship at the shrines of the official religion, and consequently were thought to be disloyal. A persecution of the Christians followed, in an attempt to make them sacrifice to the official gods.

For the next great emperor, however, the Christians were a source of strength, not suspicion. Constantine the Great came to power after seven years of internecine warfare between the Caesars and emperors, for Diocletian's rules for succession were disregarded as soon as he stepped down in AD 305. At the battle of the Milvian bridge near Rome in AD 312, where Constantine gained control of the western Empire, he saw and was guided by a shining cross in the sky. This was interpreted as a Christian sign, which encouraged him and his co-emperor in the East, Licinius, to issue the famous Edict of Milan in AD 313 giving freedom of worship and toleration to the Christians. As his reign progressed, Constantine introduced a series of laws that favored the Christians, especially after he had wrested power from Licinius and became sole emperor in AD 324. Christians were exempted from municipal obligations, and the building of churches was subsidized. The emperor himself was baptised on his deathbed, which was a common time of life to be received into the Church as there was no chance of sinning.

The reign of Constantine marked a major turning point in Christian history. The religion rose almost overnight from an insignificant but provoking cult to one of the major organized

BELOW The mausoleum of Galla Placidia, sister of the emperor Honorius. She died AD 450, but the mausoleum was set up in Ravenna *circa* AD 425.

LEFT The Byzantine and Greek Orthodox churches inherited the architectural traditions of the late empire. Small central drum church of Panayia Koudelidiki, Kastoria, northern Greece, eleventh century AD.

RIGHT Porphyry sarcophagus of Constantina (died AD 354), daughter of Constantine. It was placed in a mausoleum that later became the baptistery of the church of Santa Costanza, Rome.

BELOW The barbarian invasions of the fifth century that contributed to the fall of the western empire in AD 476.

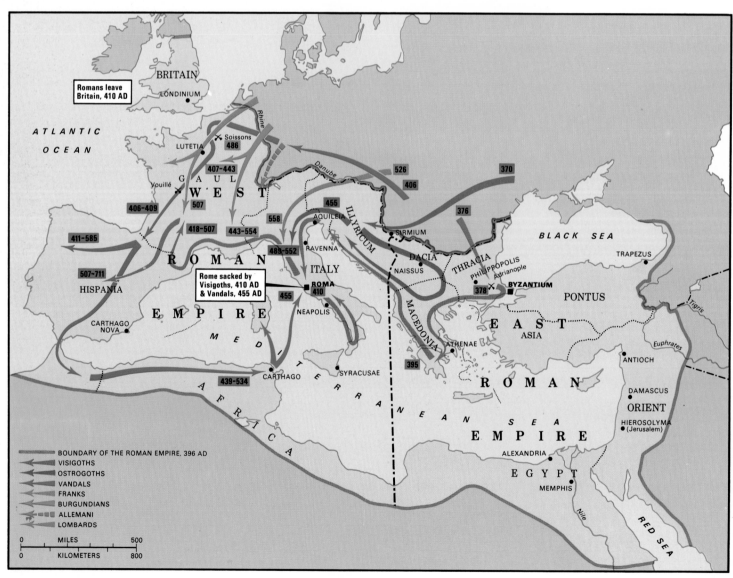

BRITAIN
Romans leave Britain, 410 AD
LONDINIUM
ATLANTIC OCEAN
Rhine
Soissons 486
LUTETIA
407-443
Vouillé
GAUL
WEST
406-409
507
Danube
526
406
370
455
418-507
558
376
411-585
ROMAN
443-554
AQUILEIA
ILLYRICUM
BLACK SEA
507-711
489-552
RAVENNA
SIRMIUM
DACIA
TRAPEZUS
HISPANIA
ITALY
NAISSUS
THRACIA
PHILIPPOPOLIS
Adrianople
EMPIRE
Rome sacked by Visigoths, 410 AD & Vandals, 455 AD
ROMA 410
455
NEAPOLIS
MACEDONIA
378 BYZANTIUM
PONTUS
EAST
ASIA
CARTHAGO NOVA
MEDITERRANEAN
395
ROMAN
Tigris
439-534
CARTHAGO
SYRACUSAE
ATHENAE
ANTIOCH
Euphrates
AFRICA
SEA
EMPIRE
DAMASCUS
ORIENT
HIEROSOLYMA (Jerusalem)
ALEXANDRIA
EGYPT
MEMPHIS
Nile
RED SEA

BOUNDARY OF THE ROMAN EMPIRE, 396 AD
VISIGOTHS
OSTROGOTHS
VANDALS
FRANKS
BURGUNDIANS
ALLEMANI
LOMBARDS

0 MILES 500
0 KILOMETERS 800

groups in the empire. Paganism was on the wane as Christian missionaries spread the newly tolerated faith abroad, gradually taking over control of the administration and the machinery of government. By the end of the fourth century, Christianity was the sole official religion, there were laws against making pagan sacrifices, and the majority of the population in the Mediterranean lands at least had been converted to the faith. However, an intellectual change accompanied the conversion to Christianity, which resulted in a different attitude toward the empire. Many men who previously would have played an active part in politics or the army now led contemplative lives, and there grew up a sense of otherworldliness that was out of tune, perhaps deliberately, with the anxieties of the age. In addition there was an emotional sense of fatalism arising from the promise of everlasting life after the miseries of the present one. As a result many people did not worry as the fourth and fifth centuries dissolved into political chaos, and the empire collapsed, for their earthly fate was of no consequence. On the other hand, it must be said that many Christians were key figures in the history of the period, leading armies or administering provinces without lapsing to the fatalistic feelings of other Christians.

The pagans, too, were demoralized by their own decline. They looked back to the golden age of Rome, when their religion and culture flourished and formed the backbone of Roman civilization. They lost faith in the future, and such things as literature, art and technical innovation were the poorer as a result. In fact, very few new developments in any of these fields took place in the later empire, save in the Christian context of church architecture and embellishment.

Constantine's army was, in his view, the most important group in the empire, and he continued to favor the troops in much the same way as emperors had done in the previous century. He also decided to make increasing use of Germans in his field army, as they were considered the best soldiers available and were skilled at fighting against their own countrymen if there were attacks across the frontier. Germans came to be employed in all ranks of the army, eventually reaching the topmost positions. By the end of the century a German commander in chief dominated the rather weak emperor of the time. This 'barbarization' of the army caused a growing rift in the relations between civilians and the military, since the soldiers were increasingly of different racial origins, with habits and customs that repelled those used to the Roman way of life. The bishop Sidonius Apollinaris, for instance, wrote of his objections to the noisy Goths, the tattooed Heruls and the Burgundians who smeared rancid butter on their hair. As German soldiers and their families began to settle within the empire, in groups known as *laeti* or *foederati*, they were kept apart from the rest of the population. Even after the German tribes had invaded in force, the provincials did not mix with them. In the long term, this failure to assimilate these new and potentially useful peoples was disastrous for the unity of the empire as the German groups kept their own identity and organization, thus forming the nucleus of the nations that were to succeed the Roman Empire.

A major development that took place under Constantine was the setting up of a second capital to administer the eastern part of the empire. The old city of Byzantium on the Bosphorus was entirely rebuilt in AD 324–30 and named Constantinople. It was modelled on Rome, with a forum, Senate and distributions of free food. Although at first it was inferior to Rome in status, it became clear that there was to be permanent transfer of power to the eastern capital. In fact, Rome was rapidly losing its status as a capital in the west too, for the administration tended to follow the emperor as he continually travelled about, and very little of its time was spent in Rome. Towns such as Milan,

Trier and Sofia were more convenient as temporary capitals since they were so much nearer the frontiers. However, Rome retained its preeminent position as the spiritual and symbolic capital of the empire; the Senate was still there, and the church tended to look to the bishop of Rome for leadership.

Since Constantine had come to power by using force, shattering Diocletian's carefully thought-out scheme for the succession, when it came for Constantine to think about his own heirs, he decided on a family dynasty as a way of solving the problem. However, at his death in AD 337 three sons and two nephews competed for power. At first there was a share out of responsibility along the lines of the old Tetrarchic system, but soon fighting broke out, ending after 13 years with Constantius II as sole emperor. He consolidated his father's reforms, especially those to do with the official recognition of Christianity, but his relative and successor, Julian (AD 360–63), followed rather a different path.

In reaction to his Christian upbringing, Julian renounced his faith, and reinstated the pagan cults. He felt that his Christian predecessors had not practiced what they had preached, because they were constantly warring against one another. Pagan philosophers had taught him as a child, and he came to despise the intellectual contortions of the contemporary Christian theologians who tried to deal with the numerous heresies that had sprung up. However, his crusade against the Christians was too aggressive to win the sympathy of most of the population, and he had little feeling for the failure of pagan religion to cater for the emotional needs of people. Christianity was restored as the Imperial religion under his pious successor Jovian.

Julian was the last of the House of Constantine, leaving no heir on his death following a wound during an expedition to Persia. The stage was set for a civil war, as had happened so often before, but none came. Jovian was elected by Julian's army, and upon his death eight months later, another general, Valentinian I, was acclaimed by the troops. A new dynasty was founded with remarkably little disturbance. Valentinian was from the Danube provinces, of partial barbarian ancestry, and he was known for his administrative and military capabilities. He promoted the cause of the poorer classes and was tolerant of different religions, especially different Christian heresies. His brother Valens was appointed Emperor of the East, restoring in part the division of responsibility set up by Diocletian. From now on the division was permanent, save for a very brief period a few years later, inadvertently making the West poorer, because it had lost the tax revenues from the rich eastern cities. Fighting in the West increased as barbarian pressure grew, which meant that the civilian population had to pay higher taxes for the defense of the frontiers. Valentinian attempted to deal with the problem of the Germans crossing the Rhine and Danube by reorganizing and rebuilding the frontier. Forts and watchtowers were built to guard the river frontiers and fortified granaries were positioned so as to ensure supplies to the field army, with the emperor himself ensuring that it was set up properly by campaigning vigorously against the barbarians for several years.

For the previous century or so, the barbarians had been kept at bay, thanks to the military leadership of such emperors as Aurelian, Diocletian, Constantine, Julian and Valentinian. It seemed that the tide of barbarians had been stemmed, and that a sort of stability could be restored to the empire. All this changed three years after Valentinian's death, when his eastern co-emperor Valens was killed at the diastrous battle of Adrianople in AD 376. The Visigoths, numbering 200,000, had been allowed to settle within the empire to escape from the attacks of a new barbarian menace the Huns. At first they did this peaceably, but they soon revolted at their treatment by the Romans and started plundering the Balkans. Valens then forced the battle, in which the entire Roman infantry was annihilated.

This shattered the reputation and morale of the army, and left a horde of hostile Goths at large within the empire. Their success also encouraged many other groups of barbarians to try their luck at crossing the frontier into Roman lands. From then on the history of the Roman Empire in the West is a decline into chaos and final collapse.

At this point it is worth considering the question of why the Roman Empire collapsed. There were both internal difficulties and external threats besetting the empire throughout the third, fourth and fifth centuries. Internally, there was major social change which led from a cohesive society in which everyone more or less willingly played a part, to one where the classes were polarized, with the military, the aristocracy and the ordinary people set against each other. The economy exacerbated these divisions because the amount of money and tax needed to pay for the army was indirectly the cause of inflation and stagnation. Social and economic problems also created a

sense of isolation in the provinces, with the result that they drifted toward independence when the opportunity presented itself. The attitude of government played its part, since the civil service was expanded to ensure that decrees were carried out, and the emperor himself became more unapproachable and despotic. Intellectually and artistically, too, the later empire marked a change from an open-minded exploratory attitude to one that was more closed and rigid, perhaps also reflected in religion, now markedly more intolerant and rooted in emotion than before. All these difficulties and changes contributed to a greater or a lesser extent to the gradual collapse in the confidence of the Roman people: the empire was no longer thought of as the guiding spirit of civilization, and it continued as long as it did for reasons of individual self-preservation as much as anything else, compounded by fear of what might replace it. The external threat, in the form of barbarians wanting to enter the empire and enjoy the fruits of its civilization,

ABOVE The silver Missorium of Thodosius, late fourth century AD.

is a much clearer reason to explain the end of the Roman Empire. But the barbarians were the agents that actually brought about its collapse – the underlying instability of the later empire being the reason why it could not withstand the barbarian onslaught.

Theodosius, the next eastern emperor after Valens, was forced to accept the Visigoths on his lands, and drew up a treaty with them. After his death, the empire was ruled by his two sons, Honorius in the West and Arcadius in the East. Both were weak personalities, relinquishing actual power to regents. In the West, the regent was a German, Stilicho, who was an active general. He harbored ambitious designs against the eastern empire, hoping to set up Honorius as the sole emperor of the Roman world, under his control. To help achieve this he left alone the Goths under their new leader Alaric, despite Gothic raids into Italy itself, since they were able to assist in his plans. This proved a mistake, due to the unforeseen events in the north in 406. The Rhine froze over, allowing a horde of Vandals, Sueves, Alans and Burgundians to sweep across Germany and Gaul. The Rhine frontier was broken permanently, and the Germans never moved out. In fact the Vandals travelled onward into Spain, eventually crossing the Straits of Gibraltar and taking control of North Africa. Britain and northern France were cut off from the empire, the former being lost soon after because the troops were removed to deal with the menace on the continent. Germans moved into eastern Britain.

Soon after this Stilicho was accused of colluding with Alaric to put his own son on the throne. Despite his appeals to Honorius at the new western capital of Ravenna, he was put to death in 408. Alaric, demanding money and land for his people, rampaged through Italy. In 410, he occupied and sacked Rome, the first time it had fallen to a foreign power for 800 years. To many, this was the end of the world as they knew it. The figurehead and symbol of all that was civilized in the ancient world had fallen to a barbarous aggressor. Nevertheless, Rome survived, for the Goths only stayed three days, and soon afterward Alaric died and the Gothic threat melted away. Alaric's successor Ataulf moved his people to southwest France.

The Vandals were the next problem for the western leaders. After they had arrived in North Africa in 429 their leader Gaiseric was granted a treaty allowing him to hold Morocco and western Algeria (Mauretania and Numidia). However, he expanded to the east, and the Romans were powerless to stop him. Carthage fell in 439, leaving Rome's vital grain supply under Vandal control. Gaiseric set up a fully independent kingdom, the first of the barbarians to do so, and his fleet proceeded to destroy Roman dominance of the Mediterranean.

Attila the Hun was the other scourge of the last days of Rome. The Huns were nomadic peoples from the Russian steppes, of non-German stock and greatly feared by the other barbarians. The Roman military leader Aetius had friendly relations with them, since he had once been their hostage and appreciated their methods of fighting. Since Aetius was in control in the West, he used some Huns as mercenaries against the Germans, while Attila and the main group of the Huns harried the Balkans and the East. However, one of the eastern emperors refused to let this continue, and cut off the large sums of gold which had been used to buy off Attila. Accordingly the Huns turned to the West for loot, and intervened in the court politics at Ravenna. Attila's proposal of marriage to the sister of the Emperor Valentinian III was rejected when he demanded half the western Empire as a dowry, thus causing him to invade Gaul. This created such alarm in the semiindependent German kingdoms of Gaul that they banded together with Aetius to confront and defeat Attila at the battle of the Catalaunian Fields in central France in AD 451. The Huns turned back, their unbeaten record now broken, and entered northern Italy. There Pope

Leo I persuaded them that there was nothing left for them to plunder, since Alaric had done so earlier, and disease and famine were ravaging the land. The Huns returned to their lands outside the empire, which were vast, stretching from the Baltic Sea to the Danube. Soon after this Attila died, the Hunnic Empire collapsed and the Huns retreated to Russia.

At about the same time Aetius and Valentinian were murdered as a result of a series of accusations and counteraccusations. Both had helped to keep the remains of the empire together; Aetius through his military and diplomatic abilities, Valentinian by virtue of being the last representative of the dynasty that his namesake, Valentinian I, had founded nearly a century before. Their deaths marked the end of the western empire.

Gaiseric almost immediately attacked and savagely looted Rome in 455, and the other German kings took advantage of the chaos in the Imperial court to make themselves increasingly independent. The Visigoths controlled Spain and southern Gaul, the Burgundians central Gaul and the Franks Belgium and northern Gaul. The Alamanni occupied the area between the Burgundians and the Franks, leaving a small area of northwest Gaul still in Roman hands, which in fact continued as nominally Roman after the western empire had collapsed. Only Italy and the Dalmatian coast were under direct Imperial control, even though they still claimed all the old territories, including long-lost Britain. A German general Ricimer was the effective ruler in Italy, although his nationality disqualified him from becoming emperor himself. A series of nominees were created emperor, culminating in a youth named Romulus Augustus (or Augustulus), who was put up by his father, one of Ricimer's successors as military commander. This emperor, with his names that recalled so vividly the great days of Rome, was in fact an usurper who was never acknowledged by the eastern Emperor. But his deposition in AD 476 (on August 28) is usually taken as the date of the end of the western empire, for no other emperors were appointed after that, and German kings took over Italy. Odoacer was the first German to do so, ruling ostensibly as the military commander representing the eastern emperor, Zeno. In fact, the lack of a western emperor made little difference to life in Italy, as the Senate continued in cooperation with Odoacer, and the Church and great landowners carried on their activities unhindered. Since Zeno was the nominal emperor of Italy, he was satisfied too, despite his realization that actual power was in German hands. The kingdom of Theodoric the Goth after 490 established Italian autonomy.

The East continued under Imperial control despite the loss of the West. Constantinople worried little about the movements of the Germans far away to the west, since the revenues of the eastern Empire were still flowing in. It changed imperceptibly into the Byzantine Empire, lasting more or less unscathed for 1000 years, until the Turks overran Constantinople in 1453.

In the West, the Germans fought among themselves for control of the old provinces. The Franks expanded to fill what is now modern France, forcing the Visigoths into Spain where they set up a kingdom. The Vandals lasted in North Africa until a Byzantine reconquest in the sixth century, to be followed in the seventh century by the overrunning of the country by the Mohammedans, who invaded and occupied Spain as well.

Out of the Frankish kingdom rose the Carolingian dynasty, whose greatest king, Charlemagne (772–814), founded the Holy Roman Empire. This was a conscious attempt at recalling the greatness of the old Roman Empire, which the Germans sought to imitate, and whose influence continued unabated throughout the centuries after the fall of the West. Of course, the memory and results of the Roman achievement still affects and influences us today.

RIGHT Byzantine mosaic of the empress Theodora, wife of Justinian, and her court.

CHRONOLOGICAL TABLE

BC

753	Traditional date for the founding of Rome
625-600	Etruscan takeover of Rome
c. **507**	Last Etruscan king expelled. Establishment of the Republic
c. **494**	Agitation by the plebs and appointment of the first tribunes
451-50	Codification of the law (The Twelve Tables)
396	Fall of Veii
387	Gauls sack Rome
378	Defensive wall of Rome built
343-290	Samnite and Latin wars
280-75	War against Pyrrhus and the Greek cities of South Italy
264-41	First Punic war
241	First overseas province set up in Sicily
238	Sardinia and Corsica annexed
225	Gauls defeated at Telamon
218-201	Second Punic war
200-168	Macedonian wars

149-46	Third Punic war
146	Carthage and Corinth razed to the ground
133, 123-2	Tribunates of Tiberius and Gaius Gracchus
91-87	Social war
81	Dictatorship of Sulla at Rome
73-71	Slave revolt of Spartacus
66-63	Pompey's campaigns in the East
60	First triumvirate of Pompey, Crassus and Caesar
58-51	Caesar's Gallic war
49-45	Civil war
44	Dictatorship of Caesar, and his assassination
43	Second triumvirate of Antony, Octavian and Lepidus
36-30	Civil war. Octavian victorious after battle of Actium
30	Deaths of Antony and Cleopatra. Egypt made part of Empire
27	Octavian hailed as Augustus, becomes first Emperor and founder of the Julio-Claudian dynasty

AD

9	Defeat of 3 legions in Germany and abandonment of offensive policy
14	Death of Augustus
14-37	Tiberius
37-41	Gaius Caligula
41-54	Claudius
41-6	Resumption of expansion with conquests of Britain, Mauretania and Thrace
54-68	Nero
66-70	First Jewish revolt

68-9	Civil war. Brief reigns by Galba, Otho and Vitellius. Vespasian, first of the Flavian dynasty, ultimately victorious
69-79	Vespasian
79-81	Titus
79	Vesuvius erupts, destroying Pompeii and Herculaneum
81-96	Domitian, last of the Flavians
96-8	Nerva
98-117	Trajan
106	Dacia conquered

117 Greatest extent of Empire reached following eastern conquests

117-38 Hadrian

122 Hadrian's Wall started in Britain. Static frontiers created elsewhere

132-5 Second Jewish revolt

138-61 Antoninus Pius

161-80 Marcus Aurelius

166-80 Wars on Danube against Marcomannic and Sarmatian aggressors

180-92 Commodus

193-7 Civil war. Septimius Severus, first of the Severan dynasty, ultimately victorious

193-211 Septimius Severus

211-17 Caracalla

212 Grant Roman citizenship to all free people in the Empire

217-8 Macrinus

218-22 Elagabalus

222-35 Severus Alexander

235-8 Maximinus Thrax

235-84 'The Soldier Emperors' and the crisis of the Empire

260 Valerian captured by Persians. German and Persian invasions

260-75 Separatist Gallic Empire

267-73 Zenobia's separatist kingdom in the East

270 Dacia abandoned

271 New defensive wall built in Rome

279 Restoration of a stable northern frontier

284-305 Diocletian and Maximian (from 286). Setting up of Tetrarchy and reorganization of the Empire

286-96 Separatist Empire in Britain

293 Constantius I and Galerius appointed as Caesars

301 Edict of maximum prices

303-11 Persecution of Christians

312 Constantine assumes power after battle of the Bridge. Founder of the Constantinian dynasty

312-37 Constantine I and Licinius (died 324)

313 Edict of Milan permitting Christian worship

324-30 Constantinople founded as eastern capital

337 Constantine II, Constantius II and Constans succeed Constantine I

360-3 Julian, last of the Constantinians, restores paganism

364-75 Valentinian I and Valens

375 Gratian and Valentinian II succeed Valentinian I as Emperors of the west

378 Valens killed at battle of Adrianople

378-95 Theodosius I

382 Altar of victory removed from Senate house in Rome, marking symbolic end of paganism

395-423 Honorius and Arcadius (died 408)

404 Ravenna established as capital of western Empire

406 Rhine freezes over, allowing German invaders in. Loss of parts of Gaul and Britain (by 410)

408-50 Theodosius II Emperor of the East

410 Sack of Rome by Alaric the Goth

413-18 Settlement of Burgundians and Visigoths inside the Empire

425-55 Valentinian III Emperor of the West

439 Vandalic kingdom set up in North Africa

451 Attila the Hun defeated in Gaul

455 Sack of Rome by Gaiseric the Vandal

456-72 Ricimer, commander of military forces in the West, sets up various puppet Emperors

475 Visigothic kingdom declared independent

475-6 Romulus Augustulus last Emper of the West, although Julius Nepos, the Emperor of the West set up by the eastern Emperor continues in exile until 480

476-93 Odoacer King of Italy

491-518 Anastasius I Emperor of the East. Conventionally regarded as the first Byzantine Emperor

INDEX

190

Acknowledgments

I am very grateful to Dr Martin Henig and Prof JJ Wilkes for their advice while writing this book, and to Profs JMC Toynbee and SS Frere for providing photographs in their possession. Judy Medrington kindly took on the onerous task of typing and interpreting my handwriting, at the same time judiciously improving the English.

I would also like to thank the following for the use of their photographs.

Andrea Caradini p 80 (below)
Antikenmuseum Staaliche Museum Preussischer Kulturbesitz p 129
Arms and Armour Press p 46 (left)
Author's Collection pp 27 (bottom), 32 (right), 38, 40 (right), 44 (top), 45 (center two), 56, 60 (both), 64 (bottom), 67, 69 (top), 71 (center), 73 (top two), 74, 75, 80 (top), 82, 83 (bottom two), 97 (below), 98 (below), 102, 103 (both), 110 (top), 115 (below), 118 (top), 123, 126, 134, 137 (below), 139, 169, 176
Biblioteca Apostolica Vaticana p 40 (left)
Biblioteque Nationale Paris p 166 (below)
Julian Bowsher pp 57, 64 (top), 73 (bottom), 101 (bottom), 146, 150–151, 159
Carlisle Museum and Art Gallery p 107 (below)
Cleveland Museum of Art, purchase, Leonard C Hanna Jr Bequest p 171, back cover
Corinium Museum Cirencester photo by P Dolphin p 144 (top)
Crown Copyright pp 61 (bottom), 68 (below)
Department of the Environment p 50–51
Deutsches Archaeologisches Instututs p 149 (right)
Dixon pp 24, 31 (below), 34–35, 47, 55, 62, 70, 86–87, 90 (above two), 108, 110 (top), 111 (top), 114, 119 (below), 119 (below), 122 (left), 124 (bottom right), 128 (top), 131 (top), 141, 148 (right), 155, 162, 163 (both right), 166 (above), 167, 178 (top)
Mary Evans pp 45 (top), 120
C Finn pp 26, 52 61 (top three), 72, 81, 117
Fishbourne Palace pp 83 (top), 92 (both), 93 (all three), 144 (bottom)
Fototeca Unione pp 13, 84
Ray Gardner p 32 (below)
Giraudon p 185
Christopher Goddard p 54 (top)
Hayling Island Excavation Project p 153 (top left)
Martin Henig pp 94, 178 (below)
Peter Horne p 153 (top right)
Israel Exploration Society, Jerusalem p 144 (center)
Institute of Archaeology, London pp 11, 18, 64 (center), 66, 68 (top), 71 (top), 97 (top), 101 (center), 110 (bottom), 118 (below), 128 (below), 131 (bottom), 145 (below)
Simon James pp 54

London Museum p 65 (bottom)
Bernard Lovell pp 14–15, 71 (bottom), 122 (right), 182 (top)
Barbara Malter p 32 (left)
Mansell pp 8 (both), 9 (top two), 12, 17, 20, 22 (both), 23 (right), 29, 33, 36, 42, 45 (bottom), 65 (top), 77 (both), 88 (both), 89, 100 (left), 112 (all three), 113 (above), 116, 124 (center right), 133, 136, 140, 145 (above), 148 (left), 149 (left), 152, 153 (below), 154, 156–57, 160, 161 (below right), 164, 168, 172, 173, 180, 187
Metropolitan Museum of Art, New York p 137 (top)
National Gallery of Art, Washington p 39
Nene Valley Research Committee p 100 (right)
Ordnance Survey p 96 (below)
Oscar Savio p 28
Penguin Books p 132, 161 (top)
du Pérac p 41 (top left)
Royal Commission of Historic Monuments p 76 (right)
Rheinischen Landesmuseum Trier pp 78, 104–05, 107 (above)
Scala pp 138–39, 183
Service National des Feuilles p 104 (above)
Sheldrake Press p 96 (top)
Society of Antiquaries pp 48, 49
Graham Sosse p 41 (below)
Hugh Toller pp 30, 41 (top right), 58–59, 69 (below)
Jocelyn Toynbee p 124 (left top and below)
Turkish Ministry of Tourism and Information p 115 (top)
Chris Unwin pp 76 (left), 163 (left)
Vatican Museum p 9 (bottom)
Verulanium Museum, St Albans, p 135 (below)
Victoria and Albert Museum p 138 (top)
Susan Walker p 130
Werner Forman Archive p 91
Jason Wood pp 23 (left), 31 (top), 37, 111 (bottom two), 158 (top), 170, 174, 175, 177, 179, 181
Roger Wood Studios p 85

Designed by Design 23
Edited by Jane Laslett
Indexed by Penny Murphy
Cartography by Richard Natkiel

Further Reading

A Boethius and J Ward Perkins, *Etruscan and Roman Architecture*, Penguin 1970
J Carcopino, *Daily Life in Ancient Rome*, Penguin 1978
R Chevallier, *Roman Roads*, Batsford 1976
M Crawford, *The Roman Republic*, Fontana 1978
D Dudley, *Urbs Roma*, Phaidon 1967
J Ferguson, *The Religions of the Roman Empire*, London 1970
M Finlay, *The Ancient Economy*, Chatto and Windus 1973
M Grant, *Gladiators*, Penguin 1971
M Grant, *History of Rome*, Faber 1979
AH Jones, *The Decline of the Ancient World*, Longman 1966

R Macmullen, *Paganism in the Roman Empire*, Yale University Press 1982
J Percival, *The Roman Villa*, Batsford 1976
D Strong and D Brown, *Roman Crafts*, Duckworth 1976
D Strong, *Roman Art*, Penguin 1976
CH Sutherland, *Roman Coins*, Barrie and Jenkins 1974
J Ward-Perkins, *Cities of Ancient Greece and Italy*, Sidgewick and Jackson 1974
G Watson, *The Roman Soldier*, Thames and Hudson 1981
G Webster, *The Roman Imperial Ary*, A & C Black 1979
C Wells, *The Roman Empire*, Fontana 1982
KD White, *Roman Farming*, Thames and Hudson 1970